FENIMORE COOPER
CRITIC OF HIS TIMES

COOPERSTOWN, FOUR CORNERS ABOUT 1850

From a Sketch by Henry L. Eckerson of an old saddle-painting.

FENIMORE COOPER
CRITIC OF HIS TIMES

BY

ROBERT E. SPILLER

New York
RUSSELL & RUSSELL
1963

"Our object has been to show, by a rapidly traced picture of life, the reluctant manner in which the mind of man abandons old to receive new impressions."

The Heidenmauer

PREFACE

IN the thirty years which followed the appearance of *The Spy* in 1821 the American nation passed through the early stages of adolescence. The civilization which European critics have but recently recognized as distinct from their own was beginning even then to become self-conscious. Political independence had been the first step toward national autonomy. Cultural independence followed slowly, hampered both by a slavish reverence for European traditions and by a premature assertion of national dignity. Cooper attempted the task which Irving deliberately avoided and which no one else seemed capable of undertaking. Without fear of consequence, he spent his life in trying to understand, to express, and to criticize the American mind. At heart a critic, he adopted the form already made fashionable by Scott, that of romantic fiction. He loved a good story of action and he appreciated natural beauty, but he had almost no other qualification of the literary artist.

Almost without exception, students of Cooper have attempted to estimate his work in terms of æsthetic principles evolved by European culture since the Renaissance, with little sympathetic attention to his background or to his own expressed objectives. The result in each case has been an attitude of apology for the very attainments which he himself believed to be the most vital. "You have appreciated my motives in regard to my own country," he wrote to his friend Horatio Greenough on May 21, 1831, "and it has given me great satisfaction. Her mental independence is my object, and if I can go down to the grave with the reflection that I have done a little towards it, I shall have the consolation of knowing that I have not been useless in my generation."

His qualities as a social critic have usually been made to appear as faults. His directness and vigor of mind caused an uncompromising attitude which often prevented the immediate effectiveness of his writings, but which tends to increase their permanent value. His appreciation of old world culture made him restless in an American environment; and the prejudices resulting from his blind idealism and his belief in American principles made him violent in his condemnation of corruption in the post-feudal society of Europe. His method, like those of Milton and Carlyle, was one of convinced enthusiasm rather than of measured logic. His writings are at once a reflection and an interpretation of the emerging American civilization about him.

His faults as an artist have been too frequently noted by Mark Twain, Lounsbury, Brownell, Van Doren, and others to need elaboration here. I have attempted instead to approach the study of Cooper as he approached that of the America of his day: to discover in the forces which made him some of the causes of his ideals and opinions, and to estimate the value of his writings for the thought they contain. The form is biographical; the result is not biography in the ordinary sense. It is a record of the evolution of a point of view.

There are three marked stages in his development. Until his departure for Europe in 1826, he thought in terms of the pioneer society of which he was a part. The social principles of aristocracy and democracy were at war within him as well as about him. He reacted to them with the vigor of youth, but he did not analyze them.

The seven years of his residence in Europe brought to him a riper comprehension of the factors in the problem. In perspective he analyzed the principles of American culture without much reference to American attainment. Confronted by the richer culture of Europe, he was guided to an understanding of European corruptions and prejudices by his friendship with liberal thinkers like Lafayette and his compatriot Samuel Morse.

On his return to America in 1833 he was dismayed by the discrepancy between ideals and facts in the civilization of his nation. For more than a decade he battled with his times in the courts and in the press, and he concluded his life in a retirement which was mental as well as physical.

With reasonable delays for the digesting of impressions, his writings follow these three stages. His early novels, up to *The Wept of Wish-ton-Wish* (1829), criticize American culture only incidentally in an enthusiastic and imaginative presentation of the immediate past. The novels of his middle years alternate between romance and the analysis of both European and American scenes in an effort to assort and define the conflicting elements in two civilizations. His final novels constitute an attempt to state his social creed. His critical writings, most of them for long almost entirely ignored, start with the second period in his development and follow through to the end. In them lies the key to an understanding of his imaginative work.

In the gathering of data for this study, and for the edition of Cooper's critical prose which is now in process of publication, I have of course referred constantly to the published *Correspondence* (1922), as well as to the Cooper family manuscripts now deposited at Yale University. In addition, I have followed most of the routes and visited most of the residences of Cooper in this country and, through the generosity of the John Simon Guggenheim Memorial Foundation, abroad. Many new manuscripts and other sources of information have turned up in the process. Friendly assistance has come from James Fenimore Cooper, Esq., Professor Marcel Clavel of Marseilles, France, Mr. John C. Pearson of Cleveland, Ohio, Miss Mary E. Phillips, and many others. The study of Cooper's relationship to his own time and to ours has scarcely commenced.

R. E. S.

Swarthmore, Pa.
July, 1931.

CONTENTS

ILLUSTRATIONS

I
1789–1826

FENIMORE COOPER

CRITIC OF HIS TIMES

CHAPTER ONE

The Retreat of the Indians

THE origin of Cooper's attitude toward the American mind of his day is to be sought in the history of the old New York frontier. The settlement and early history of Cooperstown and Otsego County furnish materials for the first chapter in a critical study of his ideas, for it was in this soil that his youth took root. Born in Burlington, New Jersey, on September 15, 1789, he was only fourteen months old when his family moved to the new home in the north. His boyhood and the beginnings of civilization in that region were contemporaneous. He was the second generation of pioneering stock in the region which he knew; the fifth generation in America; but he was not himself a pioneer. His mind and his ambitions looked downward into the soil and eastward to the older homes of culture. The son of a pioneer, he was himself rather the builder and critic of civilizations.

The history of the old New York frontier may be roughly divided into three epochs. The first began with the migrations of the fur traders at the beginning of the seventeenth century and lasted until the outbreak of the border wars. During all of this time the Indians were in rightful and complete possession. The second epoch extended from 1756 to 1783, during which the Indians were caught in the conflicts of the whites, first between the French and English, later between the English and the revolting colonists. From 1783 on, the whites alone had any real part in the history. Their complete conquest of the country was marked by the opening of the Catskill turnpike in 1802. Of the first of these epochs Cooper knew and cared little; the second deeply concerned his imagination; the lives of both his father and himself were immediately involved with the third.

There are few accurate records of the character of the Indian during the earliest epoch. Apparently he traded peaceably with the hunters and trappers of the Leather-Stocking type so long as he felt his rights were not seriously threatened, or submitted to the proselyting activities of the Jesuit, Moravian, and other missionaries. Most of those who wrote about him had seen him through the distorted perspective of personal interests or ideals of one kind or another.

The Indians of Cooper carried over some of the idealization of this period into the treachery of the period of ambush warfare which followed. With the fall of Quebec in 1759, the colonizing activities of the English grew more aggressive, and the energetic Sir William Johnson became the dominant factor in the development.

Purchase or gift from the Indians was the usual first step in the transfer of the wilderness to white ownership. It furnishes an underlying motive in more than one of Cooper's novels. The second step was the acquiring of property rights to these vast forest tracts by patents from their assumed proprietor, the King of England, and the development of manors on the traditional pattern of English feudalism. The Dutch patroons had already built up extensive estates over which they exercised absolute feudal rights at the time of the English conquest of the province, and these were absorbed into the English system. Maps of central New York State in the middle of the eighteenth century are divided into great blocks of land thus assigned to individuals. The last great act of Sir William Johnson was the negotiation of the Fort Stanwix (Fort Schuyler) treaty in 1768. By this pact, the line between property still owned by Indians and property which had legally been transferred to white ownership was fixed as running from Fort Stanwix, northwest of Cooperstown, to the Susquehanna at about the present boundary line of Pennsylvania. The complaint of Cooper's Chingachgook in *The Pioneers* that his ancestors had been robbed of their land had more of moral than of legal righteousness in it.

On the other hand, the claim of Oliver Effingham in the same novel that he had been deprived of his birthright by Marmaduke Temple had certain grounds of justification. His father, like Sir William Johnson, had been granted a royal patent to his land. The son of Sir William Johnson was, like Effingham, a royalist in the Revolutionary War, and his land was confiscated as a war-time measure. The actual Cooper patent, however, did not suffer any such experience. The transfer of this land from its royal patentee, George Croghan, to William Cooper was the result of the financial failure rather than of the patriotic sympathies of the former.

After the Revolution, the state of New York merely continued the feudal methods of land grant and land tenure which had developed under the Crown. These grants of land, Cooper explains in *The Pioneers,*

> were by letters patent under the great seal, and the term "patent" is usually applied to any district of extent thus conceded; though under the Crown, manorial rights being often granted with the soil, in the olden countries, the word "manor" is frequently used. There are many "manors" in New York, though all political and judicial rights have ceased.

Many such rights, however, survived the independence of the states, and Cooper had only to witness the power of his own father as Judge of the County Court over those who had purchased small tracts of land from him and settled within his jurisdiction, in order to comprehend the significance of this new world feudalism.

From his father Cooper early gained an understanding of the significance of the various theories of land tenure which formed the foundation of the society in which he grew up. The friendship between the Squire and Patroon Van Rensselaer provided the sharpest possible contrast between the two extremes of social theory involved. He had the means of understanding, even as a boy, the reasons why New York was, as he himself says, "the most aristocratical of all northern colonies."

Even though the foundations of a landed aristocracy were thus laid early, the actual acquirement of land was often accidental or negotiated on blind chance. Whether Cooper is speaking of his father or not he does not specify when, in *Satanstoe,* he tells of a gentleman in New York who purchased a considerable body of wild land on the faith of the map. When he came to examine his new property, it was found to be particularly wanting in water courses. The surveyor was sought and rebuked for his deception, the map having numerous lakes and streams.

"Why did you lay down all these streams here, where none are to be found?" demanded the irritated purchaser, pointing to the document.

"Why? Why, who the devil ever saw a map without rivers?" was the answer.

The heart of this wilderness was the "Glimmerglass" which Natty Bumppo came upon so unexpectedly in the opening scene of *The Deerslayer,* the lake in which the boy Cooper fished and swam with the other youngsters of Cooperstown during the years in which the Federalist John Adams controlled their several destinies from the nation's capital at Philadelphia. As the watershed of the Mohawk (and therefore of the Hudson), the Delaware, and the Susquehanna Rivers, as well as of the smaller rivers flowing into the Great Lakes, this section of New York State whispered its great economic promise to even its earliest white explorers. In 1737, Cadwallader Colden, Surveyor General and probably the first Englishman to survey that region, reported to the Hon. George Clarke, Lieutenant Governor of the Province of New York:[1]

At 50 miles from Albany, the land carriage from the Mohawk River to a lake, from whence the northern branch of the Susquehanna takes its rise, does not exceed 14 miles. Goods may be carried from this lake in bateaus or flat-bottomed vessels, through Pennsylvania to Maryland and Virginia, the current of the rivers running everywhere easy.

[1] S. M. Shaw: *Centennial Offering,* p. 6.

Forty-five years later, George Washington, after a similarly practical tour of inspection, wrote to the Marquis de Castellux[2] that he was "struck with the immense diffusion and importance" of the vast system of natural inland waterways which he had seen.

It is fitting that the first visions to be seen in this unbroken American wilderness should be those of power through economic resources. The products of these lands would move directly to the great markets of the east long before the first growth of timber was stripped from the mountains. And the mysterious inland seas which lay to the north and west were readily accessible to the hardier pioneers who fought their way through short stretches of woods and sluggish streams to Champlain and the St. Lawrence, to Ontario, Erie, to the Ohio, and to the Mississippi itself. It is not an accident that the Hudson valley provided one of the first routes of the frontier movement through the eastern mountain wall to the table-lands and the prairie rivers beyond.

The original Croghan patent occupied the entire western shore of Otsego Lake and extended in a southern and western direction half-way to the Fort Stanwix treaty line. George Croghan acquired this tract by royal patent in 1769 and added considerably to it later. As Cooper himself gives the facts in his *Chronicles of Cooperstown:* [3]

> It appears, by the documents in the possession of the Cooper family, that Col. George Croghan, who was connected with the Indian Department under the Crown, obtained a conveyance from the Indians of 100,000 acres of land, lying north and adjacent to the before-mentioned

[2] *History of Cooperstown*, p. 5.   [3] *Ibid.*, p. 3.

grant to Mr. Hartwick, and on the west side of the Susquehanna River, and of Otsego Lake, as early as the year 1768.
On the 13th of December of the same year, Col. Croghan
gave a mortgage under the Indian deed, to William Franklin, Esq., Governor of the Colony of New Jersey, to secure
the payment of £3,000; which money, as appears by the
same documents, was obtained by Governor Franklin of
certain persons in New Jersey, in behalf of Col. Croghan,
with a view to enable the latter to procure the regular
title to the same lands from the Crown. This object was
not effected until the 30th of November 1769, when letters
patent were issued by the colonial government granting
the same tract to George Croghan and ninety-nine other
persons; there existing an order to prevent grants of more
than a thousand acres at a time to single individuals.

We may conjecture with reasonable certainty that William Cooper, Esq., citizen of Burlington, was a principal
among those "certain persons in New Jersey" who took
this lien on a wilderness, for, continues his son,

on the 10th day of March 1770, George Croghan gave a
mortgage on that portion of the Otsego patent, as the
aforesaid grant was then called, which has since been
called Cooper's patent, for the further security of the payment of the said sum of £3,000; both of which mortgages,
with the accompanying bond, were regularly assigned to
the persons already mentioned, as security for their advances. On the 23rd day of March 1773, judgment was
obtained against George Croghan, in the Supreme Court
of the Colony of New York, upon the aforesaid bond.

By 1785, in addition to William Cooper, there was but
one other holder of these securities, and in this year the

new proprietor set out on horseback to discover whether his rivers and lakes were of water, or merely of ink. He left his comfortable and dignified home on the main street of the little town of Burlington, and in it his wife, his children, and his servants. He set out on the wilderness trail, a pioneer of the secondary and homesteading stamp.

The land to which he came was, however, no longer a wilderness in the strict sense of the word. The retreat of the Indian had been completed and his menace was already a problem for the historian rather than for the settler. In Cooper's own boyhood the living relics of the earlier inhabitants of northern New York were few and far less primitive than even old Indian John of the Leather-Stocking tales. "They did not," [4] says Susan Cooper,

> linger on the shores of the Otsego, as at some other points; when the white man appeared with his team, his plough, and his axe, they abandoned their canoes on the lake, gave up its choice fish to his steel hook and twine net, and followed the flying game farther toward the setting sun; or, in diminished numbers, they still wandered to and fro, over ground rendered sacred to them by older traditions connected with their lodges, and the graves of their fathers. Occasionally only they came in family groups, or in small parties, to taste the bass, or tap the maples in the forest, during the first years of the village.

As late as 1794, when James Cooper was five years old, a wandering tribe of Indians appeared in the forest near the village of Cooperstown and alarmed the inhabitants.

[4] *Pages and Pictures*, pp. 53–54.

But the days of the French and Indian wars were long past and the Cherry Valley massacre was a dim memory of twenty years previous. Women and children hid behind locked doors and closed shutters while men took down and loaded their rifles, but the wandering band of redmen disappeared as silently and as mysteriously as they had come, with harm to no one.

It is safe to say, therefore, that the picture which the novelist drew of pioneer and Indian life was almost as romantic to him as it is to us, but more vivid in that there were those still living who had experienced it. His intimate knowledge of primitive life had been gained almost wholly from such works as that of the missionary Heckewelder, even though it was set against a familiar and now peaceful background. "You have had the advantage of me," James G. Wilson quotes him as having once said to C. A. Murray, author of *The Prairie Bird*,[5] "for I was never among the Indians. All that I know of them is from reading and from hearing my father speak of them." He was too late for first-hand observation of his Indians in anything resembling their native state; but he was likewise too early for accurate historical and scientific knowledge of their racial characteristics and backgrounds. His Indians are, therefore, transmuted white men, "gone native," and restored to their vanishing wilderness.

[5] *Bryant and His Friends*, p. 237.

CHAPTER TWO

William Cooper, Esq., Federalist

THERE are no more reliable documents upon which to draw for a picture of the conditions which William Cooper faced in 1786 than the novels of his son. But as it was the latter's custom to use actual persons as the prototypes of the characters of his fiction and then to deny their identity, it may be well at this point to consider how far we may accept Marmaduke Temple of *The Pioneers* and his daughter Elizabeth as faithful portraits of Judge William Cooper and his daughter Hannah; Father Nash as Mr. Grant, the first Episcopalian rector of Cooperstown; the impetuous Richard Jones as the actual Richard Smith, the first sheriff; and even Natty Bumppo as one or another of the contending Shipmans. Whatever our decision, the spectre of the Effingham controversy and the identification of that benevolent gentleman with Fenimore Cooper himself looms in the not-distant future. *The Pioneers* and *Home as Found* are his most nearly autobiographical novels and the problem of the identity of Cooperstown and Templeton is a real one.

"There was no intention," wrote Cooper in a late preface to the former story, "to describe with particular accuracy any real characters in the book." The emphasis should be placed on the words, "with particular accuracy."

He further elaborates his theory of romantic characterization in the preface to *The Deerslayer:*

> The author has often been asked if he had any original in mind for the character of Leather-Stocking. In a physical sense, different individuals known to the writer in early life certainly presented themselves as models, through his recollections; but in a moral sense this man of the forests is purely a creation. . . . A leading character in a work of fiction has a fair right to the aid which can be obtained from a poetical view of the subject. It is in this view, rather than in one more strictly circumstantial, that Leather-Stocking has been drawn.

Those scholars who attempt to pin Harvey Birch, Long Tom Coffin, Natty Bumppo, or other classic Cooper characters down to single originals should bear this statement in mind.

To the personification of the ideal traits of a typical man of the forest, Cooper goes on to explain, are added traits derived from prejudices, tastes, and even weaknesses, in order to present a *vrai-semblance* of humanity rather than an actual individual or a paragon of virtue. A realist in his observation of detail, he was a conscious romanticist in his development of types. His use of historical facts is often misleading because of their accuracy and their profusion. But he maintains, with a vigor and determination characteristic of him in all things, the prerogative of the novelist to do what he pleases with his materials. There might be no imagined material whatever in a novel, and yet it would be unsafe to accept that novel literally as an historical record. Marmaduke Temple is beyond doubt the representation of William Cooper, but only as a puppet on strings manipulated by the hand of the son of William Cooper. He is acceptable, therefore, as a comment upon the father rather than as a literal portrait; and so of the others.

Many facts in the personal histories of the real and the imagined judge submit to a check, even in matters geneological. Among them may be mentioned the Quaker ancestry; the social position of the emigrant James Cooper, who had come over with his large family from Stratford-on-Avon in 1679 and who for thirty years was a merchant and large property owner in the prosperous town of Philadelphia; the increase in the family fortunes and position through the marriage of William, of the fourth generation in America, with Elizabeth, daughter of Richard Fenimore, also of Burlington, member of a prosperous Quaker family whose ancestors had been enrolled in the *Domesday Book*.

The characters of the two judges are similarly paralleled. The stern yet kindly justice of the fictional pioneer is reflected in the actual, as are his vigor of mind and body, his humanitarian principles, his strong sense of property, his conservative political bias, and his pride in himself, his family, and his settlement. William Cooper's *Guide in the Wilderness,* in which he merely set out to explain what he believed to be the most approved methods of settling virgin country, is in fact a record of his own successes.

The acquiring of the Croghan patent had been partly accident, partly business sagacity; but once the land had been acquired and inspected, the elder Cooper soon fixed upon the next steps. When he and his party of surveyors, after pushing their way through Cherry Valley and Middlefield, had come out upon Mount Vision at the southern end of the lake, it was he who first climbed a sapling in order to obtain a wider view of its waters. The hill bears to this day the name which he assigned to it at the moment of that vision. And once more it was the vision of an economist rather than of a poet.

By January 1786, when his full legal possession was virtually assured, he started settlements, even though the snow had not yet melted from the dilapidated blockhouse which survived from Croghan's tenure. Levi Beardsley, the son of one of his early settlers, has left a description of some of the difficulties which were to be encountered, and of the wasteful methods used by the clearers of the forests.

Hard timber, maple, beech, birch, and elm predominated in that part of Otsego County [he says],[1] the timber being very heavy. A good chopper would cut his acre and pile the brush in seven or eight days; I have known it done in less. At the age of twenty-two years I could cut an acre in seven days, but as a general average, men would be from seven to ten days, particularly if several worked together. Chopping is hard but clean work and I was fond of it. A man going into the woods with his axe soon makes an opening which, being enlarged daily, serves to encourage and stimulate him to vigorous action. The trees being chopped and brush piled, if done in May or June, should be left through July and August, by which time they become so dry that the fire frequently runs over the whole ground, burning all the brush, many of the logs, and blackening those that remain. This should be regarded as a *good burn*, leaving the soil clean of weeds and herbage.

[1] *Reminiscences,* pp. 36–37.

Then follows the logging and burning the log heaps, most dirty, smoky, disagreeable work. Three men and a yoke of oxen would log an acre per day, sometimes more if the timber was light and well felled and cut. The ashes, worth 6¼ cents, must be scraped together, and carried to an ashery to make black salts and eventually pearl of potash. All this being done, the land was ready for harrowing and reception of seed; after which the fences could be made at pleasure.

It was not uncommon to make sugar in the spring on a piece of forest land, and then clear it off for a crop of corn the same season. Several acres of my father's lands, where he afterwards planted his orchards, were thus used and cleared off; the small brush had been cut the preceding autumn. When the time arrived for making sugar, the trees were tapped and a large quantity made. As the season advanced, we cut the small timber, heaped the brush, and got everything ready to cut the large trees, as soon as sugar making was over; that being passed, we cut and burned all the timber, and cleared the land for crop.

This entire process was in full accord with the methods outlined in the *Guide*. Emphatically, William Cooper boasts that he succeeded where others had failed because he had a joy and a large interest in the game of settlement. He never kept petty advantages for himself, counting that real profits depended upon the welfare and happiness of the settlement as a whole. For the commercial future of the lands he had no doubts, indulging only in constructive and practical theories.

He encouraged others to follow the principles which he had adopted. They were, in brief: (1) Buy large tracts and sell (not give) them to settlers of all classes, but preferably to artisans and farmers, buying more as fast as these are sold; (2) Live and work with the settlers, joining hands with them in such community enterprises as local roads and bridges; (3) develop such industries as sugar and potash, as well as the more obvious lumbering and farming; and (4), keep the commercial development of the nation as a whole in mind, working for such improvements as trade highways and canals. Like Washington, he had conceived the Erie Canal project at a time when men of smaller vision were still clearing their own half acres, even though he did not live to see his dreams realized.

It was not until after the proprietor's second visit, early in the summer of 1787, in company with his wife, that the village of Cooperstown began to become an actuality. The chaise in which the two had come up the Mohawk Valley was left at the north end of the lake and the progress to its foot was made in a canoe. However, Mrs. Cooper was so much alarmed by the passage, says her son,[2]

that she disliked returning in a boat, and the chaise was brought to the place in two canoes. In order that it might reach the eastern bank, and to serve the public generally, a bridge was built at the outlet, which was the first real bridge across the Susquehanna at this spot. This bridge was composed of log abutments, sleepers, and logs laid across the latter. A road had been cut through the forest, following the direction of the lake, and coming out along the banks of Lakelands, at this bridge. It was, however, so rude and difficult to pass that when the chaise left the village, men accompanied it with ropes to prevent it from upsetting.

[2] *History of Cooperstown*, p. 11.

During this summer, many emigrants arrived, chiefly from Connecticut, and plans were made for the first Cooper home, a large frame building on the lake 'shore, completed in 1789. That winter, William Cooper kept bachelor hall in his new mansion; but when spring came again the town of seven frame houses, three frame barns, a general store, and thirty-five inhabitants was ready for the family of this new sort of American lord of the manor, a family which now included baby James, arrived in September. The following year Otsego became a county and Cooper was appointed first Judge of the County Court, with Richard Smith as Sheriff. A tavern completed the community, for many years known as the *Red Lion.*

A year after his settlement, William Cooper wrote to his "esteemed friend," Aaron Burr, on the ninth of April 1790:[3]

In the month of July last I procured a petition from the Corporation of Albany accompanied by one from the merchants of that city to the Legislature pointing out the propriety of the sum of four hundred pounds being granted to open a road from the outlet of Lake Otsego to the Mohawk River, by way of conteracting the maneuvers of the merchants of Philadelphia who have been active to secure the trade of this western country to their city. I now find that the Legislature have granted our prayer, and as I understand that thou art one of the commissioners of the Land Office, I only want to request that those moneys may not be put into the hands of any person to complete the work who is not interested in its being faithfully done. Take it for granted that those persons who have property

[3] MS. in the library of the New York Historical Society.

WILLIAM COOPER

From the painting by Gilbert Stuart.
Courtesy of James Fenimore Cooper, Esq.

the advancement of which depends on the commodiousness of this road are the only persons who will be most likely to cause every farthing of the money laid out for the advantageous purpose the legislature intended. And as [I] have 50hhd. of sugar now lying ready for market which I cannot get to Albany until this road is opened, [I] am very anxious that an order may come forward from your board authorizing some persons to set about the work and draw for the money when the business is completed. It is a delicate matter, but as my whole property is affected by the good or bad quality of this road [I] must confess that I am very desirious to have a hand in overseeing this business. As I have no acquaintance with any of the commissioners but thyself, [I] hope thee will get them together and facilitate this, and render an essential service to the state and him who subscribes himself with due respect, thy real friend, William Cooper.

Even the Quaker pronoun of Judge Cooper bears testimony to the accuracy of the portrait of the fictional Temple. And the integrity of the latter is reflected in the fact that Cooper succeeded in obtaining his money from the legislature and, there being more than was actually needed, the balance stands to this day on the account books in favor of the State, according to the statement of his great-grandson.

The route of the post road, which was soon undertaken, left the Mohawk at Canajoharie and followed Cherry Valley in a southwestern direction. Judge Cooper took an active part in its extension to within reach of Cooperstown and urged its continuation by way of the Susquehanna Valley down into central Pennsylvania, thus completing a transportation circle from the Hudson to the Chesapeake. Four years later he writes to Rufus King his delight at the promise of this highway. His was the typical attitude of the inland settler toward foreign wars, reflected in the Great War by the middle-western agrarian.

I was delighted [he says], [4] at the news of having the postoffice or road extended to Cooperstown. It ought to have been done, and not left at Canajoharie in the year '92, for being there, the people of this quarter are deprived of its utility. As to private post, they are a nuisance. Thus far, or to this place, I am very confident the revenue will be benefited; and whether by extending it to Cheningo, Tioga Point, Wyoming, from there to Bethlehem, will injure it, is submitted. Perhaps the thing is too early to bear its own expense.

Preserve the peace of America if you can, for we have *all to lose* and *nothing to win* by war. Remember that *peace* makes *plenty, war* makes *poverty.* As to the forest, why should we quarrel about what is done to ten or fifteen acres of land at Niagara when we have so many millions lying waste. Congress had better counsel together on the most eligible mode of inviting European farmers and manufacturers into the unimproved part of our country and advising ways to improve the navigation of a number of our long rivers which lead from the remote parts of the Union on the heads of which where [*sic*] their manufactories established that could make the produce of the countries round about into such shapes as would have transportation to the seaports. This would be a kind of cement to the nation, like the stone mortar of the ancients, which was stronger than the stone itself. Nothing strengthens government more than the connections of people in trade. It

[4] MS. in the library of the New York Historical Society; partly transcribed in King, *Correspondence,* I, 562–63.

is their interest, of course, their best policy, to quickly support each other and the government. Although a chain of
constitutions and good laws may be made for our common
benefit, yet they had better be but seldom tried, which may
in some measure be avoided by government wisely and
timely contemplating distant manufactories so as to interest the people in the remote parts of the country in the
welfare of the commercial towns. This would make the
mortar stronger than the stone, or the disposition of the
people stronger than the constitution and the laws. Why
is government more lasting now than of old time? Because
manufactories and commerce hath employed men so as to
interest them in each other's happiness. Why where [*sic*]
the sticklers for war at their meetings in York who spoke
and felt most for the flag of America? Why, a shoemaker,
a bankrupt, and a young lawyer of far more ambition than
wealth—in short, the real merchant is quiet in comparison
to the set that wants employ or to collect something out
of the distractions of war, a thing, should it take place,
that would at once destroy the counties of Otsego, Herki-
mer, Onondago, Ontario, Tioga, and Clinton of this state,
and injure Luzerne and Northumberland of Pennsylvania
more than the common calamities of war. *You must avoid
it,* being the least of the two evils. I feel particularly interested in preserving our neutrality, as on that my whole
fortune, which I have obtained by the dint of industry,
depends. And you will no doubt excuse so long a letter
from one of your constituents who hath spent the best of
his days improving and bringing to some sort of perfection a county where not a man was nine years ago, and
now a war would drive at least 18,000 souls from it.

Here speaks the new feudalism of democracy: power
for the manorial lord obtained through the cementing

disposition of people owning and cultivating the soil in their own right. "Some rich theorists," wrote the same benevolent despot in his *Guide,*

> let the property they purchase lie unoccupied and unproductive, and speculate upon a full indemnity from future rise in value, the more so as they feel no want of immediate profits. But I can assert from practical experience that it is better for a poor man to pay forty shillings an acre to a landlord who heads the settlement, and draws people around him by good plans for their advancement, and arrangements for their convenience, than to receive an hundred acres gratis from one of these worthy theorists; for if fifty thousand acres be settled, so that there is but one man upon a thousand acres, there can be no one convenience of life attainable; neither roads, school, church, meeting, nor any other of those advantages, without which man's life would resemble that of a wild beast.

How directly the social theory of the son was to derive from that of the father! The ideal of an American gentleman which Fenimore Cooper outlined with such conviction a quarter of a century later in his *American Democrat* was little more than a generalized portrait of this Marmaduke Temple. But the great days of Federalism were then past forever, and the newer conservatism was too frail, as the newer democracy was too gross, to appeal to the son of Judge Cooper. Times had changed, but the Cooper temperament remained the same, founded on the proud conviction that physical and mental vigor alone would provide material wealth and grant the right to rule.

That elder Cooper has been aptly termed, by Professor Dixon Ryan Fox,[5] "the mirror of partisan perfection as a

[5] *Decline of Aristocracy,* p. 136.

Federalist squire." His home was the local meeting place of his party, and he campaigned on horseback for Jay and Burr, in support of the Hamiltonian doctrines that wealth and not numbers should control government, and that the rights of property are more sacred than the genius of democracy.

On one occasion his partisan conviction was so strong that he procured the indictment of an opponent before the Federal Grand Jury of New York for circulating a petition recommending the repeal of the alien and sedition laws. In the clutches of the very law which he wished repealed, the worthy victim was roused from his bed and taken down the Hudson in the custody of the United States District Attorney. "A hundred missionaries in the cause of democracy," comments the historian Hammond,[6]

> stationed between New York and Cooperstown, could not have done so much for the Republican cause as this journey of Judge Peck, as a prisoner, from Otsego to the capital of the state. It was nothing less than the public exhibition of a suffering martyr for the freedom of speech and the press, and the right of petitioning, to the view of the citizens of the various places through which the marshal traveled with his prisoner.

"Indeed," adds the Rev. Ralph Birdsall in his account of the episode,"[7]

> the overthrow of the Federal party in this State, with the consequent success of Jefferson in the presidential canvas, is attributed to the excitement and indignation aroused by the

[6] *History of Political Parties in New York,* I, 131–32.
[7] *Story of Cooperstown,* p. 87.

spectacle of this little dried up man, one-eyed but kindly in expression and venerable, a veteran of the Revolutionary War, being transported through the State in the custody of Federal officials, and manacled, the latter an unnecessary and outrageous indignity.

In the political correspondence of Judge Cooper and his contemporaries, Mr. Cooper tells us,[8] there are frequent complaints of fraud, and of the influence and prominence of foreigners, especially the Irish, with grave expressions of fear for the future of the country and the stability of property. The Federalists describe themselves as "friends of order," and refer to their opponents as "anti-Christians," and "enemies of the country." One of Judge Cooper's friends who had removed to Philadelphia writes: "We are busy about electing a senator in the state legislature. The contest is between B. R. M., a gentleman, and consequently a Federalist, and a dirty, stinking anti-Federalist Jew tavern-keeper called I. I. But, Judge, the friends to order here don't understand the business, they are uniformly beaten; we used to order these things better at Cooperstown."

And so things were ordered at Cooperstown as long as the Squire was in control. Judge Cooper was not averse to a resort to physical prowess when matters could not be settled in other ways, and it must be admitted that his system of wrestling with his opponents was preferable to the then common practice of duelling, although perhaps not as effective in permanently disposing of a political rival. Levi Beardsley relates an incident witnessed by his father;[9] "A wrestling match was got up in front of

[8] J. F. Cooper, preface to *Guide in the Wilderness.*
[9] *Reminiscences,* p. 53–54.

the Griffins where a ring was formed, and the parties matched for the contest. Judge Cooper said he was a wrestler himself; and believed he could throw any man in the county; and further, that he wanted to find a man on his patent who could throw him, remarking that he would give any one in the company one hundred acres of land who would throw him at arm's length." Timothy Morse answered the challenge and the Judge, from his position on his back on the ground, ordered his clerk, Richard Smith, to make out the necessary papers for the hundred acres. And on another occasion, says Beardsley, he came down from the bench in order to close with his successful opponent for Congress, Major Cochran, when the latter indulged in remarks that were not to his liking.

Nevertheless, Cooper went south twice as the representative of his district in Congress, and, although ill at the time, he was carried into the session in 1800 as an elector to cast his vote for Burr when Jefferson and the Federalist had tied and all the principles which he held most sacred were threatened by a growing spirit of democracy. It was after a political meeting also that he received the blow on the head, in 1809, which resulted in his death. Such was the mettle of the elder Cooper.

CHAPTER THREE

Son of the Frontier

IF William Cooper was the personification of the spirit of the frontier, James Cooper was its son. Yet the Cooper family life, first in the Manor, then in the larger and more imposing Otsego Hall, had little of the crudity and none of the privations that one usually associates with the outposts of civilization. Of the twelve children, only seven reached maturity, and only one, a boy who died in infancy, was born in Cooperstown. But the five boys and two girls who had constituted the family when the move from Burlington was made were a happy and congenial group united by the strongest ties of affection for each other and of loyalty for their parents.

James Cooper was the youngest, and he and the village of Cooperstown grew up together in the final decade of the century. He was only James Cooper, until he adopted his mother's family name, Fenimore, by an act of the state legislature on April 13, 1826. The picture of these days which is preserved in *The Pioneers* is so detailed and so faithful that one need scarcely look further. The town was forced to depend upon its own resources for things of the mind as well as for things of the flesh. Great flocks of wild geese flew across the water to furnish target practice and good fowl for the townsmen. Huge, homewoven nets were carried out into the water and lake trout were piled up on the gravelly beach. There were always plenty of maples to tap; plenty of wood for fuel and for the hand-hewn beams of the new buildings and bridges. When a clergyman or a schoolmaster was needed, word was sent to Albany, New York, or Philadelphia. Contact with the seat of government and with the social life of the Capital was established by the leading citizen of the mountain town when he became a delegate to Congress. These people were self-sufficient for all vital things, but their viewpoint was national and cosmopolitan rather than provincial. Judge Cooper foresaw that the wilderness would not remain unsettled for many years. If he erred at all, it was in visualizing Cooperstown as too important a center in the new economic order. But his error put zest into the activities of his fellow-townsmen.

After ten years, the frame manor house by the lake shore became unsuitable to the growing dignity of the Judge and the increasing demands of his large family. In 1799 it was picked up bodily and moved down the street in order that it might not obstruct the view of the new Otsego Hall which had risen on higher ground and which was to be the home of the novelist in the years of his maturity as well as in those of his youth.

There is still in the family archives an old document, in the hand of Fenimore Cooper, which describes the new mansion.[1] Lombardy poplars, the first in the country, had been imported to form suitable avenues leading up to the new house. Stone for the foundations was taken from the fields. Bricks and lime were made from the clay and deposits of the region. Foundations, says the son of the

---

[1] J. F. Cooper, *Legends and Traditions of a Northern County*, pp. 225–27.

master, were laid in the summer of 1797; the walls and
roof completed during 1798; the family moved in during
June of 1799.

Pictures which have survived reveal this huge brick
box of a house rising from its cleared slope, surrounded
by its scrub-trees newly planted, and looking out with
a somewhat self-conscious dignity over the clear water
of the lake. Of course there was a great hall. "A piano
stood between the window and the door on the north-
east corner," continues Cooper's description,

> a side board between the two next doors, and a tea table be-
> tween the last door and the window. In the southwest cor-
> ner stood an old fashioned clock, and near it another sew-
> ing table. A long settee covered with chinz stood between
> the two doors on that side, and a large hand organ between
> the most northern of the doors and the window. There
> were two small chandeliers in the hall, and it was warmed
> by a large tin plate stove that stood in the center. There
> were also gilt branches on the door casings, and busts in
> the pediments. The window seats were generally filled
> with books.

There was a dining room, papered in straw color fig-
ured with a delicate vine pattern, which was never used
except for family festivals. The woodwork throughout
the house was tinted, but the stairs were straight and
mean. A curious mixture, this, of pioneering crudity and
remembered baronial grandeur. It is somewhat sugges-
tive of a gentleman in corduroys and a diamond stick-
pin. The tin plate stove must have had curious conversations with the plaster busts in the pedimented doorways
during those long northern winter nights.

Upstairs the two largest chambers were kept for company, but "familiar acquaintances" slept in the store-room when they came to visit. The boys had one room and the girls another. Outside there was a kitchen garden and a flower garden, as well as fruit trees. Gravel walks divided the ground into checker-board squares. Red paint was chosen for the roof and the bricks likewise were painted, but were lined in white. Life in this grand old mansion was exceedingly gay, says Cooper, at least until the accidental death of his eldest sister cast a gloom over the household.

The few anecdotes which have survived tell us that no small part of the gaiety was caused by the will and the spirit of the baby member of the family. In later years his daughter Susan prefaced her excerpts from *The Pioneers* with some notes from her father's memory.[2] Master Oliver Cory, it would seem, kept the village school in those early days. He was a laborious, upright pedagogue, firm in discipline, yet patient and kindly by nature. Latin was the staple of the week-end régime, but Saturday was devoted to morals and manners, instruction which sank deeply into the impressionable mind of the youngster.

The academy was held in a building very close to the original manor house of Judge Cooper, a hall which also variously served for political meetings, religious services, the sessions of the County Court, and the parties of the young people and of their elders. The barrel organ mentioned in the description of the new house had been brought back from the metropolitan Philadelphia by the Judge on one of his political excursions. When the strange and lugubrious sounds issued one morning from the open

[2] *Pages and Pictures,* p. 49.

windows of the Manor, the school across the way almost broke up in excitement. One may even now hear Mr. Cory, horrified but equal to the emergency, announcing in solemn tones, "Boys, that organ is a remarkable instrument. You have never heard the like of it before. I give you half an hour's intermission; go into the street and listen to the music."

Not merely pedagogues, but clergymen as well, had to be prepared for the unexpected demands of a pioneer community. Judge Cooper, in spite of his Quaker heritage, apparently early adopted the view of the New York aristocracy that there might be ways of getting into heaven other than that of the Church of England, but that no gentleman would choose any of them: "The Episcopal mode of worship," as Robert Troup once wrote to Rufus King,[3] so friendly to the government, so hostile to Jacobinism." Father Nash, the first rector of Christ's Church, was therefore Episcopalian, but his road was not easy. His task was first to convince the community of his faith, and then to adapt it to the peculiar needs of this semi-primitive life. His success, from the day of that first experimental meeting in the academy, is recorded in the person of Father Grant of *The Pioneers,* even though there seems to have been no literal resemblance between the actual and the imaginary clergyman.

Various motives prompted Judge Cooper to send his sons to the Tory rector of St. Peter's Church in Albany, after Master Cory had instilled the rudiments into them. Mental, religious, and social training were mixed in almost equal proportions. Similar motives later sent Ann Cooper to a fashionable girl's school in New York, and

[3] King, *Correspondence,* V, 37.

allowed Hannah a social fling in the Capital during a session of Congress.

The journey across the hills from Cooperstown to Albany was made by the young James under the care of a worthy farmer of the neighborhood who was taking a load of wheat from the newly cleared fields of Otsego County to the Hudson and distant markets. As they moved slowly along the broad highway on that morning in 1799, the farmer pointed out to the boy the marvels on every hand. The road had been open only a little over a year, and now there were long trains of farm wagons, heavily laden like their own, rolling eastward; there were stone bridges; and, marvel above marvels, there was a tavern for every mile all the way to Albany!

A letter to Issac, who had preceded him by a year or more, from his sister Hannah, then in Philadelphia, June 1798, tell us of the sort of school to which he was going as well as of the home which he was leaving,

> Pray, how do you like Albany, [she writes,[4]] what are your studies? and who are your companions? the last thing is of vast consequence, and I sincerely hope you may not become intimate or acquainted with the low vicious boys of which you have so many around you. Mamma is better, the boys are well, Jim has grown almost as large as William, the Doctor [Samuel] has grown also. They are very wild and show plainly they have been bred in the woods. They go to school and are learning Latin. I do not know what progress they make, but hope you will make a great improvement in your learning.

The rector of St. Peter's, Rev. William Ellison, an intimate friend of Judge Cooper's, was "a clergyman of the

⁴ *Legends and Traditions,* pp. 170–71.

true English school," Cooper many years later reminded his fellow scholar, William Jay.

> This man was an epitome of the national prejudices, and, in some respects, of the national character. He was the son of a beneficed clergyman in England; had been regularly graduated at Oxford and admitted to orders; entertained a most profound reverence for the King and the nobility; was not backward in expressing his contempt for all classes of dissenters and all ungentlemanly sects; was particularly severe on all immoralities of the French Revolution, and, though eating our bread, was not especially lenient to our own; compelled you and me to begin Virgil with the Eclogues, and Cicero with the knotty phrase that opens the oration in favor of the poet Archais, "because their writers would not have placed them first in the books if they did not intend people to read them first"; spent his money freely, and sometimes that of other people; was particularly tenacious of the ritual, and of all the decencies of the church; detested a democrat as he did the devil; cracked his jokes daily about Mr. Jefferson and Black Sal, never failing to place his libertinism in strong relief against the approved morals of George III, of several passages in whose history it is charity to suppose he was ignorant; decried all morals, institutions, churches, manners, and laws but those of England, Mondays and Saturdays; and, as it subsequently became known, was living every day in the week, *in vinculo matrimonii,* with another man's wife.

Three or more years of schooling under this worthy gentleman, both by action and by reaction, left their indelible stamps upon the forming character. It was only the death of this tutor which sent James, at the age of thirteen, to Yale.

Back home in Cooperstown, life in the new house was wholesome and happy, centering about the quiet dignity of Mrs. William Cooper, and the more colorful personality of her eldest daughter Hannah. It was even rumored many years later that, during her brief visit to Philadelphia, this young lady had been the object of a certain flirtatious regard on the part of a Virginia gentleman, William Henry Harrison, later the President of the United States, but at the time a mere delegate to Congress. In a letter to Rufus Griswold, dated from the Hall a few weeks before his death,[5] her brother tells us that she "was very highly appreciated and is very generally known in Philadelphia," an entirely suitable nominee for Mr. Griswold's album of beauties of the Capital, except that she held sway during the administration of Adams rather than that of Washington. And when he was accused of representing this sister, whose memory he cherished "with a reverence that surpassed the love of a brother," as Elizabeth Temple, he took occasion to deny the sacrilege.

Nevertheless, there is little of the anointed saint in the Hannah Cooper who speaks through the few letters which have survived. As the feminine head of the new generation she reported the homely doings at the Hall to her absentee men-folk. To her father in Philadelphia she writes, April 28, 1800: [6]

Saturday last,—the onions and strawberries were put out. —This morning—Bilderbeck and Howard are employed in making the sweet potato bed. By noon they will be in the

[5] Griswold MSS., Boston Public Library.
[6] MS. in the possession of Miss Katherine Livingston Mather of Cleveland, Ohio.

ground. The seeds we can now sow at our leisure, but they shall be done as soon as possible. On Friday last we had a heavy snow storm; it remained upon the ground long. Mamma thinks you had better purchase the two boys, Samuel and James, some summer stockings—cotton they must be. We are almost tired of asking you to make purchases, but so large a family cannot be provided for without trouble. We are at a loss to know what to do for summer clothes for the children; the spring goods have not come yet,

and the hasty note concludes with a dutiful adieu.

Two months later she sent a similar report to young William at Princeton, July 12, 1800: [7]

Dear Brother. It is very late at night. Nobody in the house is up save myself and Mamma, who is playing upon the organ. This amusement engages her every night after the family have separated, and very pretty effect it has, being not unlike a serenade, which you know is the manner of courting with the Spaniards. It must be charming for the Spanish belles, but very toilsome for their beaus. The weather is now uncommonly warm here; our Fourth of July passed very brilliantly away. There were not any fireworks, but the Masonic Hall was handsomely illuminated. The lads and lasses repaired in the evening to our house, and we had quite a large party to dance, "rallying round our liberty." Sister Nancy has not returned from Sister Mary's yet. We expect her in a day or two. Mr. Fitch has Richard's farm; he removed there shortly. Doctor grows quite tall; is nearly as large as James. The family desire their love. Good night—may your dreams be sweet. Your loving sister, Hannah Cooper.

[7] *Legends and Traditions,* p. 174.

Two months later almost to the day, she left the Hall with her brother Richard, on horseback, to visit the Morrises at the Butternuts across the hills. The fall which brought her life to a close at the age of twenty-two left one of the deepest of all impressions upon the mind of the boy James. She was, he said later, "esteemed and loved by all who knew her. Few young women of her age ever died more lamented." Her family never entirely recovered from the shock and the loss.

On the twelfth of September the body was removed to the Hall, her brother records,[8]

and placed between the two southern doors on the east side, leaving room for a row of chairs next the wall. The Rev. Mr. Nash preached a sermon, standing near the pantry door, and the hall was filled with people. Judge Cooper, Richard Fenimore, Samuel, and James Fenimore, were all the members of the family present, Isaac being in Philadelphia, and William being at Princeton College. Mrs. Cooper and her daughter Ann were in the room of the former. The procession left the house by the front door, and the body was interred in the present family burying ground. A slab was placed over the grave, made of the common stone of the country (quarries had been opened) and the inscription on it was written by Judge Cooper.

So great was the grief of the father that he could not bring himself to write out his daughter's name on the stone. In his grief alone was to be preserved the memory of the laughing girl whose name had been the subject of an acrostic by the great Talleyrand during his visit to the wilderness town some years before:

[8] *Ibid.,* pp. 227–28.

"Amiable philosophe au printemps de son âge,
Ni les temps, ni les lieus n'alterant son esprit;
Ne cedent qu'à ses gouts simples et son étalage,
Au milieu des deserts, elle lit, pense, ecrit.

Cultivez, belle Anna, votre goût pour l'étude;
On ne saurait ici mieux employer son temps;
Otsego n'est pas gai—mais tout est habitude;
Paris vous deplairait fort au premier moment;
Et qui jouit de soi dans une solitude,
Rentrant au monde, est sur d'en faire l'ornement."

Assuredly *"Otsego n'est pas gai,"* especially during the
long winter months, except for the gaiety which a few
high spirits, nourished on the vigorous life of the woods
and trained to the best culture available, could make it.
With a wisdom unusual in the wilderness homesteader,
Judge Cooper realized that the next step in the process
of civilization was the training of his children to bring to
the new settlement from the seats of culture in the east
those indefinable elements which he had left behind him.
The next step was assuredly not more pioneering. The son
of the frontier must reëstablish the severed links with tradition.

CHAPTER FOUR

Latin and Life

IT was entirely in keeping with William Cooper's view of
life that his youngest son should profit by the family
increases in fortune and social position. William, Jr., and
Isaac had been students at Nassau Hall in New Jersey, but
James was sent to Yale, an older college. Cooper, however,
in *Santanstoe,* gives other reasons why the change in the
family policy might be interpreted as a disadvantage to
himself. "I should have sent Evans to Yale," he makes
Mrs. Littlepage explain,

> had it not been for the miserable manner of speaking Eng-
> lish they have in New England, and I have no wish to
> have a son of mine who might pass for a Cornishman.
> We shall have to send this boy to Newark, in New Jersey.
> The distance is not so great, and we shall be certain he
> will not get any of your Roundhead notions of religion,
> too.

The course of study at Yale at this time was borrowed
from the century-old Harvard tradition, the origin of
which was English, although modelled on British secondary school rather than university curricula. It was
predominately classical in content, learned and professional in its aims, and dogmatic in its methods. Latin was
the language of ordinary conversation, and the Fresh-

37

man year was devoted to the study of Greek and Hebrew. Logic was included in the second year, physics in the third, metaphysics and mathematics in the fourth. "The tongues" continued throughout, as did weekly exercises in rhetoric, ethics, and theology, together with declamations in either Latin, Greek, or Hebrew on Fridays. Cooper did not hold the colleges responsible for whatever intellectual deficiencies he may have had, even though he thought little of American educational standards in his day. The hero of *The Chainbearer* "got a degree and what is called an education," and Cooper confesses in his preface to *Lionel Lincoln* that he himself soon forgot what little the colleges had bestowed upon him. The colleges are probably mentioned in the plural because this was in 1824, the year in which Columbia conferred upon him an honorary M. A. "Learning," he concludes in *The Chainbearer,* "advances in this country on the great American principle of imparting a little to a great many, instead of teaching a good deal to a few." In this remark, as so often, he seems almost to be describing our day rather than his own.

So excellent had been the training of the Church of England Rector of Albany, however, that most of the burden of the classic disciplines was child's-play for him, even at the age of thirteen. With the exception of James Hillhouse, his companion in school at Albany, he was the youngest in his class, but his precocity was not phenomenal. The college course of those days was planned for the age levels of the present secondary school. John Trumbull had, some years previously, passed the entrance examinations for Yale at the age of seven.

"I could wish you to mention me to Mr. Day and Mr.

Kingsley," [1] Cooper wrote to his favorite master Benjamin Silliman, the youthful professor of mineralogy and geology. [2]

I dare say I should say Dr. Kingsley, but of this I am in the dark. I remember the latter with affection. He did his duty, and more than his duty by me; and could I have been reclaimed to study by kindness, he would have done it. My misfortune was extreme youth. I was not sixteen when you expelled me. I had been early and highly educated for a boy,—so much so as to be far beyond most of my classmates in Latin; and this enabled me to play— a boy of thirteen!—all the first year. I dare say Mr. Kingsley never suspected me of knowing too much, but there can be no great danger now in telling him the truth. So well was I grounded in the Latin that I scarce ever looked at my Horace or Tully until I was in his fearful presence; and if he recollects, although he had a trick of trotting me about the pages in order to get me mired, he may remember that I generally came off pretty well. There is one of my college adventures which tickles me, even to this day. I never studied but one regular lesson in Homer. The poor bell, or a cold, or some letter had to answer for all the others. Well, when the class reviewed, I clapped another sixty or fifty lines to the old lesson, and went to recitation. The fact was notorious,—so notorious that the division used to laugh when I was called on for a Homeric excuse. Examination came at length, and Mr. Stuart,[3] between whom and myself I cannot say there were any very strong

[1] Jeremiah Day, Professor of Mathematics, Natural Philosophy, and Astronomy; and James L. Kingsley, Professor of Hebrew, Latin and Greek.
[2] G. P. Fisher, *Life of Benjamin Silliman*, I, 336–37.
[3] Moses Stuart, tutor at Yale and Professor of Sacred Literature at Andover Theological Academy.

sympathies, was examining. I had calculated my distance, and by aid of the Latin Translation, which I read as easily as English, I was endeavoring to find out what Homer meant in a certain paragraph that I anticipated would fall to my lot. I remember that I sweated. The examiner was not disposed to give me the benefit of my recent application, but skipped me over the whole book. I found the new place amid a general titter, and lo! it was in the very heart of my two lessons. As we sailors say, there was plenty of sea-room, and I had half a mind to ask the examiner to take his pick. As it was, I got through admirably, and believe greatly to the astonishment of the examiner; and I know it was highly to the amusement of my own tutor, whose laughing eyes seemed to say, "This is what my boys can do without study." If I ever write my memoir, the college part of it will not be the least amusing.

The ingenious youth has triumphed over the frowning and black-robed examiner before this instance,—and since, but the triumph is usually short lived. The difficulty is that no really high-spirited boy is satisfied with a single engagement, however victorious. The letter continues:[4]

On one occasion, a tutor of the name of Fowler[1] was scraped in the hall. Now I was charged with being one of his assailants, *by himself,* and was arraigned before you all in conclave. You presided, and appealed to my honor to know whether I scraped or not. I told you the truth that I did not, for I disliked the manner of assailing a man *en masse.* You believed me, for we understood each other, and I was dismissed without even a reproof. You told me you believed me, and I was not a boy to deceive anyone who

[4] G. P. Fisher, Life of Benjamin Silliman, pp. 337–38.
[5] Bancroft Fowler, Professor of Sacred Literature at Bangor Theological Academy.

had that sort of confidence in me. This little court made a pleasant impression on me which I remember to this day.

Later, however, he faced another academic court and came from it with an impression which he tried to forget and succeeded in leaving as something of a mystery. The wonder is not so much that Cooper was asked to leave Yale in his Junior year, but rather that, with such a liberal attitude toward authority, he was permitted to stay so long. The explanation of both mysteries is solved in the personality of President Dwight.

The elder Timothy Dwight had been elected to the Presidency of Yale in 1795, and it was this Timothy Dwight who wrote, "The spirit of infidelity has the heart of a wolf, the fangs of a tiger, and the talons of a vulture. Blood is its proper nourishment; and it scents its prey with the nerves of a hound." But it was also this Timothy Dwight who remarked, "I would rather be sometimes cheated than not to trust in those around me." Under his direction Yale tripled its size of something over 100 students, added to its faculty, among others, Silliman, Day, and Kingsley, the three professors whom Cooper remembered with real affection, laid the foundations for separate schools of Medicine, Law, and Theology, and took the first steps from the status of a college to that of a university. Further, the ghostly head of infidelity, product of the French Revolution, was laid low by his sledgehammer blows. The power and consistency of this man shaped the Yale of a century following his death, and is felt in no little measure today. "The moral and religious atmosphere of the college was wholesome," writes the biographer of Noah Porter, an undergraduate of the

decade following Dwight's death.[6] "The spirit of the
instructors was reverent, the old Christian faith was held
with unshaken steadfastness, God was honored by daily
morning and evening prayers in the chapel and by two
services for preaching on Sundays." Services at six o'clock
on cold winter mornings and in the midst of games at
five in the afternoon furnished severe tests for academic
as well as theological discipline. The dogmatism of
Dwight, coming as it did on the heels of a period of
rationalism and doubt, was more powerful in the nineteenth century even than the traditional Calvinism of Harvard, because it had gone into dire battle with its two-
headed dragon foe and come forth completely victorious.
To these three years of discipline we may safely attribute
at least some of the roots of Cooper's religious convictions, as well as to the Quaker ancestry of his father and
the Church of England training of the Rev. Grant and
the Rev. Ellison.

Tradition has it that Cooper was a high-spirited youth
who was galled by all restraint and preferred walks in
the Connecticut hills to studious application in his room.
His presumed silhouette, now at Yale, reveals a profile
not to be lightly crossed, and his later writings show
both will and wilfulness. The curriculum or the religious
régime of the college would either one have provided
enough restraint to threaten trouble. The only surviving
letter from Cooper during his college days is further revealing of his character. It incloses a statement from one
John Mix, who, says Cooper, is impatient for his money
because he is about to go to New York. "If you have any,"

[6] W. W. Andrews, "Student at Yale," in G. S. Merriam, *Noah Porter*, p. 13.

he suggests to his father,[7] "and if it is agreeable to you to pay, you would I believe much oblige him. I have not a copper of money and am much in want of a little." Regulations adopted by the Corporation the autumn of the year of his dismissal tell the rest of the story:

Whenever the College Faculty shall be satisfied, that any student is guilty of frequent absence from prayers, public worship, or any college exercises, established by law; or of disorderly behavior when present at any of them, or in the dining hall; or of unreasonable expensiveness in living or company keeping in his rooms or elsewhere; or of idleness, or profane language, or profaning the Sabbath; or that he has gone out of College limits without leave; or has attended a dancing school, or dancing assemblies; or procured or received meals, or other entertainment, in any tavern, or boarding-house; or frequented such house or houses; or that he absents himself from his room after 10 o'clock at night; or is frequently absent from his room in study hours; or has been guilty of any loose conduct, or of disrespectful behavior to any officer of this college—He shall be admonished of his misbehavior by his Instructor, or any other member of the Faculty: and if he shall continue unreformed, his case shall be made known by his Instructor to his parent or guardians. If he continue still unreformed, he shall be sent home; and shall never be readmitted, except by a major vote of the Faculty.[8]

The popular rendering of this rule comes to us from one of Cooper's classmates. Having done away with petty pen-

[7] M.S. in possession of Miss Katherine L. Mather, of Cleveland, Ohio.
[8] MS. Yale Corporation Records, September 13, 1804, A. P. Stokes, *Memorials of Eminent Yale Men,* I, 137.

alties, the President of this "little monarchy" and his privy
council, the professors and tutors, "will admit almost anyone however bad into College as it were upon trial, and
then if we play any tricks which they don't like, instead
of inflicting any other kind of punishment, they excom-
municate us, or like the Quakers, spew us out of their
mouth." [9]

Whatever the circumstances, Cooper left Yale in this in-
elegant manner in the summer of 1806. Lounsbury tells us
that "a frolic in which he was engaged during his third
year was attended by consequences more serious than
disfavor. It led to dismissal." If, according to the college
ruling already quoted, we accept the "scraping" of Tutor
Fowler as a first offense, the fight with his classmate, John
Boyle, in May will serve as an excellent second. We are
told that Boyle, a native of Maryland, was "considered a
young man of considerable energy of mind, of much
political information, and strongly attached to Republican
principles." [10]

What happened to his opponent, Cooper, we do not
know, nor do we know the circumstances of the fight,
but the records tell us that Boyle stood bound for his
appearance at court in two sums, one $80, and the other
$200; that he was tried and dismissed from college; and
that the next year he was readmitted, and allowed to
graduate a year later with the class of 1807.

The family tradition holds that Cooper's dismissal was
caused by an explosion set off in a friend's room by pushing a rag containing powder through the keyhole. If this

[9] *Ibid.*, I, 137.
[10] MS. letter of J. H. Trumbull, May 1874, quoted by F. B. Dexter,
*Biographical Sketches of Yale College with Annals of the College
History*, VI, 96.

happened to have been on the Fourth, Cooper was not alone in wishing to celebrate his country's independence in spite of a strict college prohibition. His classmate, Daniel Mulford, quoted above, confesses that "about 20 of us however collected in Connor's room immediately after dinner, drank wine and sang songs till 3, when we were dispersed by one of the tutors." [11] The making of rules had once more failed as a means of restraining youth; but in spite of the efforts of his father, who came valiantly and vigorously to his defense, Cooper returned about this time to the wilderness lands without honors and with no settled ideas as to a career. His spirit, however, remained undulled.

[11] A. P. Stokes, *Memorials,* I, 141.

CHAPTER FIVE

Afloat

THE unexpected homecoming did not help to solve the problem of a career for the son of an American country gentleman. Running races around the square with a small child on one's shoulder will demonstrate manliness, physical prowess, fleetness of foot, and good sportsmanship, but it will not prepare one to earn a living. Walks to Mount Vision might store up images for unwritten stories, but at the time their practical value was not evident. So far, the only hint of a literary career had been a tale of "knights, and squires, and horses, and ladies, and castes and banners," a few chapters of which had been set up during a schoolboy vacation on the press of the *Otsego Herald*. European visitors to the Hall, from the great Talleyrand to the Scotch mason Jamie Allen, brought social theories and amusing anecdotes which were discussed and recounted many years later in such novels as *The Heidenmauer* and *Wyandotté,* but accidental education of this sort led to no immediate objective.

The navy was an obvious choice. "It will be remembered," Cooper wrote many years later, in his *History of the Navy,*

> that in the year 1807, America possessed the experience of three naval wars; that by the force of things, she had created a corps of officers, which, small as it was, had no superior, in any other country; that her artisans put on the

ocean as fine vessels of their class as floated, and that the
conviction of the necessity of an efficient marine, was deep
and general.

England was even then threatening war daily by her
constant impressment of American seamen, and it would
have seemed only logical for the young nation to bend
every effort toward naval supremacy; yet, continues
Cooper,

> the government was empowered to employ no more than
> 1,425 seamen, ordinary seamen and boys, in all the vessels
> of the navy, whether in commission or in ordinary. The
> administration felt that this number was insufficient for the
> common wants of the service, and early in 1808, the Secre-
> tary asked for authority to raise 1,272 additional men, to be
> put on board the gun-boats, that were now ready to re-
> ceive them. The necessary law, however, was withheld.

It was not until after January 1809, that the total was
raised to 5,025 men, with some 2,000 officers, midshipmen,
and members of the marine corps. By 1810 there were a
dozen cruisers and a number of gun-boats in the service.
A quarter of a century passed before there was any sort
of school for midshipmen in the nation, and the Naval
Academy at Annapolis was not founded until 1845. In
1806, there was an obvious career in the navy, but, for the
moment, no very obvious means of qualifying for it,
either by enlistment or by schooling. Judge Cooper did
as many fathers of wayward boys did in those days; he
articled his son to the captain of a merchantman. This
was in the autumn of 1806 and Cooper was a lad of seventeen.

Again we must turn to the reminiscences of later times

for the record of this year on the Atlantic and the Mediterranean. "Excuse the liberty I take in addressing you,"
wrote Edward R. Meyers on January 23, 1843, to James
Fenimore Cooper, Esq., author of *The Pilot, The Spy,* etc.,

> but being anxious to know whether you are the Mr. Cooper
> who in 1806 or 1807 was on board the ship *Sterling,* Cap.
> Johnson, bound from New York to London, if so whether
> you recollect the boy *Ned* whose life you saved in London
> dock, on a Sunday, if so it would give me a great deal of
> pleasure to see you, I am at present at the Sailors' Snug
> Harbor, or if you would send me your address in the city,
> I would call upon you.

The letter was answered and in the resulting visit to
Cooperstown an earlier Trader Horn dictated his story
to his old shipmate. It was a tale of risks and hardships,
and the worn-out adventurer, old before his time, wished
it recorded so that it might "have some effect in causing
this large and useful class of men to think on the subject
of their habits," to avoid drink and irreligion, and to pray
to God for mercy.

There was no other single year of Cooper's life which
went into more novels than that recalled by the visit of
Ned Myers. In middle life he toured London with a cul-
tured English friend and the quaint comments of his
earlier guide, a cockney custom house official, kept recur-
ring to his mind. And in the year before his death the
flavor of the Spanish grapes of Almeria, which he had
tasted in his youth, was still fresh in his memory.

"Tell about that day you first shipped with us," Myers
probably said, and the swift hand of the novelist covered
his great folio sheet of white paper:

The *Sterling* soon began to take in her cargo. She was to receive a freight of flour, for Cowes and a market. Not only was the hold filled, but the state-room and cabin, leaving barely room to climb over the barrels to reach the berths. A place was left, just inside of the cabin door for the table. Passengers were not common in that day, while commerce was pushed to the utmost. Our sails were bending when the consignee, followed by another merchant, came down to the ship, accompanied by a youth, who it was understood, wished also to be received in the vessel. This youth was named Cooper, and was never called by any other appellation in the ship. He was accepted by Capt. Johnson, signed the articles, and the next day he joined us, in sailor's rig. He never came to the cabin, but was immediately employed forward, in such service as he was able to perform. It was afterwards understood that he was destined for the navy.

Captain Johnson was a native of Wiscasset, Maine, but the crew was composed of Portuguese, Scottish, Canadian, Prussian, Danish, Spanish, and English, as well as American, sailors, and there was one passenger, the master of a wrecked English vessel. Yet the adventures of the young novelist were very different from the stern glimpses of a harsh world which Melville so pitifully recounts in Redburn's first voyage. A few stupid, greenhorn mistakes and the active and determined character of Cooper asserted itself. If Ned's story be accurate, there were few scrapes or adventures in which his shipmate was not conspicuous.

The first stop was at St. Helen's Roads, Cowes, Isle of Wight, where Captain Johnson received his order to proceed to London. Meanwhile, a British man-of-war's cutter came alongside and impressed an American sailor who was unfortunate enough not to have proofs of his nationality about him. A second sailor escaped because he could prove his case, only to be impressed a few days later in London. Even Captain Johnson himself, probing the secrets of Old London in a blue long-tog, drab-breeches, and top boots, was detained by the press gang until Cooper arrived with his desk and papers to prove his identity. And finally "Philadelphia" Bill, really a native of Falmouth, was forced to bid a tearful farewell, pack up his sea chest and do his part to hold Napoleon clear of British shores. If we wish to seek origins for Cooper's later belief in a large and powerful navy, of his jealousy of the British ownership of Bermuda, and of his deep-rooted antipathy toward everything English, from the English character to the Isle of Wight butter, we may safely start with these incidents.

We catch numerous glimpses of the young sailor on the voyage through Gibraltar and back to London: when Ned Myers fell overboard, his shipmate was after him in a flash; when a pirate felucca brought the *Sterling* to a halt off the coast of Portugal, Cooper was with the party in the jolly-boat prepared to surrender her papers when a squall and a frigate intervened to save the day; it was Cooper who on a dark night made one leap down the steps for the cabin lantern, thereby avoiding a crash with a two-decker in thick westerly weather off Cape Trafal-gar; and it was Cooper again who tried to persuade Ned to call on his godfather, the Duke of Kent, when the two young sailors were on shore leave, cruising around the West End of London.

Twice the *Sterling* was anchored in England's busiest

harbor, and Cooper lost no opportunity to avail himself
of her stores of sights and adventures. His visit to St.
Paul's gave the kindly lie to his scorn for antiquity. "Well
do I remember," he wrote later, "the impression it made
on me, when, an uninstructed boy, fresh from America,
I first stood beneath its arching dome. I actually experienced a sensation of dizziness, like that one feels in looking over a precipice."

Sometimes it was "Philadelphia" Bill, sometimes Dan
McCoy (who had once even been to Russia), sometimes
the old custom house official, and sometimes Ned himself
that Cooper took with him on "many a drift" about the
parks, palaces, and churches. Once he and his stalwart
Kennebunk Port companion, Stephen Simpson, were hesi-
tating at the gates of Green Park when a friendly citizen
approached them and said, "Go in, my lads, this is a
free country, and you have as much right there as the
King." One wonders whether it was actually the blunt
Stephen at the time, or the critical commentator writing
thirty years later, who remarked dryly, "What queer
notions these people have of liberty. They think it a great
matter to be able to walk in a field," and the occasion is
sufficient illustration for even the boy's mind of the contrast between English and American theories of popular
sovereignty.

The first perception I had [concludes Cooper] of the
broad distinction that exists between political *franchises*
and political *liberty,* dates from that moment. Young as
I was then, I knew enough about royal *appanages,* and the
uses of royal parks, to understand that the public enter them
as a favor, and not as a right; but had it been otherwise,
it would have left ground for reflection on the essential

difference in principle, that exists between a state of things
in which the community receive certain privileges as concessions, and that in which power itself is merely a temporary trust, delegated directly and expressly by the body
of the people.

A youthful and irresponsible sailor in quest of adventure
would have been content to leave this incident in its immediate and circumstantial aspects only; the social critic
probed deeper to the principles of human liberty which
underlay the event.

Almost two months of stormy seas brought the *Sterling*
once more into the familiar waters of New York harbor,
and on the 18th of September Cooper once more stepped
ashore. But the taste of the sea which this experience had
brought already had created a life-long love which was
to rival even the love of his native forests. We can imagine
him, a tanned, healthy young American, being welcomed
in his home village, strutting about the streets, telling of
his adventures in the evenings at the *Red Lion,* rousing
the envy of the less fortunate boys who must stay at home.
But early in the new year he was off again, down the
river to New York, to take his oath as midshipman and
prepare himself for the inevitable war with England
which was to decide the supremacy of the sea, at least in
so far as American waters and American rights were concerned. "I take the earliest opportunity of returning the
oath as you have directed," he wrote to the Secretary of
the Navy on February 20, 1808.[1] "I shall remain in New
York until I receive your order." His commission, signed
by Jefferson, was dated January 1, but the first definite as-

[1] This unpublished letter and others to the Secretary of the Navy,
here quoted, are in the Navy Department in Washington.

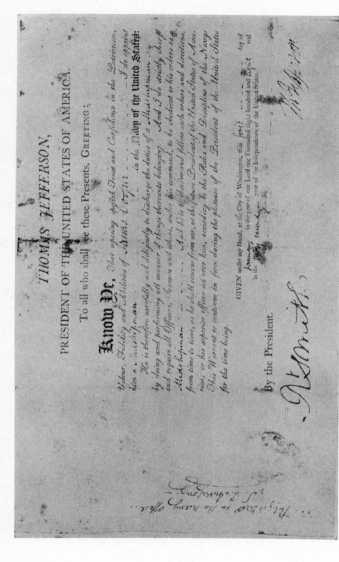

Courtesy of The Stirling Memorial Library, Yale University.

COOPER'S WARRANT AS MIDSHIPMAN, SIGNED BY JEFFERSON

signment of which there is record sent him back to his forests in July. Obviously, if a war was to be fought with Great Britain, some part of it would center about Niagara and along the Canadian border. By way of preparation, the Navy Department ordered three ships, suitable for inland waters, to be built, two on Champlain, and one on Ontario, under the direction of Lieutenant Melancthon T. Wolsey, an officer only seven years Cooper's senior and quite his equal in good spirits and desire for adventure.

The small detachment of which Cooper thus became a part, established its headquarters late in 1808 at Oswego on Lake Ontario, a village of some twenty rude houses along the lake shore on the edge of a thirty mile wilderness. The *Oneida,* a vessel of about two hundred and forty tons measurement, pierced for sixteen guns, the only real brig of war of the three, was laid down immediately and was ready for service the following spring. Five American officers and, as Cooper himself tells us, a strong gang of ship carpenters, riggers, blacksmiths, and other workers created a great commotion in the inland port. For the first time actual money took the place of barrels of salt as the standard medium of exchange when Lieutenant Wolsey set up housekeeping, and the "mess" became the social as well as the commercial center of life for the traders, boatmen, smugglers, and mechanics who composed the more permanent element in the population.

During the dreary winter days which followed, Cooper and his companions more than once amused themselves by crawling out on the roof of the adjoining house and dropping snowballs down the chimney to cool the village doctor's pot of soup. Later, when a small detachment of the old Sixth Infantry under the command of Lieutenant Christie swelled the official family by taking up headquarters in the old fort, the doctor was invited to meet the newcomers and was introduced by Cooper to Ensign Gardner.

"By the way, Galen," said the young gentleman fresh from the classical environment of Yale, "let me make you acquainted with our neighbor, Hippocrates." The doctor advanced and held out his hand, not at all abashed by the amused smile of the educated gentlemen present. "Don't mind what Cooper says, Mr. Galen," he explained. "He is always up to some foolery or other."

Cranberries were the staple commodity of the mess, but salmon, bass, venison, rabbits, squirrels, wild geese, and ducks graced the table of that "notable caterer" and the excellent conversationalist, Lieutenant Wolsey. By Christmas the old bar, for the house had once been a tavern, was a well stocked larder.

Once an official ball was arranged and the surrounding country was scoured for ladies to form the grand march, who were brought in by boat and cart. Social precedence was immediately established, and those with both shoes and stockings led the Virginia reel while those without either took part in the country dance. On another occasion it was reported to the mess that a stranger had arrived and departed after a careful examination of the new brig. It later developed that this gentleman was a member of the British Provincial Navy on a scouting expedition to determine how large a vessel should be laid down on the other side of the lake.

In this way the winter passed. Cooper wrote to his elder brother Richard that he expected—one might almost say "hoped"—to share service with the British during the following summer, but by April he became impatient. "I have taken the liberty," he wrote to the Secretary of the Navy,

> of addressing you, to request (if that request should not be improper) a removal from this station to one of actual service. This importance of such a removal to *myself,* as affording an opportunity of acquiring experience; and a desire of improving in my profession, will, I hope, be a sufficient apology for troubling the Department with this request. Should there be any prospect of such an opportunity's offering on this station, it would afford me pleasure to remain with Lieut. Wolsey, my present respected and esteem'd Commander.

The request was not granted, but when Wolsey went to Lake Champlain early in June to lay up the gun-boats there built, he left Cooper in command of the Oswego port; and after his return, the two set out with a small party on an expedition to Niagara. The midshipman's restlessness was allayed until September.

The Niagara trip was one of the most enjoyable of Cooper's early experiences—one never to be forgotten, and to be recalled almost a quarter of a century later as background for the love story of Leather-Stocking, *The Pathfinder,* certainly one of the best tales of the series, especially in its forest descriptions.

Cooper himself gives a full account of the journey in his life of Wolsey: Four days out provisions failed and the launch was pulled up to a beach where it was easy to land. The party was about to bivouac supperless when Cooper came upon a hedgehog which he killed with the sword of a cane. This piece of luck provided the supper, and in the morning a forage was undertaken. When after an hour the hungry men came upon a log hut and found two loaves of bread, some milk, and the proverbial pie, but no owner present, tramp instincts asserted themselves to be balanced by the gentlemanly act of leaving behind two silver dollars to pay for the feast. Cooper also tells of an amusing argument with a transplanted London Cockney, one of whose precious sheep was bargained away from him while the diplomatic Wolsey silenced the protests of his wife by waxing ecstatic over the lady's fine children, "three as foul little Christians as one could find on the frontier."

On the Fourth of July, fittingly enough, the little launch entered the Niagara River and proceeded to Newark, bearing the American ensign for the first time on a man-of-war's boat into these waters. A deputation from Fort Niagara greeted the party and some days were spent in inspecting the region. The return journey to Oswego was made in two days, but the rumor of war had been silenced and the commissioning of the *Oneida* was indefinitely postponed.

These were interesting adventures, but they did not satisfy the restless Cooper. The Indians with which he peopled the country in *The Pathfinder* are not mentioned in the actual record. Killing hedgehogs was not sufficient sport to prevent his writing again to the Secretary of the Navy on September 13, when the prospect of a second wilderness winter loomed. "I have the honor of addressing you," he wrote, "to request a furlough for the purpose of making a European voyage. I trust, Sir, you will more readily excuse this liberty, when I inform you, that I have never been attached to any vessel in commission since I have had the honor of belonging to the Service."

This furlough was granted, but the young midshipman's plans were altered as soon as he reached New York. On November 8, he again addressed his superior from that city. "The difficulty of procuring a berth on any ship bound for Europe," he explains, "as well as the advice of several officers of rank in the navy, have induced me to relinquish the idea. Capt. Lawrence of the *Wasp* has been so obliging as to inform me that he would receive me on board his ship. I therefore take the liberty to request that I may be attached to that vessel." An indorsement on this letter tells us that Midshipman Mountain of the *Wasp* had, two days before, requested a furlough for the merchant service. Cooper's positive reasons for his request are more convincing than his negative, and he was allowed to spend the final year of his naval service under the command of Lawrence.

The *Wasp* was a sloop of eighteen guns, one of the smaller vessels in the regular service; but she contributed her share of captures in the American victories of 1812–14, only to disappear finally in foreign waters and never again be heard of. During Cooper's winter of service on her, however, there is no record of any event to relieve his tedium. One circumstance of value to him, however, it is necessary to note—his friendship for the Shubricks. William Shubrick became his most loyal messmate in the service, as the dedications of *The Pilot* and *The Red Rover,* as well as much later correspondence, will testify.

On one brief furlough home, the young naval officer appeared in full uniform, with a *queue* after the fashion of Napoleon and Nelson. He was the talk of the village, and apparently not the pride of the family, for he was soon persuaded to cut it off. Uncle Isaac, however, rescued his pig-tail and that evening when Coopers of every connection sat down to a family dinner of the grand old style, the *queue* was hanging from a chandelier over the table.

Two letters of May 1810 complete the story of Cooper's naval experience, the one official and the other to his brother. The first is dated from the *Wasp* on May 3. "Owing to the recent death of my father and the consequent necessity of my attending, immediately, to my private affairs," he explained to Secretary Hamilton,

> I must take the liberty of asking the indulgence of a furlough for a year—attached to the service. I have thought it better to make this request in preference to an entire resignation of my warrant, of which I otherwise would be compelled to desire your acceptance should you think it proper, Sir, to grant this indulgence. I should consider myself bound to pay that much attention to my profession, as would not leave me destitute of what little nautical knowledge I may have already attained.

The furlough was granted on May 9; but a year later, May 6, 1811, Cooper resigned from the service. The nature of the urgent private affairs to which he felt impelled to devote his undivided attention are described somewhat more confidentially to his brother a week after his furlough had been granted. "I have bowed," he confesses, "to the influence of the charms of a fair damsel of eighteen."

CHAPTER SIX

Ashore

SUSAN AUGUSTA DeLANCEY is said to have sat for the portrait of Lucy Hardinge in *Afloat and Ashore*. "She was all woman," we may believe,

there being nothing about *her* to create any miraculous expectations or fanciful pictures; but she was fast getting to be a very lovely woman. Honest, sincere, full of heart, overflowing with the feelings of her sex, gentle, yet spirited, buoyant though melting with the charities; her changeful, but natural, and yet constant feelings in her, kept me incessantly in pursuit of her playful mind and varying humors.

"I loved her like a man and told her of it like a sailor," Cooper continues in his letter to his brother Richard.

As you are coolly to decide, I will as coolly give you the qualities of my mistress; Susan DeLancey is the daughter of a man of very respectable connections and a handsome fortune—amiable, sweet tempered, and happy in her disposition. She has been educated in the country, occasionally trying the temperature of the city to rub off the rust— but hold a moment. Like a true Quixotic lover, I made proposals to her father. He has answered them in the most gentlemanly manner—You have my consent to address my daughter if you will gain the approbation of your mother.

He also informs me that his daughter has an estate in the
County of Westchester in reversion, secured to her by a
deed in trust to him, and depending upon the life of an
aunt, *Aetat.* 72—so you see, Squire, the old woman can't
weather it long. I write all this for *you*—you know I am indifferent to anything of this nature.

Nevertheless, Cooper was human enough to be glad
that his dream had substance, and he was willing to conform to a social code which, in the interest of delicacy,
forbade his visits until Squire Richard, now head of the
house of Cooper, should "take pen and write to Mr.
DeLancey stating the *happiness* and *pleasure* it will give
all the family to have this connection completed."

The wedding took place on New Year's day, 1811, in
the drawing room of Heathcote Hill, the old DeLancey
mansion on a sloping lawn overlooking Long Island
Sound at Mamaroneck, about twenty-five miles from the
town of New York. The white shingled magnificence of
this old colonial house has been sadly insulted in these
later and more commercial times by a move down to the
side of the Boston Post Road and conversion into a gaso-
line service station; but Susan Cooper has left us a charming picture of its earlier nobility. Giant peach trees shaded
its covered porches and a row of locusts screened the
road at the foot of the hill. Cherry trees, apricots, and
willows broke the smooth green of the lawn. To the
south one could see many sails carrying their cargoes in
and out of the busy harbor of New York, and in the rear
the hillside sloped down to the red gate and the road to
the village of Mamaroneck, close at hand. A cluster of
lilac bushes, the garden, and the barns were but a step

from the door, the rolling hills of Westchester County farm lands with their tenant cottages and well-marked fields in the distance. The "Neck" too—now a cluster of fine old houses—was then a part of the DeLancey farm. The son of William Cooper was linking his name with that of a family worthy of the father's social ambitions.

The wedding was a simple one. As the furlough of the young midshipman did not expire until the sixth of the following May, it is possible that he was still in the naval uniform. Only William, of the Cooper brothers, was present, as well as the family of the bride. The Rev. Mr. Asgill read the Church of England service with a nasal drawl. "Wilt thou—hum—ha—have—hum—ha—hum— this woman to thy wedded—hum—ha—wife?" The jolly black Mammie—then probably still enjoying the idyllic security of slavery—bustled about the kitchen preparing the wedding supper, her daughter Harriet eavesdropped at the hall doorway, and her son Henry busied himself grooming the spirited horses always to be found in the DeLancey stables. Colored children romped on the lawn at the rear of the house. After the ceremony, Cooper and his bride played chess until supper. If the scene had been laid in Virginia, it could scarcely have had more of the plantation atmosphere about it. Westchester County was at this time still perhaps the most aristocratic bit of American soil. The DeLanceys inherited Huguenot blood, the Dutch patroon system of land tenure, an American Tory political philosophy, and the property of the Heathcotes with whom they had intermarried. William Cooper had bought land in large tracts and sold it in small; the DeLanceys had inherited land in large tracts and rented it in small. To both land was the measure of wealth and of worth, and both families had much of it.

It is a pity to interrupt a romance by discussion of such sordid realities as property, inheritance, and social doctrines. But his marriage was more than a romance to Cooper—more even than an acquirement of a certain added share of this world's goods along with a devoted and charming wife. Susan DeLancey's influence undoubtedly augmented his natural tendencies toward social conservatism, even though his political convictions remained undisturbed. He had married a social system similar to that which his father had sought to establish in the wilderness, but far more deeply rooted in the soil and more nearly feudal in structure. For the fifteen years during which he brought to the world a family of four daughters and two children who died in infancy, we find him, gentleman farmer and prominent citizen of the metropolis, treading a triangular path between Cooperstown, Mamaroneck, and New York City.

With the Tory strain in his wife's family, Cooper never admitted any sympathy, and for their pro-British survivals in the New York society of the day, he had the utmost scorn. "They still admired, as the provincial can only admire," he writes in *Afloat and Ashore,* "and they worshipped, as the provincial worships; or at a safe distance. The strange medley of truth, cant, selfishness, sophistry, and good faith, that founded the political hostility to the movements of the French Revolution, had as ardent believers in this country as it had in England itself."

But the Tory tradition in the DeLancey family was no such groveling political and social subservience as this.

Susan DeLancey's Uncle James, and his father of the same name, had led the party of the King for almost a century in New York. The elder James had been Lieutenant Governor of the Colony until his death in 1760 and had married the eldest daughter and co-heiress of Colonel Caleb Heathcote, lord of the manor of Scarsdale and owner of the original mansion on Heathcote Hill. He sent his eldest son to Harrow for his schooling, and at Greenwich the boy prepared himself for His Majesty's Colonials. Before the war he led the Church of England "DeLancey Party" in city politics, against the Presbyterian or "Livingston" party. The Livingstons represented the tradesmen, shipwrights, small farmers, and artisans; the DeLanceys, the merchant, crown officers, and men of professional life. The distinction was religious, social, and economic as well as political. The younger DeLancey pledged his following to the King and to the Church of England.

His younger brother, John Peter DeLancey, Cooper's father-in-law, was a captain in the Royal Irish Regiment and Major of the Pennsylvania Loyalists. After the war he went to England, where he was married in 1785. Four years later he returned to America and settled on the Heathcote estates at Mamaroneck, which he had inherited from his mother. The new frame house was erected on the foundations of the old brick manor house of his maternal grandfather. His wife was as aristocratic as himself. She was the daughter of Colonel Richard Floyd, member of an old Suffolk County, Long Island, family. His sons were trained for the law and the Church, his daughters for marriage.

Although the DeLancey lands were confiscated by the

young republic, the maternal estate remained in the
family. An original deed, dated 10 June 1701, records the
sale by Patthunck, Brope, and Wepetuck, Indian proprietors, to Colonel Caleb Heathcote and others, of a tract of
land on Mamaroneck River.[1]

This tract included the whole of the present town of
Scarsdale, for which Colonel Heathcote immediately obtained letters patent from the British crown, securing to
him that territory, and constituting the "lordship" or
manor of Scarsdale.[2] It was a part of this land which
Cooper inherited through his wife. He thus became, by
adoption, a somewhat modified patroon.

The connection of the English with the Dutch system
of land tenure in New York was chiefly one of imitation.
The varying social systems in the American colonies were
shaped largely by the accident of primitive conditions
coupled with social theories imported from Europe. Theo-
cratic Massachusetts reflected the parliamentary oligarchy
of Cromwell, aristocratic Virginia, the modified feudalism of the English Stuarts, Pennsylvania and Rhode
Island, various shades of separatist middle-class English
democracy. New York was founded on the more rigid
feudalism of the Dutch patroon and the English manorial systems. When it was taken over by the English the
Dutch patroonships were preserved and erected into English manors in the Hudson Valley and along the Sound.
The grantee established his manor farms like a thirteenth
century English baron. Both religious and social convictions, therefore, underlay Cooper's life-long antipathy for
all things of New England, but particularly for those of

[1] R. Bolton, *A History of the County of Westchester*, I, 475–76.
[2] C. W. Baird, *History of Rye, Westchester County, N. Y.*, p. 155.

Connecticut. The same background will explain his respect for the Dutch, particularly in his later novels.

The most famous of the Dutch patroons was the lord of the manor of Rensselaerwyck. The holdings of the Van Rensselaers included all of the territory about Albany, although the greater part of them were on the eastern bank of the Hudson. Founded on a practically unrestricted grant from the West India Company, this manor, as well as those of the Cortlands and the Livingstons, were each entitled to representatives in the Assembly. Besides these which enjoyed political privileges, there was the almost equally powerful and extensive Phillipse Manor, and families principally of Dutch origin like the Schuylers and Cuylers owned or rented great tracts of land which they leased out to small farmers. The lords of these manors held a position more akin to that of the old world nobility than anyone else in the American colonies. They had the power to hold courts, civil and criminal, and to fortify their holdings. Constituting one of the strongest strands in American Federalism, they were almost the last vested interests to give way in the early nineteenth century before the rising tide of Jacksonian Democracy.

The elements of a strong sense of social structure had been embedded in the mind of Fenimore Cooper by his father's activities and his own early training. His wife's social position and promise of inherited property removed the necessity of his searching for a trade or profession upon which to build his career. During the first decade of his married life, therefore, the personal problem which demanded his most absorbed attention was the stabilizing of his own and his family's position in a social structure fraught with conflicts and inconsistencies, and founded upon sharply contradictory traditions and theories. No longer was the navy or the law of importance to his future. Whatever particular kind of a gentleman he might be, one fact was established: he would be an American gentleman.

In the year 1811, Cooper could not have defined the essential requisites and characteristics of an American gentleman: in the year 1838 he published a small text book on the subject. The intervening years were spent in discovering and defining that social portrait.

The one point upon which he never seems to have had any doubt was the identity of wealth and land. There were for him, therefore, two clearly marked alternatives: either he must establish his family at Cooperstown where he might take a tract of land and build his manor adjoining that of Otsego Hall, or he might build upon the Heathcote foundations and take a tract of pleasant farm country in Westchester County. He tried both. Fenimore Farm on the western shore at the lower end of Otsego Lake was the first experiment; Angevine Farm in Scarsdale was the second; his residence in New York City and his trip abroad provided an extended interlude during which his political ideals shaped themselves to his social convictions; his final residence in the remodeled Otsego Hall was the consummation of his plans and hopes. But social America had meanwhile developed on an exactly contrary pattern.

For a time the bride and groom were absorbed into the DeLancey family at Heathcote Hill. A brief experiment at home building was made at Mamaroneck in "Closet Hall," a small cottage up the hill of the Boston road on the further side of the town. There the first child, a daughter who died in infancy, was born. But the experiment in housekeeping was evidently not a success, for the return was soon made to the paternal roof.

The first move toward Cooperstown was the construction of a small frame house on Fenimore Farm, a temporary residence while the stone manor house was being built. Here the recollections of Susan Cooper begin.

I used very often to trot along between my Father and Mother about the grounds; and I remember distinctly going with them to the new stone house, then building. In that house they expected to pass their lives. But in fact it was never inhabited. Your grandfather [she was writing for her nephews and nieces] one day chose an even stone to be placed in the wall, and carved on it his own name and that of your grandmother, with the date—1816. The position of that house was charming, on a rising knoll, commanding a lovely view of the lake and village. . . . The garden at Fenimore was then placed in the meadow just beyond the road leading to the barn at the farmhouse. I remember walking there with your grandfather, who was always fond of gardening.

The nurse Nanny, an old English family servant, had been brought from Heathcote Hill, together with her stout young daughter who was to do the cooking, and Fred, a slave who had been given to Susan DeLancey by her father, but to whom Cooper paid wages. Sam Brimmer, the coachman, was the son of a Hessian soldier. His task was to care for the two gray family horses and the carriage of which the upper deck had been removed and which was therefore dubbed the *rasée* by the former midshipman.

Cooper lost no time in laying the foundations, not only of his new house, but of his new life as a gentleman farmer. He became Secretary of the County Agricultural Society, a vestryman of the local Episcopal church, and Secretary of the County Bible Society. The hill behind the house was assigned to some fine Merino sheep which he imported from Europe. Mrs. Cooper began the education of the girls by sitting them on little stools at her feet to spell from their primer and to sew on their samplers. Later the pupils donned aprons—or *pinafores,* as Nanny insisted upon calling them—and adjourned to the pantry. The second daughter, Caroline Martha, had been born soon after the move to Fenimore, and the third, Ann Charlotte, not long after. With her husband, Mrs. Cooper often rode as far as the top of Mt. Vision on horseback or went boating on the lake. Family lake parties were frequent at the Three Mile Point—later the subject of much controversy—and there was still good hunting for bear, deer, and wolf in the hills. In his idle time, Cooper learned to play the flute, and in winter there was skating and sleighing on the ice. The life within the family and between the various Cooper households in the vicinity was happy and industrious. Living was an art worthy of cultivation.

But at last the day arrived, in the spring of 1817, when the move back to Mamaroneck had become a certainty. The reasons for this change of plan are somewhat cloudy, but at the time it seemed only temporary. When the little girls went over to Otsego Hall to say good-bye to their grandmother, they found her sitting by her little table in the great hall with the "Governor," the old negro butler, at the door. The old Judge had been dead these half dozen years or more, and her eldest son was also gone. All of her other children had either died or left her. She herself lived only until the following December.

Before leaving, Cooper took his daughter's hand and led her through the Fenimore lands, across the brook, to the enclosure where her older sister Elizabeth had been buried, a few years before. Then the whole party embarked in the *rasée* for the long climb up the Vision road, pausing at the top to gather a huge bunch of the wild roses of Otsego. Seventeen years passed before they returned once more to Cooperstown.

The summer passed with the DeLancey brothers on the farm, but when fall came, the inducements for a permanent settlement at Westchester obviously became too strong. The land at Scarsdale had always been allocated to Susan DeLancey, and her husband's desire to settle permanently in his own country were overcome. He determined to abandon the Fenimore Farm project and to build at Angevine, a name adopted from the family of Huguenot tenants who had worked it previously. Once more on a hill overlooking distant water, the site was one which invariably appealed to Cooper. Of his temporary homes in Europe, all but those in a city's heart were of this description. There was a great house-warming at Angevine that winter, and a few years later the new stone house at Fenimore was burned to the ground.

The Westchester County Agricultural Society now claimed his loyalty, but it was necessary to drive to Rye or to New Rochelle in order to worship in an Episcopal church. On one of these drives, the favorite horse "Bullhead" stumbled on the hill going down from the farmhouse and the children were thrown out of the gig. A

pair of black horses had supplanted the grays for the
rasée, and "Bull-head" was sold. The family had grown
so large that an assistant nurse was employed, but Fred
the slave boy deserted.

Cooper's life, therefore, at Angevine was not unlike
that at Fenimore, except perhaps for the greater degree
of conventionality demanded by the more cultivated society in which the family now moved. Governor Clinton,
Susan tells us, made her father his aide-de-camp about
this time with the rank of Colonel, and he made a handsome picture in full blue and buff uniform, cocked hat
and sword, mounted on Bull-head and setting forth for a
military review. On July 20, 1819, he was appointed
Quartermaster of the Fourth Division of Infantry of
New York State, and on September 10, he was made pay-
master.

But his most ambitious undertaking at this time, in
addition to the management of his farm, was the purchase of a two-thirds interest in a whaling vessel, the
Union, in partnership with Charles T. Dering of Shelter
Island, who had married Mrs. Cooper's cousin, Eliza
Floyd Nicoll. Although the venture was primarily commercial, Cooper himself often sailed in his vessel on short
passages and spent much time at Sag Harbor when she
was in port. It is said that he was the first to originate, at
least in the vicinity, the plan of purchasing a whaling
vessel by forming a small stock company, and he, as the
largest shareholder, took charge, on behalf of the others,
of equipping and manning the boat, as well as of market-
ing the oil when the whaler returned from a voyage.

During the three years in which he was concerned in
the venture, he frequently stayed at the tavern of Peletiah

Fordham,[3] otherwise known as "Duke Fordham," at the foot of Main Street, Sag Harbor. Captain Jonathan Osborne, of Wainscott, was placed in command, and the vessel had already returned from her first voyage before the end of the summer of 1819. Cooper took charge of refitting her, and the following July she was again in port with a cargo of 900 barrels of oil after capturing twelve whales, which was not considered an especially good showing. There is no further evidence of Cooper's association with her, although she made two successful voyages under the command of Captain Osborne to the coast of Patagonia in 1821 and 1822, and there is a record in the Sag Harbor Custom House of her return from a whaling voyage on June 16, 1827. Her captain, and presumably her ownership, had meanwhile changed.

The experience gained by this venture furnished Cooper with the background for *The Sea Lions,* which was not written until many years later. He gives in this novel a vivid description of the isolated harbor town with its pride of place and its community of interest in the great adventures of pursuing the whale and the seal. "Thither the youths of the whole region resorted for employment," he writes, "and to advance their fortunes, and generally with such success as is apt to attend enterprise, industry, and daring, when exercised with energy in a pursuit of moderate gains. None became rich, in the strict significance of the term, although a few got to be in reasonably affluent circumstances."

Doubtless the lack of profit in the venture influenced Cooper in his abandonment of it; but there was at least one other cause. He had discovered a new outlet for his

[3] A. Mulford, *Sketch of Sage,* pp. 28–36.

energies and his imagination. During his spare time at
Angevine and Sag Harbor he had been amusing himself
by writing his first novel, *Precaution*.

The phenomenon of a young American gentleman
suddenly turning to authorship after thirty years of dis-
like even of letter writing was sufficient to cause a ripple
on the none too placid cultural waters of the young nation. Washington Irving, author of Knickerbocker's burlesque *History of New York*, had been producing his
Sketch Book in parts during the preceding year, but
Bryant's first volume of poems did not appear until 1821,
and as yet America had boasted but one professional
novelist, Charles Brockden Brown of Philadelphia. Maga-
zines willing to publish literary efforts were few, and
even these subsisted largely on an imported diet. The total
lack of any American copyright protection for English
authors made it practically impossible for native writers
to reach their own public because imported books could
be published in America at a price so low as to make the
payment of royalties to native authors impracticable. As
long as the book stores were flooded with cheap American reprints of Scott, Campbell, Maria Edgeworth, and
Byron while the British ink in the volumes of these popular authors was still wet, there was little chance that the
American publishers would subsidize native genius or that
the American public would pay a double price for its
novels and its poetry in order to encourage home talent.
The hue and cry after a national literature had already set
in, but the demands of patriotism and the demands upon
the individual purse made an orator practice less than he
was all too eager to preach.

Cooper's venture into literature, however, had no commercial intent. The story of his self-imposed challenge to improve upon an English novel which he was reading to his wife has been told and retold. The similarity of his experiment to Jane Austen's *Pride and Prejudice* has led some to believe that this was the book which he laid down with the remark, "I could write you a better book than that myself," but there is only the similarity of the stories to support the supposition. As the world was full of lady novelists at the time, this is not conclusive evidence. Susan Cooper suggests that it might have been one of Amelia Opie's "or one of that school," whereas Anna Mulford, who relies upon the local tradition of Sag Harbor rather than upon internal evidence,[4] asserts definitely that the novel was *Discipline,* a very popular work by Mrs. Mary Balfour Brunton, published in 1814.

Mrs. Cooper laughed heartily at the idea, but after the first few pages had been written, she encouraged him to finish and even to print it. The scene was laid in an English village as a matter of course, even though the author's experience was limited to his few short walks about the streets of London in 1806. The style, too, was closely imitative of his model.

The work successfully passed its first test when Susan, hidden under the writing table during the reading, burst into tears. The second test was a reading to the venerable John Jay and his family at Bedford. "Father, Mother, Susie, and *Precaution*" set out in the gig and the event took place in the parlor. The authorship was not disclosed and a friend of the Jays who was present asserted that she was sure she had read it somewhere before. This was indeed assuring. Finally, Charles Wilkes, one of Cooper's

[4] A. Mulford, *Sketch of Sage,* p. 30.

most intimate friends in New York, was consulted and, on his advice, the book was put to press. A bad manuscript and inexperienced proof-reading led to an almost unreadable text, and the author later apologized to his public both for the imperfection of his tale and for its careless dress. "More than this the public will feel no interest in knowing," he wrote later, "and less than this the author could not consent to say on presenting to the world a reprint of a book with so few claims to notice." The new edition was but a slight improvement over the first, and commentators upon Cooper, from Bryant to the present time, have striven to avoid a judgment upon the quality of the work. Seldom has there been a less promising first novel.

It served its main purpose, however, in proving to Cooper that he could write a book and enjoy doing it. With his usual energy, he set to work almost immediately upon *The Spy*, which appeared the following year. Every chapter was read to Mrs. Cooper and every detail of plot and character was discussed with her as the work advanced. Susan tells us that this was his practice during the entire thirty years of his literary life.

The idea for the new novel was furnished by Governor Jay who told Cooper an anecdote about a spy in the "neutral ground" during the Revolution. Even in his own day, efforts were made to identify Harvey Birch, but as Cooper himself apparently did not know the name of the original upon whom he had patterned his hero, such efforts would seem to hint of misdirected energy. If Enoch Crosby were proved conclusively to have been the man in Jay's mind when he told the story, the identification might add something to the fame of that worthy adventurer, but it would have little bearing upon the literary method or ability of the author. It was Enoch Crosby and the promoters of the dramatic version of the story rather than Cooper or his friends who were eager to prove the identity. The significant fact about the novel, however, is that in it Cooper first turned to his native soil for material and never again for long interrupted his analysis of America and her problems.

CHAPTER SEVEN

Bread and Cheese

BOTH business and social attractions frequently drew Cooper from his Scarsdale farm to the metropolis. Often he walked the twenty-five miles into town and came home exhausted. Usually he would go by stage or in his own gig and occasionally he would take ship through the narrows and Hell Gate, landing on the lower East River. But in 1822 he decided that his daughters would have better schooling and he could supervise the publication of his books more advantageously if the whole family became city dwellers. A new house on Broadway above Prince Street was rented and the move was made. Susan tells us that she and her sister Cally were sent next door to a boarding school where she wore a pig's foot about her neck when she was disobedient and where she was assigned, much to her father's disgust, a theme on the differences between the characters of Franklin and Washington.

New York in the early twenties was already outgrowing its provinciality and finding its place as the commercial capital of the nation. A day's journey by steamboat and stage would bring the traveler from Albany or Philadelphia to the docks near the Battery. The harbor was filled with the ships of all nations, unloading goods for the wholesale markets and merchandizing establishments in the neighborhood of Pearl Street. The town boasted ten daily public journals, nine theatres, ten public schools, and innumerable churches of all denominations. There were two medical schools, and Columbia College occupied an entire block on Church Street between Barclay and Murray, near Broadway. The older residential district extended from Broadway to the Harbor with its brick and stone front houses. The more thickly settled part of the city was below Bleecker and First Streets, but blocks were laid in checkerboard fashion as far as Fourteenth, and already the enterprise of John Jacob Astor and others had lined Broadway and the Bowery with fine new residences as far as the boundary.

The City Hotel, at the corner of Wall Street and Broadway, was one of the favorite gathering places of the town. There one might dine with the intellectual and aristocratic citizen as well as with the sailor, the salesman, or the visitor. Just around the corner on New Street was the book-store of Charles Wiley, which, like Murray's in London, was a rendezvous for the writers as well as the purchasers of books. At Washington Hotel, or Hall, one might attend great dinners, public meetings, or balls in honor of distinguished foreign guests; at the Park or Lafayette Theatres one might see Kean, Matthews, or Macready as Lear or Shylock; at the New York Institution by the City Hall one might attend meetings of the Literary and Philosophical Society, the American Academy of the Fine Arts, or the Lyceum of Natural History. In 1820 there were 20,000 houses in the city and a population of over 100,000 whites and 10,000 blacks. It was a city to hold the foreign visitor for more than the day of his arrival in the new land.

To Cooper, New York City was something more than

a mere port of call. He was, said George Bancroft in 1851,[1] "emphatically a son of New York, born in your vicinity, educated almost in your midst, receiving his inspiration among you, pursuing his career among you, trusting to you for that blame and that praise, without which there is no literary success. His career belongs emphatically and peculiarly to New York." And Cooper, in a moment of intense patriotism and civic pride, wrote, "It is only necessary to sit down with a minute map of the country before you to perceive at a glance, that Nature herself has intended the island of Manhattan for the site of one of the greatest commercial towns of the world." Like his father before him he saw clearly that the vast unexplored resources of the nation, the commercial disposition of the people, the absence of serious rivals, and the natural superiority of the harbor dictated its destiny. He had been brought up to a knowledge of the land which looked to New York as its commercial capital; and there was hardly an inch of its water which he had not sailed. Few men know their city as Cooper knew his. When, in *The Water Witch,* he carried his readers back more than a century, he warned them that by "the Manhattanese who is familiar with the forest of masts, the miles of wharves, the countless villas, the hundred churches, the castles, the smoking and busy vessels that crowd his bay, the daily increase and the general movement of his native town, the picture we are about to sketch will scarcely be recognized." To him it was sufficient that the New Amsterdam of this continent already rivaled its parent of the other. The future would rank her on a level with the proudest capitals of Europe.

[1] *Memorial,* p. 74.

He already had many friends in the city, principal among whom were Charles Wilkes and Charles Wiley, with both of whom he had business dealings as well. There was a small room in the back part of Wiley's bookstore which Cooper christened "The Den." [2] Wiley, with good business sense, had the name written up over the door, and the comfortable good companionship of the impromptu club drew such men as Fitz-Greene Halleck, then the first of American poets, Morse and Dunlap, the artists, Irving's friend Henry Brevoort, and many other congenial souls. Even in this early glimpse we find Cooper dominating the group with his strong personality and fine talk. At dinner at the home of Robert Sedgwick a year or so later, Bryant tells us that he met him, together with Halleck, Sands, and some other literary gentlemen. "Mr. Cooper," he says,[3] "engrossed the whole conversation, and seems a little giddy with the great success his works have met with."

Bryant's feelings toward Cooper were always somewhat mixed. "I saw Cooper yesterday," he wrote to Dana on September 1, 1824.[4]

He is printing a novel entitled *The Last of the Mohicans.* The first volume is nearly finished. You tell me that I must review him next time myself. Ah, Sir! He is too sensitive a creature for me to touch. He seems to think his own works his own property, instead of being the property of the public, to whom he has given them; and it is almost as difficult to praise or blame them in the right place as it was to praise or blame Goldsmith properly in the presence of Johnson.

[2] J. G. Wilson, *Bryant and His Friends,* p. 190.
[3] P. Godwin, *Bryant,* I, 189.   [4] *Ibid.,* I, 221.

A quarter of a century later he recalled [5] the "inexhaustable vivacity of his conversation and the minuteness of his knowledge, in everything which depended upon acuteness of observation and exactness of recollection." The poet was a man of naturally shy disposition, with the quiet of the Berkshire Hills as his background, and the blunt frankness of the more vigorous man made him somewhat ill at ease.

Foreign reviews of *The Spy* and *The Pilot* were already making their appearance, and native writers were pointing to the new star in the western sky. Never again did Cooper bask in such unshadowed public favor. To his social and literary successes must also be added his vigorous health. It was not until the time of his departure for Europe that even the slightest hint of physical limitations of any kind became apparent. The country life had been good for him; success was even better.

Much of his home life has found its way into Susan's revealing pages. That spring he moved to No. 3 Beach Street, more in the heart of the older residential district and only a few blocks from the river. The house, which belonged to Mrs. Cooper's cousin, Henry Floyd Jones of Fort Neck, was a typical brick-front city dwelling, with marble steps, wrought iron railings, massive oaken doors, and many deep windows shaded by Venetian blinds and awnings.

It was at this time that he became interested in journalism. His friend Colonel Gardenier had started a paper called the *Patriot* and Cooper was asked frequently to contribute to it. He also wrote occasionally for the *New*

[5] "Discourse," in *Memorial*, p. 50.

York American, edited by Charles King, later President of Columbia College.

But the short residence in Beach Street was not without its vicissitudes. The house was very much out of repair and was somewhat too well populated with rats for comfort. Added to this scourge was one of the most serious outbreaks of yellow fever which New York had known.

As yet the cause of this dread disease was a mystery to medical science. Cooper himself advances some interesting conjectures about it, no doubt based on his conversations with John W. Francis, his consulting physician for the greater part of his life, and James DeKay the naturalist, one of his most intimate friends. He alligns himself with those who believed that the disease was infectious rather than contagious and that it resulted in some way from the breathing of impure atmosphere in a temperature of more than 80°. It was believed rightly to have been imported, probably from the West Indies, and to be easily controlled by isolation of infected districts rather than of cases. He tells of one interesting instance of the contraction of the disease, an anecdote which is repeated by his daughter. It seems that a high board fence had been built around the infected neighborhood of Pearl Street and the docks. A young man of one of the prominent families which had removed for safety to a temporary home outside the city returned one day on a brief errand to the family home and a few days later developed the fever. The case caused much perplexity until it was discovered that curiosity had prompted the young man to climb up the side of the fence in order to see the deserted streets of the isolated district. No doubt a mosquito

had done the rest, but no physician then living was able
to say so.

During the summer, however, the Cooper family followed the prevailing exodus and took a country house at
Turtle Bay. One more winter was spent in Beach Street,
but in May the move was made to 345 Greenwich Street,
just around the corner, and there they lived until the
departure for Europe in 1826.

It was in 1823, at a dinner party at the home of Charles
Wilkes in St. John's Square, that the idea for *The Pilot*
was suggested. The conversation turned upon the authorship of *The Pirate* and several of those present insisted
that it could not have been written by a landsman.
Cooper, however, detected too many nautical errors in
the book and argued that no seaman had written it. He
even went further and insisted that more of the narrative
could to advantage have been located on shipboard. No
one agreed with him. Wilkes shook his head. Once again
a challenge led Cooper to the subject for a novel. On the
way home he outlined the plot and then discussed it with
his wife. The first thorough-going sea tale in the English
language was the result.

The Cooper household was managed upon comfortable
lines. There were negro servants and governesses, usually
French, for the girls. Cooper expressed the belief also
that the future commercial relations between North and
South America would make the mastery of Spanish an
essential to an American education. His experiment with
his own family was only partially successful, but the study
of French survived every vicissitude. At one time three of
the daughters went to school where all the pupils except
themselves were French and where no English was

spoken. He and Susan walked three times a week to the home of Monsieur Monesca, a refugee from San Domingo, in Liberty Street. Always, the idea that before long the entire family would go abroad was in his mind. But, if one may judge by the accuracy of the French words and phrases which have found their way into the pages of Cooper's later works, one may only hope for her sake that Susan's youth gave her an advantage and that she mastered the language more fully than did her father. Among the American manuscripts are many letters from the daughter to her French friends, written in a fine, fluent hand, but the French manuscripts of Cooper are improved, as Mark Twain has put it, by being retranslated back into their native tongue.

The democratic aspect of New York society was apparent to the astute observation of Cooper. "The general society of New York," he makes his fictitious English traveler in the *Notions of the Americans* write to his imaginary French correspondent, "bears a strong impression of its commercial character." The Revolution swept away many of the older families—no doubt he has the DeLanceys immediately in mind—and the rapid growth and progressive changes in the city made for less social stability than in Philadelphia, for example.

The traveling bachelor's letters of introduction threw him first among the mercantile men—doubtless such men as Brevoort and Wilkes. "It was my lot frequently," he writes, "to occupy a seat at a banquet between some fine, spirited, intelligent individual, whose mind and manners had been improved by travel and education, and, perhaps another votary of Plutus (one hardly dare say of Mercury, in this stage of the world), whose ideas were never above the level of a sordid calculation, and all of whose calculations were as egotistical as his discourse."

Cadwallader, the American gentleman however, upon his return to the city introduced the visitor to a more select circle. "His connections," continues the latter, "were strictly of New York, and they were altogether among the principal and longest established families. Here I met with many men of great leisure and large fortunes, who had imparted to their children what they had received from their fathers. . . . I am inclined to think that the doors of those who are secure of their stations are guarded with the customary watchfulness." Of course, Cooper was attempting to write from the point of view of an English gentleman of large leisure, but it is impossible not to detect a genuine note of approval and respect for this latter class. The same is not, however, to be discovered in his comment of two decades later, after he had himself experienced both the closed and the open doors of English society in its own strongholds. When social aristocracy was of purely native origin and growth, Cooper had profound respect for it; but when it subsisted on imported notions, he scorned it with the bitterness of a native and a democrat.

During this early New York period Cooper apparently mingled more with the literary and commercial society of the city than with the old families. There are no intimate references to the Van Cortlandts, the DePeysters or the Livingstons in his letters or in Susan's memories, and when a committee of prominent citizens was organized to welcome Lafayette, he was not of their number.

There is ample testimony, however, to his dominant position in the group with which he associated. The

"Bread and Cheese" lunch club which he founded and which often was referred to as the "Cooper Club" included as intelligent and diversified a group as its more famous prototype, the Club of Johnson. Bryant, Dr. Francis, Philip Hone, and James Grant Wilson, as well as Susan Cooper, have left records and notes of the meetings of this fellowship, all of which bear witness to the power of Cooper's personality. Cooper himself testified that its founding was one of the acts of his life in which he took great pride.

The impromptu meetings in Wiley's "Den" apparently first suggested the idea. The club itself took shape in 1824 and continued active for some years after Cooper's departure for Europe. Chancellor Kent, Henry D. Sedgwick, J. DePeyster Ogden, and Charles King were among the men of "ability and character" who belonged. Jarvis, Durand and Morse, the painters, DeKay and Francis among medical men, the scholars G. C. Verplanck and Henry James Anderson, Sands and Halleck, the poets, and numerous army and navy men were also at one time or another included.

Accounts vary as to the place of meeting. Abigail Jones, a famous colored cook in her day, supplied the stuff of which good conversation is made, and Bryant and Francis agree in their statements that Washington Hall was the gathering place at the time the club was most active. The purpose of the club was strictly social and most of the distinguished visitors to the city were entertained at its dinners, Webster, Starrs, W. B. Lawrence, and the French minister Hyde de Neuville among them.

On one occasion when Daniel Webster and Henry

Wheaton were present, Dr. Francis produced the skull of the actor George Frederick Cooke, which had made an emergency appearance at the Park Theatre the evening before in *Hamlet*. The phrenological skill of those present was called upon and the skull was pronounced "capricious, the functions of the animal amply developed; the height of the forehead ordinary; the space between the orbits of unusual breadth, giving proof of strong perceptive powers; the transverse basilar portion of the skull of corresponding width."

Cooper was always acknowledged as the leader of conversation, and due credit was given him by the members. On the occasion of the celebration of the opening of the Erie Canal, the parade passed the house in Greenwich Street and one carriage was occupied by a group of the members. As they went by they waved in the air canes on the ends of which were slices of bread and cheese.

Records vary again as to how long the Club continued after Cooper went abroad. With their "Constitution," as the founder was affectionately dubbed, absent, the Commission worked valiantly to keep up the spirit of the organization. A mock official report followed him to Paris on November 25, 1826, and reported that "at the appointed hour twenty-seven members were seen to surround the stately Loaf that sublimely surmounted the majestic Cheese, while six decanters of Madeira poured forth a rich and joyous libation to our ever honored *Constitution*."

The election of Philip Hone is announced and that of His Most Christian Majesty proposed for honorary membership as an expression of gratitude for his "most distinguished attention" paid to the *Constitution*. A branch lunch in Paris, under His Majesty's immediate patronage, to be known as "Le Morceau du Pain et du Fromage," is recommended as a useful scheme for the promoting of amicable relations between the two nations.

Wilkes, Harvey, and others kept Cooper posted as to their activities during the winter and official letters were addressed from the rue St-Maur to the Club. In acknowledging one of these on May 14, 1827, Jacob Harvey wrote, "The Lunch, on the whole, was well attended during the winter, and *you* were often the topic of conversation— we heard of you frequently through some of our members, and we took much interest, as in duty bound, in the attentions which you received from the great men of Europe."

Meanwhile, the Cooper family was living quietly and preparing for its European hegira. The schooling of the girls was continued and a boy, Paul, the only son to survive to maturity, who had been born during the winter in Beach Street was toddling about the house and experimenting with two languages. Summers had been spent in a farmhouse at Bay Side, near Flushing, and at Hallet's Cove in a farmhouse belonging to Colonel Gibbs. Cooper was always near water when he could manage it. Even when in the city, he kept the private sloop *Van Tromp* anchored at a wharf near the house for excursions on the river and out into the harbor. It was from this sloop that his family watched the naval maneuvers in the bay in honor of Lafayette on the occasion of his memorable visit in 1824.

When the god of the new liberty returned to New York after his tour of New England, the city went into a furor of welcome. The saturnalia opened with a dinner

given by the Society of the Cincinnati at Washington
Hall, on his birthday, September 6, 1824. Two days later
the veteran visited the forts in the harbor and, at that
which had been named in his honor, there was a colla-
tion, or *déjuener à la fourchette* arranged in an upper
room. Cooper was not present at the first occasion, not
being a member of that patriotic order, but among the
many toasts proposed upon the second was his own ingenious tribute, "The fortress and its name; the former is
durable, but the latter is imperishable."

Other dinners and receptions followed, but the climax
of the week was the ball given at Castle Garden, a fortress
on the battery transformed by a canvas roof into a gigantic tent, and by banners, transparencies, pillars, and chandeliers into a fairyland of light and color. Planned for
the 13th, it was postponed on account of bad weather to
the following night. Meanwhile Mr. Lewis, an engraver
of No. 3 Wall Street, struck out "an exquisite miniature
likeness of General Lafayette, warranted in fine gold or
silver," in differing models for ladies and gentlemen.
Numerous firms offered for sale "ladies' and gentlemen's
white kid gloves, ornamented with a miniature likeness
of the General." At the theatre Mr. Richings sang, between the two plays, *Welcome Lafayette,* with words
by Samuel Woodworth, of *Old Oaken Bucket* fame.

Doubtless Cooper had heard much talk of Lafayette—
had perhaps even met him—at the home of his friend
Charles King, editor of the *New York American,* for
Mrs. King had known the family of the Marquis in
France and Lafayette had honored her with a call on the
occasion of his first visit to New York a few months before. The Frenchman who had taken a leading part in

all the popular uprisings in his own country and who had worshipped liberty (or adventure) enough to try his life in the struggle of idealists on the other side of the world, was a household god in more than one American family. To Cooper he had many claims to reverence. The Lafayettes were allied to the greatest families of France and had a hint of Bourbon blood in their veins; Cooper was born into one of the oldest families of the respectable colony of New Jersey. The Lafayettes were landed, though poor, proprietors in idyllic Auvergne; Cooper had married into the Huguenot family of DeLancey who, because of Tory symapthies in the Revolution, had been deprived of their lands within what is now the city of New York. But, above all, Lafayette, himself a gentleman and a Marquis, had chosen to volunteer in the popular cause, and now, having almost lived his three-score and ten, was, more than any living man, the personification of the new order, the liberty which had swept the corrupt *ancien régime* from its European as well as its American strongholds. Louis XVI and George III had both bowed to his fiery idealism.

Cooper's enthusiasm for the god of the new order took the form of supervising the hanging of gay-colored bunting and the swinging of lanterns. Castle Garden was ready for the welcome, and Cooper and his friends were tired. The gay crowds arrived and the dancing began at 8 o'clock. In two hours the hero and his party would come. Meanwhile "the American fair" held undisputed sway.

The arriving gallants and their ladies passed first through a seventy-five foot pyramidal arch surmounted by a brilliant star. The narrow way from the shore to the gigantic squat cylinder in the harbor was covered with canvas and lighted dimly so that the blaze of glory inside the hall might burst suddenly upon the astonished eyes of the company. Once within the fortress, all was light and color. A circular tier of seats rose to thirty feet against the walls. Over the main entrance was a triumphal arch reaching to the canvas roof, adorned with wreaths of laurel and oak, and garlands of flowers, crowned with a colossal bust of Washington and resting on pillars of cannon. At the top, flags of America and of France were joined, and in the center was a painting of the Goddess of Liberty holding a scroll with the inscription "To the Nation's Guest." Beyond were columns, more draperies and festoons, chandeliers brilliantly lighted and, at the fortress side, flanked by two brass pieces taken at Yorktown, was the General's pavilion. Outside, the water was studded with small craft—steamboats, sail-boats, skiffs, each with its lanterns and gay company. Between eight and ten o'clock five thousand people had assembled.

The arrival of the honored guest was, of course, the moment of climax for all these weary hours of preparation. His party was escorted from his lodgings by Generals Fish and Morton, and was met at the gate by the committee of the militia and leading citizens. In stately procession, the distinguished company passed through the awed ranks of beauty while the band played the familiar Lafayette march. When the revolution-scarred veteran had taken his place of honor, a transparency lighted before his astonished eyes. La Grange, the feudal castle in far-away France, was revealed in a gigantic picture. Over this masterpiece of American art and craftsmanship were the simple but touching words, "His

Home." The General wept. The apotheosis was complete.

In the early hours of the morning, Cooper sat in the office of his friend Charles King and wrote for the *New York American* an account of this brilliant, if somewhat sophomoric, exhibition of the national enthusiasm. No more glowing description appeared in any contemporary record. As yet he was only the observer; later he was to become the critic.

The final demonstration of civic pride which Cooper witnessed before his departure was that in celebration of the opening of the Erie Canal in the fall of 1825. The gigantic task had been completed on October 26 and the canal boat *Seneca Chief* left Buffalo on that day with two ornamental casks of Lake Erie water, Governor Clinton, Patroon Van Rensselaer, and other notables aboard. There was a great commotion when the party passed Albany on the thirtieth, but the real celebration occurred when it reached New York City and the Lake Erie water was officially emptied into the harbor. The ringing of bells, martial music, and the thunder of cannon awakened the citizens on the clear morning of November 4. As Cooper watched the aquatic procession pass down the harbor, he saw the dream of his father realized. The "American Mediterraneans" were at last linked with the sea.

Before his departure, a testimonial dinner was given to Cooper by the Lunch. His thanks for the honor were contained in a letter to William Gracie: [6]

Sir,—I accept with great pleasure, the invitation to meet the "Bread and Cheese" on Monday next. I have always

[6] *N. Y. American,* May 30, 1826.

taken a deep interest in the prosperity of our Club, and few things could afford me more satisfaction than to be able to interchange those good feelings which have always existed among us, once more, before I leave the country.

The honor the gentlemen are disposed to confer on me is much enhanced by the obliging manner in which you have been pleased to communicate their wishes. With much respect, yours, &c.

J. FENIMORE COOPER.

The members and guests assembled at the City Hotel on May 29 at five o'clock. Chancellor Kent, as Caterer of the Day, was in the chair, with Peter Jay, Chairman of the Committee of Arrangements, beside him. Among those present were the Governor, Bishop Hobart, Robert Y. Hayne of South Carolina, Commodore Chauncey, and General Scott.

Charles King first offered a toast to Cooper couched in the florid rhetoric of the period.

I will ask your permission [he said] to detain you a few minutes, while I glance at the claims which this gentleman has upon the regard and the admiration of his countrymen generally, and upon the particular regrets of this Association whose founder he was, whose pride he is, and to whom now that they are, though only for a season, to lose him, they look with increased interest. To the author of *The Spy* and *The Pioneers* we are indebted, not only for much individual gratification, but for much and enduring national renown. It had been said again and again, and repeated until it had almost acquired the weight of a demonstration, that under our system of government, and in a state of society where there is so much equality of condition and of employment—where there are no hereditary statesmen, nor richly endowed scholarships to patronize or to force the growth of literature; where all are engaged in pursuits of necessary industry, and idlers are unknown—it had been said, that the flowers of fancy, and the inspirations of genius, could find no aliment. It was conceded that we might have good lawyers, skillful physicians, ingenious artists, because all these were called for by the every day wants of a growing and prosperous country; but the regions of fancy, the domains of fiction and of invention, were, it was contended, shut out from our approach. It may be the just boast of this Association that it comprises among its members more than one who has falsified these assertions. As a lyric poet there is now before us one whose genius and fine taste have graced with laurels the laurelled flag of his country—who has in verse as beautiful as the beautiful scene that inspired him, added something even to the "Storied Percy's" pride; and in the glowing lines of Marco Bozzaris, given to liberty another battle-cry. To the· works of Mr. Cooper we may in like manner refer as evidence that if fine, vigorous, and original conception, a quick and happy perception, and exquisite delineation of the beauties of nature— a power hardly surpassed of portraying the deep and strong passions of the human heart—a capacity to excite and to sustain the most breathless interest in the fortunes of those whom he brings upon the scene—if any or all these constitute genius, it may be claimed for him. Praise indeed can hardly go higher than by merely alluding to the fact that the works of our associate and guest whom we referred to, are, if it be desired to class them, almost instinctively compared to those of the Great Enchanter of the North, who from his Scottish hillside has so long exercised his potent spell over the whole reading world. To have sprung thus full-grown into existence, and to have taken a place at once, if not beside, at least in close approach to, the Great Master of the art, *proximus a primo,* is glory enough. It would, indeed, seem that the great events of our revolutionary contest, the wild and peculiar habits of our early settlers, and the deeply interesting, and alas! rapidly vanishing aboriginal race of this continent have inspired the pen of the American novelist, and that he has looked with a poet's fancy and a painter's eye upon the grandeur and magnificence of our mountain scenery, the varied tints and glorious sunshine of our autumn skies and woods, our rushing cataracts, and mighty rivers, and forests co-eval with nature. But it is not my purpose, nor can it be necessary in this place to enter into a detailed notice of the works of our distinguished associate. In referring to them as has been done, the chief object was to show that in refuting, as by their well-earned popularity they have had the effect of doing, the zealously inculcated notion that on our soil "fancy sickens and genius dies," a national benefit has been conferred. Let us hope that in visiting the countries where his reputation has preceded him, our friend will find the same disposition to receive with kindness the author, as has been shown with respect to his books, and that he may experience in his own person, that the republic of letters is co-extensive in its courtesies with education and knowledge. One other hope, before I sit down, I may be allowed to express, that our associate will not permit absence to render him, unmindful he can not be, but indifferent, even for a time, to the just expectations of those he leaves behind. We shall not be content that his pen should be unemployed, even though to indulge us he be compelled to snatch some hours from the gratifications that may surround him in other lands. His first duty is here—and when the discharge of that duty results in cementing friendship and adding to fortune and to reputation, it may not be neglected.

Cooper's reply to this praise was characteristic in its blunt egoism. It is especially interesting, however, as an announcement of his intention to devote his principal energy to the writing of a naval history, an ambition not to be realized for more than a decade. Even now, when success as a novelist gave him as much distinction among his fellows as any man could wish, his thoughts were already turning to the forms of writing which seemed to him of most lasting value.

I have been termed [he said] the Founder of this Club. I feel certain, Sir, that I may appeal with confidence to the distinguished strangers who have this day favored us with their company, to know if there is reason to be ashamed of my work! It is not a little to have been the instrument of collecting from the materials of general society, such a mass of intelligence and reputation as is here assembled, and to have brought it, in this manner together, in free, social, unpretending, pleasurable, and, I may add, profitable communion. It is one of the acts of my life, Sir, in which I take great pride. I leave you prosperous and harmonious as an association, and I sincerely pray, that when the period allotted for my absence shall have passed, that I may be permitted to return, to find each individual among you filling his place at our board, as respectable, as happy, and as well disposed toward his associates, as when I left him.

The gentleman who has addressed you, has been pleased to express a wish that the pen which already has inflicted so much on the public, may not be unemployed during the temporary absence of its owner. On this subject, Sir, I affect no reserve. It is certainly my intention that it shall not be idle. Of those works of fiction, to which my friend has so obligingly alluded, I shall only say, it is probable that the reading world will be the first to tire. But, Sir, if there be a man in this community who owes a debt to the Muse of History, it would seem to be the one who has now the

honor to address you. No writer of our country has invaded
her sacred precincts with greater license or more frequency.
Sir, I have not been unmindful of the weight of my trans-
gressions in this particular, and I have long and seriously
reflected on the means of presenting an expiatory offering
before the altar of the offended Goddess. The apparent
tardiness of this repentance ought not to be ascribed to
want of diligence or want of inclination, but is merely an
additional evidence of the vast disparity which is known to
exist between truth and its opposite quality. Encouraged
by your kindness, Sir, I will, however, take this opportunity
of recording the deeds and sufferings of a class of men to
which this nation owes a debt of lasting gratitude—a class
of men among whom I am always ready to declare that
not only the earliest but many of the happiest days of my
youth have been passed.

I shall have great pleasure in discharging this duty, Sir,
for duty, under these circumstances, I do really consider it;
because the nearer my approaches to the sacred quality just
mentioned, the more certain I shall feel of contributing to
the renown of many of my nearest and dearest friends.

The toasts which followed, with one exception, waved
the Stars and Stripes over the head of the patriot author.
It would have been well for Cooper if he could have
turned a deaf ear to them all and listened only to the
quiet sophistication of Professor Renwick: "Irony and
raillery," he offered, "the pastime of the Lunch. May they
be the serious pursuits of the nation." But neither the
nation nor its favored author had reached an age at which
such pursuits could be taken seriously.

II
1826–1833

CHAPTER EIGHT

To Europe

THE reasons for Cooper's long-cherished plan to take his entire family to Europe have perhaps been sufficiently indicated. A letter to John Miller in 1826 states them more explicitly. "My object," he writes, "is my own health and the instruction of my children in the French and Italian languages. Perhaps there is also a little pleasure concealed in the bottom of the cup." To these motives might be added the desire to discover a way of making foreign publication of his novels realize substantial additions to the family coffers. On this score alone the trip fully justified itself.

At the time of his departure a fever had reduced Cooper to rather poor health, and the numerous portraits made of him during his first two years in Europe reveal a face more nearly of the conventional type of the man of letters, thin and with the sensitive qualities which the French know so well how to appreciate and to depict. Frequent colds, which resulted from low vitality, also interrupted his activities for the next few years.

"As is always done by good Manhattanese," he tells us, "the town house had been given up on the first of May, since which time we had resided at a hotel. The furniture had been principally sold at auction, and the entire month had passed in what I believed to be very ample preparation." Nevertheless, at the last moment Mrs.

Cooper discovered an alarming shortage of towels in the family equipment; and her husband had to ship off to the care of his friend Shubrick some fifty or a hundred books and pamphlets which could not be included in his civilian baggage, but which were to be delivered to him later by the man-of-war *Lexington*. The family nurse Abby was left at home and Mrs. Cooper assumed the responsibility of her children until foreign servants could be engaged.

The trip across the Atlantic in the days immediately before the advent of steam was little more of an adventure than it is today. Regular service was maintained between the principal ports of the old world and the new in large and well-appointed sailing packets. The crossing ordinarily took thirty days and, in spite of winds and storms, a fairly regular schedule was maintained.

As soon as the deck of the London packet began to rise and fall beneath Cooper's feet, the old zest of the sailor for the sea returned to him. There was a flat calm as the Hudson dropped down the bay, but the sails soon filled and the beloved New York and Connecticut shoreline faded from sight.

The harbor was, as usual, full of ships. One fine vessel tacked directly on their quarter and an Englishman of Cooper's acquaintance called a greeting.

"How long do you mean to be absent?"

"Five years."

"You will never come back."

These were the last words which he heard on leaving America and, although not literally a true prediction, they were an omen of something very near to the truth. In his introduction to the last volume of his travels, he quotes Jefferson as having once said that no American should leave his country for more than five years lest he get behind it. He admits the possibility, but only with respect to facts. His conviction was that his opinions might develop, with the advantage of the perspectives of time and distance, so that in theory he might well be in advance of his countrymen after the experience of travel. He was absent something over seven years, and, in his own conviction, progressed considerably beyond his country. He was always out of accord with the transformations wrought by Jacksonian democracy. He never came back—to the America he left. Those years served as a wedge between the new Cooper and the new America, the one deeply moved by the culture, the ideals, and the corruptions of old world society; the other grown vigorous and vulgar with the restless strength of the open west.

In his pocket Cooper carried his commission as United States Consul at Lyons, dated May 26, 1826. He apparently never had any intention of serving in person as a foreign representative of his country, although he had written the Secretary of State, Henry Clay, on May 3,[1]

> May I recall Lyons to your recollection? The situation is in some degree mercantile, but should there be nothing in which it might be thought I could serve the Government, it would answer all my views to fill such a consulate. If nothing unforeseen occurs, I shall sail for London on the first of June. My stay in England will not exceed ten days, after which I shall proceed direct to Paris.

The implication that the appointment would be a convenience to him as a passport is unmistakable, and the

[1] MS. in the archives of the State Department, Washington, D. C.

commission was so used by him, a resident of Lyons having been appointed to act in his absence. He held the post until April 10, 1829, when he was succeeded by Cornelius Bradford, who likewise appointed a substitute to act for him.[2] The practice seems to have been fairly general at the time. Cooper himself justifies the appointment by explaining:

> The consulate of the writer was given to him solely to avoid the appearance of going over to the enemy during his residence abroad. The situation conferred neither honor nor profit, there being no salary, and, in his case, not fees enough to meet the expense of the office opened by a deputy.

Carefully locked up in his baggage were some twenty letters of introduction, pressed upon him by his friends. Unlike Irving, Willis, and other Americans, however, he used none of them. "I have a strong repugnance," he explained, "to pushing myself on the acquaintance of any man." The practice had been so abused that his national as well as his personal pride made him shrink from it. Such trifles are sometimes profoundly revealing of character.

Early in the morning of June 30, Cooper came on deck and

> a glorious view presented itself. The day was fine, clear and exhilarating, and the wind was blowing fresh from the westward. Ninety-seven sail, which had come into the Channel, like ourselves, during the thick weather, were in plain sight. The majority were English, but we recognized the

[2] Letters to the Department of State, III, 102. Archives of the American Embassy at Paris.

build of half the maritime nations of Christendom in the brilliant fleet. Everybody was busy and the blue waters were glittering with canvas. A frigate was in the midst of us, walking through the crowd like a giant stepping among pigmies. Our own good vessel left everything behind her also, with the exception of two or three other bright-sided ships, which happened to be as fast as herself.

The next day the fields of Dorsetshire lay behind a range of low cliffs not far distant, and in the afternoon, a mass of dark herbage was pointed out as Carisbrooke Castle on the Isle of Wight. The ship put into Cowes, and on July 2 the Cooper party went ashore, to be met by an old friend, the United States Consul Robert R. Hunter.

Cooper's first observations on the English relate to manners rather than to scenery. Freed from the isolation imposed by the Napoleonic wars, the people seemed to him, even in such superficials as costume, to be less provincial than they had been in 1806. Nevertheless, they were still even more emphatic about the excellence of English things and English ideas than the cosmopolitan French or the imitative Americans. From the moment of his first glance, Cooper never ceased to be slightly irritated by this fact and to generalize on English pride whenever he caught the slightest manifestation of it. The absence of salt in Isle of Wight butter likewise brought home to him the realization that this was not his own country, even though he was broad minded enough to smile at his American brand of provinciality.

In his comments upon his first views of old world ruins lies the key to another fundamental factor in his reaction to European culture. So great was his delight in the fine old village church below Carisbrooke Castle and in the remains of a ruined priory close by, that he turned his horse and drove back to the Fountain Inn for the rest of the party in order that they might all enjoy the experience together. But his Jeffersonian sense of practical values moved him later to remark upon the crumbling walls of Netley Abbey: "Had we seen Netley Abbey, just as far advanced toward completion as it was, in fact, advanced towards decay, our speculation would have been limited by a few conjectures on its probable appearance, but gazing at it, as we did, we peopled its passages, imagined Benedictines stalking along its galleries, and fancied that we heard the voices of the choir, pealing among its arches." The social critic had already come to grips with the romancer in the mind of the novelist who was to write his Europe into *The Bravo* and his America into *Satanstoe*.

Perched on the high seat by the coachman, Cooper soon rode up to London in order to set his business with the publishers to rights. Once more his comments upon the scenery are casual, and again he notes an event that probes into the national character. While the assizes were sitting at Winchester, the royal troops had been sent down and billeted upon the inhabitants of Southampton, thereby inflicting a serious private wrong in order that, in form at least, an abstract and perfectly useless principle might be maintained. The custom had developed justly and logically from the needs of a feudal society; even when those needs were no longer present, the custom was maintained for centuries. The maintainance of such traditions, thought Cooper, was one of the reasons why England was "so much in arrears in many of the great essentials."

Familiar but somewhat altered sights met his curious eye as the coach rattled into London and pulled up at the Adam Street Hotel, Adelphi, just off the Strand at Charing Cross. He was not long in getting in touch with John Miller, who had been his English publisher ever since his unsatisfactory negotiations with Murray in 1821-23.

All available evidence points to his hope at this time that personal investigation of the situation might result in substantial payment for the English rights to his novels. Washington Irving, on the plan of dividing profits with his publisher, had netted over a thousand pounds in the English sales of each of his most recent works, *Bracebridge Hall* and *Tales of a Traveller,* whereas Cooper's first two novels had been published in England without any return whatever to their author. With Irving's aid he had tried the profit plan with Murray on *The Pioneers,* but had received only £134. John Miller had then taken over the English publication of his work, with what results we do not know, but Miller was more bookseller and literary agent than publisher in his own right. *The Prairie,* upon which Cooper was working at the time of his journey to London, was issued by Henry Colburn, Murray's most successful rival, on April 21, 1827, almost a month before its appearance in the United States. This was his last work to be published in England on a profit-sharing plan, and when Richard Bentley took over the Colburn business in 1832, Cooper was regularly selling English rights for cash payments of from two to thirteen hundred pounds for each work, and American editions were being delayed in order that the English publisher might profit by the somewhat informal copyright regulations of his own nation. *The Last of the Mohicans* had just been issued from the press with Miller's imprint upon it when Cooper appeared in London in July 1826. We may assume that he discussed its sales with Miller and decided that subsequent dealings with him were undesirable. He then entered into negotiations with Colburn and laid the foundations of the business agreement which held, even during some stormy interludes, throughout his quarter-century association with this firm.

This business completed, he returned to his family at Southampton. A few friends had meanwhile been discovered, among them Mrs. Cooper's sister, Anne De Lancey, who had been born in England during her Tory parents' exile and who had never been in America. She had married the "colossus of roads," J. L. McAdam, and now saw her sister for the first time. With her the children could indulge to their hearts' content in that state which their father called "toosey-moosey," a kind of excitement especially provoked by the sight of ruined arches and ivied walls.

As soon as the head of the family had returned from his more important concerns, they all set out in a "small, rickety, jerky, dirty steamboat," as Susan described it, for the native province of their de Lancé ancestors. A disabled boiler, Cooper explains, delayed their passage and caused a flutter among the women passengers, but he set their fears at rest by assuring them that they were not all going to be drowned, as a well-swaddled elderly gentleman had warned them. A female *commissionaire* engineered the party through the customs at Havre and an American-owned steamboat took them up the Seine

AN AMERICAN AND A FRENCH PORTRAIT OF COOPER

*From the painting by John W. Jarvis, New York, 1822;
and the engraving by Johannot, Paris, about 1827.*

to Rouen. There Cooper bought a traveling *calèche,* piled his family into it, and took the road for Paris.

Before they had proceeded far, an elephantine French *diligence* came thundering down upon them, and, there not being enough windows in the carriage to accommodate all the heads, the whole family got out to look at the marvel of transportation with its passengers and trunks piled high on its clumsy body. The curiosity was mutual, for the American party, with its flock of white-clad, lively girls, was not an everyday sight on the French roadside.

From the top of the hill, they surveyed the old world landscape.

The Seine [writes Cooper] comes winding its way, through a broad rich valley, from the southward, having just before run east, and, a league or two beyond, due west, our own Susquehanna being less crooked. The stream was not broad, but its numerous isles, willowy banks, and verdant meadows formed a line for the eye to follow. Rouen in the distance, with its ebony towers, fantastic roofs, and straggling suburbs, lines its shores at a curvature where the stream swept west again, bearing craft up to the sea on its bosom. These dark old towers have a sombre, mysterious air which harmonizes admirably with the recollections which crowd the mind at such a moment! Scarce an isolated dwelling was to be seen, but the dense population is compressed into villages and *bourgs* that dot the view, looking brown and teeming like nests of wasps. Some of these places have still remains of walls, and most of them are so compact and well defined that they appear more like vast castles than like the villages of England or America. All are gray, sombre, and without glare, rising from the background of pale verdure, so many appropriate *bas reliefs.*

The attention to details of direction and distance in this sketch, coupled with the feeling for tone and the dim recollection of historical associations, are characteristic of all Cooper's impressions of European scenery. Certainly this was a different world from that of the forests, the fields, and the towns of clean frame houses in which he had spent his boyhood.

The party stopped for the night at Vernon, and when evening came again the following day, the dome of the Hôtel des Invalides "rose like a glittering beacon" in the sunset after a light shower, and proclaimed Paris. Down the Champs Elysées their carriage took them, past the place where, within the memory of many then living, Louis XVI and Marie Antoinette had been beheaded, into the boulevards and the narrow winding streets of the city, and finally to the door of the Hôtel Montmorency, rue St-Marc, where they stayed until permanent quarters were taken on the other side of the river.

A home for them all and a suitable school for the girls were Cooper's first thoughts. It was his habit during all his years in Europe to patronize public coaches and hotels as little as possible. He bought and sold, or rented, carriages for all long journeys, and he rented spacious apartments or villas for all residences of a month or longer.

The first of his Paris homes is today almost as he left it, but most of the others in which he lived for extended periods have long since disappeared. Of his many incidental residences, a few can still be identified. "We were not a fortnight in Paris," he writes, "before we were quietly established, *en bourgeois,* in the Faubourg St-Germain." A century has made few changes in the rue de l'Abbé Gregoire. Leaving the glaring plate glass windows of the Bon Marché, with their displays of modern luxuries and comforts, we may turn off the rue de Sèvres into a narrow street walled by high and somber buildings. Only the modern paving and lighting have altered its appearance since Cooper first ventured down "the narrow, gloomy rue St-Maur," as Susan describes it, "with its muddy gutter in the center, and a melancholy oil lamp swinging from a rope." The *porte cochère,* before which he stopped to inquire for the select "institution" of Mesdames Trigant de la Tour and Kantz, still retains the dignity of its antiquity. Even though this imposing entrance to the courtyard is not shown on the plans of Paris which Monsieur J. Parrang has discovered in the national archives and library of Paris, it is probably very old.

Father Parrang is the local authority on this one-time aristocratic quarter, and his findings are not to be questioned. The notes which he has kindly furnished enable us to enter the courtyard of the Hôtel de Jumilhac with a memory not only of Cooper and his friends, Lafayette, Scott, and others, but also of grocer Pierre le Jay who, with his wife Geneviève Quantin, purchased this land in 1644 from the Abbey of St-Germain des Près, on the condition that they open two streets and build residences.

By 1700, when the Dames de St-Maur took up their retired lives in the house across the court, the Hôtel d'Ecquivilly, which was later to be renamed the Hôtel de Jumilhac, was already an outstanding feature of the neighborhood. A perspective plan of the parish of St-Sulpice, drawn in 1696, shows its façade, recognizable today in spite of alterations, and the garden which Susan Cooper described two centuries later. "The ducal dignitary of the days of Louis XIV" to whom Susan Cooper refers, was Monseigneur René de Froulay, Comte de Tessé, maréchal de France, Grand d'Espagne, French Ambassador to Rome, etc. Not a few gay lords and their ladies drew up in their gilded carriages and mounted the marble stairs in these festive days; nor were the following years barren of spectacle. Other nobles succeeded the Comte de Tessé, among them, in 1766, Pierre-Joseph Chapelle, Marquis de Jumilhac, whose name the old house still bears.

But the Sisters of St-Maur in their convent next door saw little of this pageantry. Theirs was a different and seemingly a more enduring sort of life, for in 1824 the rich old Hôtel de Jumilhac passed quietly into their hands. Today it is a *pension de famille,* a religious school, and a convent. The corner plot on the rue du Cherche Midi has been sold, the Hôtel de Jumilhac itself (now actually No. 14, although entered by No. 12) has been extended to include No. 16 as well, the secluded gardens have been enlarged by the removal of dividing walls, and a chapel and new buildings in the convent proper have been erected. But we may still pass through the same *porte cochère* which admitted Scott in 1826, we may still ascend the spacious old marble staircase, we may pause on the first floor at the door of the grand salon which Susan Cooper describes as a sort of dormitory during her school days, and we may continue up to the Cooper apartment, of which four of the five rooms are unaltered, the salon having been cut in two. Time has made few changes here.

"How may one explain," asks Father Parrang, "the presence of a man in a house for two years the property of a convent?" The answer is not difficult. Cooper's prejudices against a Catholic education for his daughters were so strong as to prevent any identification of the "institution" of Mesdames de la Tour and Kantz with that now conducted in the house. The rooms were obviously rented out, as they are today, and Cooper accepted, as the visitor may still accept, the hospitality of the old Hôtel de Jumilhac.

"The two lower floors of the hôtel," explains Cooper, "were occupied as a girls' boarding-school; the reason of our dwelling in it, for our own daughters were in the establishment; *au second,* there was nothing but our own *appartement,* and above us again, dwelt a family whose visitors never came in carriages." Susan, the eldest of the daughters, gives a somewhat more graphic picture of the

pleasant furnished apartment, *au second,* in a fine old *hôtel,* once occupied by a ducal dignitary of the days of Louis XIV. Towards the street it was a most gloomy looking building, blank grey walls. But, once within the *porte cochère,* all was changed; there was a lovely garden of more than an acre, with other adjoining gardens, all surrounded with stone walls at least twelve feet high, while groves of fine trees appeared above the walls. The *hôtel* itself was on a grand scale—a noble stone stairway, with elaborate iron railing, rooms with very high ceilings, wide doorways, with pictured panels above and gilt lines over the woodwork—large windows, and parquet floors of course.

Here the Cooper girls, then ranging from seven to thirteen in age, learned those refinements of education which were unattainable at home before the days of the Troy Female Seminary and other such pioneer establishments. Bottin for 1828 lists Madame de la Tour at this address, but by 1832 the school had been taken over by Madame Liot and had moved to the rue Richer, No. 14. Cooper is still listed as its patron, however, and we may assume that his daughters continued their training in "music, drawing and dancing," as well as in French, with only vacation interruptions during at least five of their seven years abroad. The link with the past was restored in the grandchildren of the pioneer.

CHAPTER NINE

The End of Despotism

COOPER'S reputation had gone before him and letters of introduction were not necessary to provide as much sociability as was desired. For the first winter their friends were chiefly in the American circle, the Hunters who frequently came over from Cowes, Dr. and Mrs. Jarvis, the American Envoy James Brown and his wife, and many others. The two notable exceptions were Lafayette and the Russian *emigré* Princess Barbara Galitzin. Lafayette heard early of the arrivals and wrote from his *château* La Grange at Rozoy-en-Brie, near Melun and Meaux, in the broad valley between the Seine and the Marne. The letter is dated July 24, 1826:

> With much pleasure I hear that Mr. and Mrs. Cooper and their family are expected last night in Paris. How long they intend to remain there before they take the road to the South I do not know. But I hope it will not be out of their line of arrangements to grant some time to the inhabitants of La Grange. My daughters, granddaughters, and son join in the request; and I, who, although Mr. Cooper was one of the first New York friends I had the gratification to take by the hand, have much regretted not to have more opportunities to enjoy his company.

Such an appeal Cooper found irresistible, for he never failed to respond to hospitality and friendship offered with an open hand. The renewal of his casual relationship with Lafayette led to the most important single shaping influence in his entire European experience. The two men were intimate friends for seven years, even though Lafayette's repeated invitation to the entire Cooper family to visit La Grange was never accepted. Cooper went out alone for several visits of nearly a week each and on one occasion Mrs. Cooper accompanied him.

The story of his third visit is recorded in detail. The *château* is among the less pretentious of those fortified memorials to feudalism, only too few of which have survived the ravages of the revolutionary era. Lafayette had acquired it by inheritance through his wife and had modified it to suit his republican principles. The moat was filled in on two sides and the western façade was altered to resemble an English country house. The grounds were laid out as a park and thrown open so that the neighboring peasants could approach to the very door of their aristocratic advocate. On the east the semblance of a fortress was maintained, with the willow-shaded moat, the moss-stained walls, the five coned towers, and the drawbridge entrance.

Subtly, perhaps, but none the less effectively, this curious mixture of the traditions of the feudal past with the principles and hopes of the democratic future found a responsive chord in Cooper's consciousness. As he crossed the moat on the stone bridge which had supplanted the draw and entered the low-arched portal, he left the present behind him, only to find it spread out before him again in the fields and park beyond.

Carp from the moat furnished the breakfast for the first day, as they may well for the modern visitor when the hospitality of Lafayette's descendant, the Comte Louis de Lasteyrie, makes it possible for him to see the tower room where Cooper slept and the cheerful circular library on the floor above, with a number of Lafayette's books still on the built-in shelves. As many as thirty people were often in the *château* at one time, including the large family, the servants, and the innumerable visitors who were continually coming and going. In the cabinet adjoining the library the American and French idealists sat for hours discussing the state of world affairs and hoping that some day American principles would free social France from her inherited bondage, and that old world culture would soften the sharp edges and enrich the shallow surfaces of American culture.

When in town, Lafayette also met Cooper frequently at the home of James Brown. One of the first great social events which Cooper attended was a diplomatic dinner given by the American Envoy in honor of Canning who was then in Paris. Cooper's impressionable mind made notes of the brilliant costumes and decorations of the men, and of the silks and jewels of the ladies. The French prime minister, M. De Villèle, Lord Viscount Grenville, the Papal Nuncio, and the Ambassadors of Austria, Spain, and Russia were among the guests.

"They make quite a lion of him," wrote Mrs. Cooper to her sisters on November 28, "and Princesses write to him, and he has invitations from Lords and Ladies. He has so many notes from Princess Galitzin, that I should be absolutely jealous, were it not that she is a grandmother."

"The moment I see 'American Novel by Cooper,'"

Princess Galitzin had written, "my heart leaps." Her repeated invitations were welcomed and her *soirées* were
among the most frequent and enjoyable of the Coopers'
social experiences. On Sundays the Princess gave parties
to her grandchildren, but Mrs. Cooper is proud to note
that her own children did not need a hint that on this
day at least such entertainments should be refused.

Perhaps the most interesting of all of Cooper's experiences, however, during those first years in Europe was
his first meeting with Sir Walter Scott, not more than
ten days after his arrival in the rue St-Maur. A carriage
had been ordered for a drive and Cooper had reached
his door when a second carriage rattled into the little
court and a large heavy-moulded man alighted and
limped slowly up the grand stairway with his cane. As
the Americans were the only people in the building
likely to receive such a visitor, Cooper turned and followed the stranger to the first landing.

"Est-ce Monsieur Cooper, que j'ai l'honneur de voir?"
he asked in French of Scottish flavor.

"Monsieur, je m'appelle Cooper."

"Eh bien, donc—je suis Walter Scott."

Still *parley-vousing,* he explained that the Princess
Galitzin had given him Cooper's address. The drive was
abandoned and the two most widely admired novelists
then living took each other's arm and climbed one more
flight of marble stairs.

"I'll tell you what I most like," said Scott as soon as
he had seated himself in the comfortable *bergère* which
Lafayette had left only a few moments before, "and it
is the manner in which you maintain the ascendency of
your own country on all proper occasions without de-

THE HÔTEL JUMILHAC, PARIS, AND THE
GRAND STAIRWAY

scending to vulgar abuse of ours. You are obliged to bring the two nations into collision, and I respect your liberal hostility."

The conversation turned chiefly upon copyright in America and the translation of English works into French, the subject of a letter from Cooper which was the cause of Scott's visit. Both men were then dealing directly with the Parisian publisher Gosselin—a gosling, added Scott, that laid golden eggs—but there were no American fowl ready to bestow like favors on British authors. The result of the talk was that Cooper subsequently made a sustained but ineffectual effort, both by correspondence with his own publishers and friends in America and by letters to the press, to work out some arrangement whereby Scott and others might profit by the sales of their writings in the United States.

"We saw Sir Walter Scott repeatedly while he was in Paris," wrote Mrs. Cooper to her sister, November 28, 1826.

He was with us several times, and treated Mr. Cooper like a son or younger brother in the same vocation. He is a giant in form, as he is one in literature—to you who are craniologists, I must mention that his head is uncommonly high and narrow. He is very gray—and has a fine florid, healthy appearance. He talks a great deal and quotes old ballads and Shakespeare very happily and pleasantly—and to this I will add that he has quite a rustic appearance— and still further, but this is for your private ear alone, that he put me in mind of one of our own country Presbyterian parsons.

The Princess Galitzin gave a reception in which the

Scotch and American lions took the field together, but, as Susan adds, "of course Sir Walter was the lion-in-chief."

"I'm as good a lion as needs be," Scott confided to Cooper on this occasion, "allowing my mane to be stroked as familiarly as they please, but I can't growl for them in French. How is it with you?"

"The manner of Sir Walter Scott," wrote Cooper later, "is that of a man accustomed to see much of the world without being exactly a man of the world himself. He has evidently great social tact, perfect self-possession, is quiet, and absolutely without pretension, and has much dignity; and yet it struck me that he wanted the ease and *aplomb* of one accustomed to live with his equals."

Scott entered in his journal, November 3, 1826: "Visited Princess Galitzin, and also Cooper, the American novelist. This man, who has shown so much genius, has a good deal the manner, or want of manner, peculiar to his countrymen." Scott's biographer, Lockhart, did not help matters by quoting the word as "manners." Cooper's resentment made itself felt in his review of the book in the *Knickerbocker Magazine*.

Curious, and perhaps amused, reflection may well result from the reading of these comments. Obviously, the two lions were from different jungles. Their mutual love of romance was completely over-balanced by their differences in social and political convictions. They discussed business rather than novels and they were unimpressed by each other's manners. Scott was a British Tory; Cooper an American liberal.

By the second winter in France, the circle of Cooper's Parisian acquaintances was so great that on a single evening he visited a half-dozen houses, commencing with a dinner party at the *hôtel* of the Lord High Chancellor of France and concluding with a legation ball given probably by the Count Pozzo di Borgo, Ambassador of Russia. Among his visits was one to the venerable M. de Marbois, who vied with the Princess Galitzin in the number of his attentions to the American novelist. The ease of French manners on such great occasions had a decided appeal to Cooper and he frequently comments upon the natural grace with which social distinctions and usages are observed, contrasting them with both the heavy English society manner and the confused uncertainty in the drawing rooms of his own land where an inherited caste system was lacking and where sometimes there seemed to be no rules whatever for correctness and taste. Again it is difficult to decide, from his comments, whether he admires most the polished form of an organized society or the free principles of democracy. In these early social adventures he seems principally impressed by the very enjoyable results of the former and to have reserved his doubts for more mature thought. He was, however, much troubled by the *roué* air of some fine dowagers who had survived from the *ancien régime* and by the loose standards of morality which were revealed in the light conversation of the ladies at the dinner table or in the drawing room.

Similarly, his early comments on French politics show him to have been entirely ready to accept the government of the Bourbon Charles X and his exceedingly unpopular minister Villèle with little question. An occasional thrust, however, penetrates to the rotten core of the situation. Once he attended some horse races at the Champ de Mars and was almost mortified by the sullen silence with which the royal children were met by the French people. It was obvious to him that the King and his family were honestly scorned by the populace and that peace was preserved only by latent military power. A demonstration mock battle on the plain of Issy served to show the mailed fist, but the forced shouts of *"Vive le Roi"* when the King and his party appeared were suddenly punctuated by a vehement *"A bas les ministres"* from the National Guard.

The next day, April 29, the National Guard was disbanded by royal decree, and censorship of the press was established. Law and medical students thronged the streets shouting the same cry under the very windows of the ministers. A group of them was gathered about the column in the Place Vendôme when Cooper happened to pass. A detachment of royal troops dismounted and marched single file into the mass, straight to the base of the monument. By describing increasingly larger circles, they drove the insurgents into the narrow streets and effectually broke up the demonstration. Cooper seems to have been more impressed by the skill of the military maneuver than by sympathy for the rebellious students.

"The catastrophe is to come," he wrote after witnessing a public dinner of the royal family. During the perfunctory display, the crowd gathered behind the rail was silent and orderly, but the instant the King's back was turned, all was confusion. Little by little the meaning of events taking place about him became clear. "I know not what to tell you of the political condition of France," he wrote to Professor Silliman on May 12, after he had been in Paris almost a year.[1]

I do not think there is much danger from conspiracies—the Frenchmen dare not trust each other enough to conspire with success. Then the Government is very decided in all its steps, witness the manner in which the National Guard has been disbanded. But as this is a fierce people and one altogether governed by impulses, it is hard to pronounce on the future. The Government seems chiefly impressed with the truth that the Revolution was produced by, or rather might have been prevented but for the imbecility of Louis XVI. It appears determined not to fail by a similar fault. All this decision might do if it were well regulated. The effect of their policy is, undoubtedly, to sour the public mind. An unfortunate measure might kindle a flame they could not extinguish, by raising the nation *en masse*. It is, however, more probable that a change of ministers will give a new direction to public feeling and lessen the danger. Then there is the constant probability, or I should say liability, to foreign wars, a step that the ministers would at any moment take rather than lose their places. The vapid vanity of the nation is constantly furnishing them with opportunities—witness the absurd question of Count d'Appiny and the military titles, this winter. An artful minister might easily have produced a war from that foolish business which would momentarily have appeased the mortified pride, or rather vanity, of this trivial people. To sum up the whole, with a nation so little governed by reflection it is impossible to predict anything with certainty, though it is well known that all restless tempers are anxious for change at any hazard.

[1] A. P. Stokes, *Memorials of Eminent Yale Men*, p. 144.

A visit to the Chamber of Deputies, in order to hear his friends Lafayette and Benjamin Constant, further clarified his ideas and pointed to the principles underlying the situation. He now recognized that the weakness of the government lay in the legislative initiative of the King, which made the Chamber a mere *lit de justice* unless it wished to assert arbitrary authority and overthrow the monarchy. The crisis in which this action would inevitably be taken seemed to Cooper only a matter of time. "France has gained," he writes in his *France,*

> beyond estimate, by the changes from the old order to the present system, but it is in a manner to render further violent changes necessary . . . The mongrel government which exists neither can stand, nor does it deserve to stand. It contains the seeds of its own destruction. Here, you will be told that the King is a Jesuit, that he desires to return to the ancient régime, and that the opposition wishes merely to keep him within the limits of the charter. My own observations lead to a very different conclusion. The difficulty is in the charter itself, which leaves the government neither free nor despotic; in short, without any distinctive character.

One morning Cooper awoke to learn that there had been fighting in the city and that about fifty had been killed or wounded. His recent predictions, growing doubtless out of his many long conversations with Lafayette and other members of the Opposition, were now completely supported by events.

None of these concerns, however, materially disturbed his own way of life. His regular habit of devoting his mornings to writing allowed him to complete *The Prairie,*

The Red Rover, and the *Notions of the Americans* before
he left Paris in February 1828. Much of the last two
books was written during the summer of 1827, which was
spent in a rented villa overlooking the Seine on the outskirts of Montmartre. Unfortunately, this house disappeared many years ago before the onslaught of modern
progress. Industry, represented by Petrol, has absorbed the
entire region into its domain, and a huge garage now
stands on the site of three country houses. Miss Phillips
has incorrectly supposed Cooper to have rented the
Château de ma Folie, not far away. This villa, which was
next door but one to Cooper's home, is of almost identical type of location and is of such similar size and general appointments that we can easily recreate the demolished from the remaining house.

The move to St-Ouen was made early in June. When
spring came, even the one acre garden behind the walls
in the gloomy rue St-Maur was not enough, and Cooper
made a tour of the *banlieu* in search of a more pleasant
place to spend the summer. Auteuil, Passy, and other
nearby villages were dismissed for one reason or another,
the search finally ending in the little market square of
St-Ouen. There was nothing princely, or even aristocratic, about this "cluster of small, mean stone houses,
stretched along the right bank of the Seine," which here
loops back upon its course so far as to seem almost
another river. After passing through the most imposing
porte cochère on the little square, however, Cooper found
the house for which he had been searching.

On one side of the gate [he says] was a lodge for a
porter, and on the other, a building to contain gardener's

tools, plants, etc. The walls that separate it from the square and the adjoining gardens are twelve or fourteen feet high, and once within them, the world is completely excluded. The width of the grounds does not exceed a hundred and fifty feet; the length, the form being that of a parallelogram, may be a hundred or a little more; and yet in these narrow limits, which are planted *à l'Anglaise,* so well is everything contrived that we appear to have abundance of room. The garden terminates in a terrace that overhangs the river, and from this point the eye ranges over a wide extent of beautiful plain that is bounded by fine bold hills which are teeming with gray villas and *bourgs.*

The house, which he also describes in detail in his *France,* was large and comfortable. In the center was a drawing room thirty feet long, where, according to tradition, the Prince de Soubise, Grand Veneur of Louis XV, was accustomed to serve his master the fruits of the chase; and on each of the two floors there were seven or eight good-sized rooms devoted to a variety of purposes. A carriage house, which was soon occupied by a private cabriolet and a riding horse, completed the ensemble, and the family settled down to a leisurely and pleasurable five months. For all of this Cooper paid one hundred dollars a month in rent, and enjoyed the services of a gardener and a porter without extra charge. The rent was low, considering the advantages of the property, because the town was admittedly unfashionable, but there was an expansiveness and a repose about the house and a view which appealed to the owner of Angevine and Fenimore. His modest inherited wealth was amply reinforced by returns from a handful of successful novels and there were two books then in the mill. There was, therefore, no reason why he should not have the comfort and enjoyment which he could so thoroughly appreciate. With well assorted neighbors—one unusually musical and the other unusually quiet—and with free access to the parks and gardens of his landlord, the Baron Ternaux, who owned most of the surrounding property, there was plenty to occupy the children as well as their parents. Historical associations also helped. M. Ternaux, a wealthy manufacturer, lived in the famous Petit Château, built in 1756, bought soon after by the great financier of the Revolution, Necker, the father of Madame de Staël, and only demolished a very few years ago. Not far away also was the site of the *château* where Louis XVIII had paused on his way back to Paris with the Bourbon crown, and an earlier Louis had installed his Madame de Pompadour. Memories and slightly faded magnificence had taken the place of the royal presence in Cooper's day, but the little village on the bank of the Seine was still a desirable place for one who cared more for the fine than the fashionable.

CHAPTER TEN

American Notions and English Facts

BY the end of February 1828, Cooper had finished the manuscript of his *Notions of the Americans, picked up by a Travelling Bachelor,* and with Mrs. Cooper and Paul he set out once more for London to see it through the press. There is every reason to believe that he considered this book the most important of his works up to that time, and he wished no accident to impede its publication in the England for which it had been written. "The author has far less ambition to be thought a fine writer," he assures us, "than to be thought an accurate observer and a faithful narrator of what he has witnessed." He had adopted semi-fictional machinery for the presentation of his case, and he justifies the method by his belief that "a close and detailed statistical work on the United States of America could not keep its place as authority for five years." Yet the need for answering the great mass of superficial impressions and incorrect conclusions which European travelers in America had been producing for the two previous decades seemed to him pressing. Two purposes must be served: the misinformed and prejudiced criticism of the English must be silenced; and the slavish mental dependence of the American mind upon British opinion must be brought to an end. "The American who gets the good word of England," he writes in his *Gleanings,* "is sure of having that of his own country, and he who is abused by England will be certain of being abused at home. . . . If the craven and dependent feeling which exists so strongly in what are called the better classes of America, on the subject of Great Britain, existed in the body of the nation, our political union, or political independence, in my opinion, would not be worth ten years' purchase."

The two books which most immediately provoked Cooper's answer to the English travels in America were Adam Hodgson's *Letters from North America* (1824) and John Fredrich De Roos's *Personal Narrative of Travels in the United States and Canada* (1827). At the time he wrote, Captain Basil Hall was across the sea collecting impressions and facts for his *Travels in North America* (1829), and the more famous castigations of Mrs. Frances Trollope and Charles Dickens were still to come; but the war between English and American writers had already been waged for more than a quarter of a century. Some forty-odd pretentious works of almost identical title had already appeared. Each recorded the impressions of an Englishman on a short tour of the eastern states, with condescending comments upon the ideals, institutions, and manners of their inhabitants. The peak of production, however, was not reached until the early thirties when five years witnessed the appearance of twenty-five such volumes written by all classes of men and women, from ex-barbers to clergymen, and reviewed at length and with enthusiasm by the leading journals of England.

American answers to this barrage were less numerous. A few, like Robert Walsh in his *Appeal from the Judgments of Great Britain* (1819), proceeded to the defense with legal poise, but most of the replies take the form of angry protest and burlesqued travels. Royall Tyler, C. J. Ingersoll, and James K. Paulding had already produced travel accounts written by fictitious Englishmen before Cooper adopted the method in 1828. All of these works, however, were characterized rather by the power of their feelings than by their literary excellences:

"It is with feelings of deep regret that I observe the literary animosity growing up between England and America," wrote the gentlemanly Irving in 1819, but Cooper was not a man of gentle and melancholy mood. "I have little doubt," he asserts,

> that most of the books of travel that have been published in England, and in which America has been held up to ridicule, have been addressed to the prejudices of the nation; written in that particular vein, because it has been believed that it would be more likely to please than any other. Very few of them discover honesty of intention, a trait that is usually detected even in the midst of blunders.

None of this bitterness, however, finds its way into the pages which he filled in his garden study overlooking the Seine valley during the summer of 1827. His years abroad were dedicated to the defense of American principles and the American character against European, but particularly English, criticism. The foundation book for the defense was a review of the status of his native government and society, glamorous perhaps in the perspectives of three thousand miles and a year of absence, but accurate in most of its facts.

Cooper has adopted the rather original device of a club of gentlemen, representative of the leading nations of Europe, whose time is their own and whose purpose in life is the impartial observation and judgment of the civilizations of the world. With no motive other than the improvement of their minds by the critical observation of mankind, they were unprejudiced, but in no sense idle, travelers. Their social bias was in every case aristocratic, a fact worthy perhaps of more than casual mention, and the American John Cadwallader who directed the anonymous English author during his travels was in every sense eligible for membership. He is Cooper's first portrayal of his ideal American gentleman, a personage to be described in the abstract once more in *The American Democrat* and to be reincarnated in the Edward Effingham, the Miles Wallingford, and the Mordaunt Littlepage of the later novels. "Society in America is constituted as in every other Christian country," writes Cadwallader in one of his notes of explanation to his guest, "breeding, education, family alliances, and wealth exerting most of their customary influences." All of these the ideal American gentleman possessed, but he could boast a further quality which his European compeers might only envy. The "political freedom and high rational refinement" with which he was endowed, in common with his fellows, by the liberal social and political régime under which he lived, had cultivated in him a species of "common sense" unknown in Europe. He could regard the absence of fixed rules of caste with mild assurance that the power of his own intelligence, refinement, and wealth would guarantee him social ascendency as long as he deserved it. In spite of the Catholic Abbate Giromachi of Italy, who objected to the preponderance of the Protestant interest, and of the British

Baronet, Sir Edward Waller, who was a little jealous of having a member who might introduce a dialect of his mother tongue, the American was finally elected to the exclusive club of gentlemen of the world in reward for his services to his English guest. There is a touch of satire in this, but there is also an unmistakable admission on Cooper's part that an American aristocracy of worth was a desideratum of the new social order.

The bachelor's tour was restricted to the eastern states with which Cooper himself was familiar, from Boston to Washington, with an extension to Cooperstown. His method is that of the narrative travel record, liberally expanded by comment of a more or less philosophical nature. His arrival in New York was opportunely timed so that his first experience with the American people was his observation of their welcome to the *Cadmus* in 1824, just arrived with Lafayette and his party. In contrast to the sophomoric ecstasy which contemporary newspapers reflect, the national greeting seemed to him dignified and restrained, characterized by vast but well ordered crowds, tasteful display, and cordial personal welcome by the Vice President. Twice later, in Washington and in Boston, his route crossed that of Lafayette and again he was impressed by the tasteful restraint self-imposed upon the American enthusiasm.

The reserve of the national character was somewhat of a mystery to him but Cadwallader gave him the solution: "In the tossings and agitations of the public opinion," he explained, "the fine and precious grain of truth gradually gets winnowed from the chaff of empiricism and interestedness, and, to pursue the figure, literally becomes the mental aliment of the nation." Nourished on such wholesome matter, the national mind attained to a poise and self-reliance which gave to the stranger a sense of reserve. Democracy in government, explained Cadwallader further, was not to be confused with general social leveling. The American feared and hated monarchy, but admitted social inequalities as long as they resulted from natural superiority of the individual and not from a rigid and inherited caste system.

All of the various social institutions and activities of the nation were examined with the closest scrutiny. Inheritance of money or land, he concluded, must be accompanied by an inheritance of merit, for "nothing is easier than for a member of any circle to forfeit the privileges of caste." In such a society there is provided a greater flexibility and therefore an almost complete freedom for the individual. The position of women reflected this freedom. "A young American dancer chats, laughs, and is just as happy in the saloon, as she was a few years before in the nursery. It is expected that the young men would seek her out, sit next her, endeavor to amuse her, and, in short, to make themselves as agreeable as possible." Whereas such conduct would prove dangerous for the lady in European society, it was only dangerous in America to the foolhardy youth who indulged in the language of gallantry and found himself suddenly confronted with the alternatives of marriage or social ostracism.

Americans lived according to English standards of comfort in their households, the bachelor reports, except to a small extent in the quantity of carpets and other conveniences available. Industry had raised them far above the level of the primitive. In cultural amenities they were not far from that of European attainment.

General education had created a public receptive to the
arts and to study and, although less attention was paid
to classical learning than in Europe because there was
too much still to be done in the national life, nevertheless the higher branches of learning were on the increase.
Since the turn of the century, the exodus of young men
to European universities had fallen off somewhat, and in
1820 there were 8000 graduates of the twelve oldest colleges in the country, of whom one thousand were clergymen.

In spite of the fact that America could as yet boast few
men who had devoted their lives to literature or scholarship, her attainments in these fields were not negligible.
Contending on unequal terms with English authors, the
nation had produced Irving, Halleck, Bryant, Percival,
Brown, and Sprague, and had generously patronized visiting English actors like Cooke and Matthews. In addition to the obstacle presented by the absence of international copyright protection, there was also what seemed
to Cooper a poverty of materials. His comments in this
difficulty point forward to the experiments which he later
made in such novels of manners as *Home as Found* and
Satanstoe.

> It certainly would be possible for an American to give
> a description of the manners of his country, in a book that
> he might choose to call a romance, which should be read,
> because the world is curious on the subject, but which
> would certainly never be read for that nearly indefinable
> poetical interest which attaches itself to a description of
> manners less bald and uniform. All the attempts to blend
> history with romance in America have been comparatively
> failures (and perhaps fortunately), since the subjects are

too familiar to be treated with the freedom that the imagination absolutely requires.

After thus disposing of his previous literary efforts, Cooper suggests the solution to the problem in the success of those authors who had trusted most to their own conceptions of characters and to qualities that are common to the rest of the world and to human nature. Further, the American might find a certain literary distinction by portraying those aspects of the national life which were connected with his distinctive political opinions. Here, then, we find Cooper's own justification for his treatment of his characters as more or less universal types and for his motivation of so many of his later novels by social or political theories.

Equally interesting in the light of his later experiences are Cooper's notes on the press.

> The public press in America is rather more decent than that of England, and less decorous than that of France [he says]. The tone of the nation, and the respect for private feelings, which are, perhaps, in some measure, the consequence of a less artificial state of society, produce the former; and the liberty, which is a necessary attendant of fearless discussion, is, I think, the cause of the latter . . . . Actions for injuries done by the press, considering the number of journals, are astonishingly rare in America.

This fact seemed to him to furnish "irresistible evidence of the general tone of decency which predominates in the nation." Ten years later he discovered that these conclusions could not be counted upon to result from his premises. His analysis of the elements in the case persisted; his confidence in human decency was shaken.

In his comments on the army, the navy, and the institution of slavery he is similarly optimistic. The American character furnished the materials for excellent armed forces, but the disposition of the people made such forces unnecessary. On the question of slavery his position is equivocal although he never materially altered it. He cannot justify it in moral principle, but he finds the slaves themselves to be generally well treated, and he anticipates a gradual adjustment of the evil by natural and imposed limitations on its spread and by gradual emancipation. In this he was merely reflecting the opinions and actions of northern slave-owners he had known.

During his visit to Washington, the bachelor attended the session of Congress and furnished Cooper with an opportunity to explain and eulogize the political structure of the country. His comments are so objective that it is difficult to detect a partisan bias except in his rather more cordial admiration for Washington and for others who had. upheld the doctrines of Federalism than for those who espoused republicanism. It would seem, however, that this was rather more of a social than a political bias. The principle of manhood suffrage was affirmed equally by both parties and this alone seemed of fundamental importance to Cooper.

The adverse criticism of the Americans which finds its way occasionally into this book is so completely overweighed by patriotic enthusiasm that it is almost wholly lost. That the permanence of the Union was already threatened by slavery, Cooper recognized; he also sensed the danger in the enactment of more rigid laws curtailing individual liberty as corruptions advanced with the complications of civilization; but his final conclusion is that the spirit of greatness was in the nation and the means of greatness were within her grasp. A new era, he believed, was about to dawn. America had ceased to creep; she had begun to walk erect among the powers of the earth.

With this manuscript in his bag, Cooper landed at Dover on the morning of February 17, 1828, and, after a pause at the Adam Street Hotel, settled his wife, his nephew William Cooper, and his small boy in a comfortable house in No. 33 St. James's Place, a stone's throw from Piccadilly and almost in the yard of the Palace. Letters from Mrs. Cooper to her daughters, and contemporary maps, allow us to locate the house accurately as that on the further corner of a small court on the left, just before the narrow street widens to the tiny square in front of Spencer House. Cooper's door was, therefore, only a step from that of Lord Althorp, who is frequently mentioned in his letters. The arrangement he made with the owners of the house provided for service and the use of a tiny drawing room, a dining room, and three bed rooms.

The location was an admirable focal point in the intellectual and social life of the city, close by Mayfair, which, in the quaint provincialism of Sydney Smith, contained "more intelligence and human ability, to say nothing of wealth and beauty, than the world has ever collected in such a place before." Cooper's province bordered upon this Elysian preserve; and his neighbors were worthy of the rarified atmosphere. Among them were George IV, the Bishop of London, Earl Spencer, and the poet Samuel Rogers. "It was but a step from my door to that of Mr. Rogers," writes Cooper. "His house stands near the head of the place, there being a right angle between his dwelling and mine." His introduction to Rogers had been the result of letters forwarded, without his consent, by the dilettante poet William Spencer, youngest grandson of the Duke of Marlborough whom he had met in Paris, to the author of *The Pleasures of Memory*.

William Godwin was, however, the first Englishman to call. Under the impression that he was acquainted with the novelist's father, the quiet little old man appeared in the drawing room of No. 33 St. James's Place one morning while Cooper was busy writing. After explanations, the social philosopher sat down, and the conversation turned upon American politics, prospects, and literature.

"I have seen something of Dwight's, Humphrey's and Barlow's," volunteered Godwin, "but I cannot say that they pleased me much."

Cooper laughed. "We can do much better than that now," he assured his visitor, and proceeded to quote a passage from Halleck's *Alnwick Castle*.

Godwin was polite, but he was obviously not deeply impressed. His first visit was also his last.

With Rogers there is a different story to tell. It was at the *petits déjeuners* and dinners in his comfortable home that Cooper met most of those English men and women who invited him to their balls, receptions, and dinners, among whom were Earl Grey, Lord Lansdowne, and the Duke of Devonshire. The famous dining room in this miniature museum, much altered by subsequent owners, still looks out on a trim garden to the grassy stretch of Green Park beyond.

Rogers told Cooper the story of a visit one day from Chantrey, the sculptor. Among the treasures in the dining room was the carved wood pedestal of an antique vase.

"Do you know who did this carving?" he asked, and mentioned an elder sculptor.

"Yes," said Chantrey, "he had the job, but I did the work."

The artists and writers whose treasures were about the walls were entertained at the table. Among Americans before the time of Cooper's visit, George Ticknor and Washington Irving had enjoyed the hospitality of this quiet little connoisseur who was striving to keep alight the flame of eighteenth century wit and taste in a world that already contained but did not boast the more vigorous fires of Shelley, Coleridge, and Charles Lamb.

Wordsworth was in town for a brief visit in the winter of 1828, and Cooper was invited to meet him at Rogers's home, but a cold prevented his going. He met Coleridge at a dinner at Sotheby's and failed to be overwhelmed by an oral dissertation of more than an hour on the unity of Homer, which was punctuated rarely by gentle observation from the host and an occasional "Eloquent!" "Wonderful!" or "Very extraordinary!" from Scott. Once Cooper caught a hint of suppressed amusement in the eye of Scott's son-in-law, Lockhart, and he was himself impressed with the beauty rather than the logic of Coleridge's eloquence. Later, the American went with Sotheby to Highgate to call upon both Coleridge and Johanna Baillie, whose *Plays on the Passions* were still the talk of London's literary circles. His remarks are inclined to be more appreciative when speaking of such people of taste as this retired old lady or the powerful Sir James

Mackintosh, than when he mentions such eccentrics as Coleridge or Godwin. The wit of Sydney Smith, Joseph Jekyll, or Horace Smith seemed to him to be rather more desirable in civilized society than the eloquence of Coleridge, even though the famous conversational ability of Richard Sharp failed to live up to anticipations. Cooper was not alone among American writers of romantic literature to be blinded to their fellows on the other side of the water by the fading excellence of the older English writers. Irving, Willis, Halleck, and others sought out and praised Campbell, Montgomery, and Rogers rather than Byron, Hazlitt, or Keats.

The friendship with Scott did not prosper upon its renewal in London. One day Cooper recognized his carriage in the street by the coat of arms painted on its door; Scott later paid a formal call, and the paths of the two men crossed at several social gatherings. But again Cooper's political rather than his literary sympathies predominated, and he discovered a growing estrangement. Scott was courteous but distant; Cooper was silent or abrupt. In this case, as in so many, Cooper seems to have been super-sensitive, for his record of Scott's attention to him would leave little to be desired. But political and social bias was fundamental in the American.

For the same reason, Cooper found himself both welcomed and at home in the best Whig society in the city. Political sympathies at the time seem to have divided social London into two clearly defined camps, and, with the exception of Scott, Cooper made no friends among the Tories.

The ice once broken, as Cooper puts it, many distinguished hands were laid upon his knocker, and the incessant fire of invitations attendant upon the session of Parliament brought a few random shots in his own mail. At a dinner at Lord Grey's he met his neighbor Lord Althorp, Lord Durham, Lord John Russell, and Lord Holland. These gentlemen were already agitating in the House of Commons the reforms in the electorate which became the law of the land during the Grey ministry in 1832.

Some of Cooper's most pleasant evenings were spent in this society, leavened by some literary guests as well, at Holland House. Dinners at the fine old country house on the outskirts of the city, were among the most sought after of London's invitations. The sharp—almost rude—social manner of Lady Holland offset the milder hospitality of her consort and created the atmosphere of a truly British *soirée*. Cooper never felt fully at ease in such gatherings and, whereas he was quite ready to take his place at the foot of the table in the dining room of Envoy Brown or the Princess Galitzin, he resented the same experience in that of the Duke of Devonshire or Lord Lansdowne. His feeling was partly the result of the difference in the manners which prevailed in the social life of the two cities, but it may be more fully explained by a deep-seated hostility toward England which consistently motivated his conduct and colored his remarks.

The assertion of the contemporary American press that he accepted the hospitality of the English when he was with them, only to knife them in the back with his criticisms, is patently absurd.

"I hope you think worse of England than it deserves," wrote Charles Wilkes from New York on May 16, 1828, in reply to a letter from Cooper, and the real feeling of the latter is admirably summarized in the concluding statement of his own book on England:

> a country that I could fain like, but whose prejudices and national antipathies throw a chill over all my affections; a country that unquestionably stands at the head of civilization in a thousand things, but which singularly exemplifies a truth that we all acknowledge,—how much easier it is to possess great and useful, and even noble qualities, than it is to display those that are attractive and winning; —a country that all respect, but few love.

His passionate conviction that the cultural development, and even the political existence, of his nation depended upon a sharp break with her inherited past, was stung by the willing subservience of the American press to British opinion, by the prejudiced and superficial criticisms of English travelers in America, and finally by a British social attitude which accepted him and his country willingly, but, as it were, at arm's length. What he believed to be American principles and American aspirations rather than what he saw of English life and English manners absorbed Cooper's mind during those four months in London.

CHAPTER ELEVEN

Interlude: Switzerland and Italy

IN the last week of May 1828, when the *Notions* was well through the press and Cooper's business arrangements with Colburn promised well, he left London for Paris by way of Rotterdam, The Hague, and Brussels. He remained in the French capital only long enough to complete his plans for the summer and, on Monday, July 14, he set out for Switzerland accompanied by his entire family in a traveling carriage bought for the purpose, with a team of three horses and a booted postilion.

The first day took them as far as Melun, where they visited the Palace of Fontainebleau; the next to the Auxerre; the next to Dijon; and the fourth to Salins. On the following morning they started their climb across the Swiss border through a misty rain, but it soon cleared to reveal their first view of Mont Blanc at seventy miles distance.

I shall never forget the thrill of that moment [writes Cooper]. There is a feeling allied to the universal love of the mysterious that causes us to look with pleasure at any distant object which insensibly leads the mind to the contemplation of things that are invisible. The imagination steals down the sides of distant peaks into the valleys, which it is apt to people with creatures from its stores of recollections, or perhaps by its own creative powers.

As the country became more hilly, Cooper got out of the carriage and joined a peasant who was laboring up the ascent.

"Monsieur vient de Paris?"

"Oui."

"Apparemment, Monsieur est Anglais?"

"Non. Américain."

"Ah! Anglo-Américain, n'est-ce pas, Monsieur?"

This strange European conception of the Americans as a mixed and foreign race, largely negro and very little English, haunted Cooper, and he mentions frequent evidences of it. Next to American pride in themselves, European ignorance of America was, to him, the greatest obstacle against which the culture of his nation had to contend. That evening they arrived at Neuchâtel; and another day's stage brought them to Berne, where they settled until October.

Following his usual custom, Cooper's first thought was the finding of a home for his family. Berne had obviously been chosen for its central location and convenience rather than from any real knowledge of its charms. The party stayed at the principal inn, the Fauçon, only long enough to explore the neighborhood and to select a home on the fringe of population. The Villa La Lorraine, to which they moved, was probably the most imposing country-house in the neighborhood, in spite of Susan Cooper's disparaging comments on its cramped and uninteresting garden. It was situated half a mile down the Aar valley, in what was then open pasture land, but which today is a crowded manufacturing district, and is the only property in this vicinity which is shown on contemporary maps. From the terrace behind the house the eye could follow the river's course in a wide sweep around the close-crowded roofs and steeples of the town to the distant range of the Oberland Alps; and the drive down to the shops and to the beginnings of the main roads across the country in all directions was only a matter of minutes.

After circling around three sides of the old city of Calvin, with its bears and its wood-carvers, the river Aar turned, in Cooper's day, to flow between green fields and high embankments.

> Our house [says Cooper] is about as large as one of the ordinary boxes of Manhattan Island. It is built of stone, and, on the whole, is sufficiently comfortable. We found both house and furniture faultlessly neat. The place had just been occupied by the Spanish Minister, but it is the property of the Count Pourtalès of Neuchâtel, who is another Monsieur Tonson as regards landed estates, his name meeting you at every turn.

The Comte Louis de Pourtalès had owned this property for some years, and did not dispose of it until 1845, even though he never lived in it. In the opinion of Dr. Ed. de Reynier of Neuchâtel, an intimate friend of the family, he acquired this property in Berne in order to be able to accept the title of citizen of that aristocratic and powerful city, an honor which had been awarded him. Cooper sublet it from General de Toledo.

Even at that time the Villa La Lorraine was very old. It existed in the 15th century under the name "Kleiner Wyler," but in 1635 it was acquired by the Junker Johannes Steiger, Baron de Mont le Vieux et de Rolle, Captain in the French army, Garde Suisse in Paris. The villa was

then named La Lorraine because its new owner had
fought in the Regiment d'Erlach in the Lorraine against
the Austrian and Spanish armies. Since that time the villa
had given its name to the entire quarter.

Again we must turn to Susan Cooper for a description of the life of the family in their picturesque home.

> Close at hand [she says] was a common, with a sort of
> natural terrace, higher than the house, which became a
> favorite evening walk, where parents, and children also,
> with hoops, kites, and jumping ropes, found much enjoy-
> ment. This natural terrace formed the regular quarterdeck
> walk of the author; like other sailors, he never lost the
> habit, formed in naval life, of pacing to and fro over the
> same ground, either alone, or with a companion. From
> this common there was a very grand view of the Ober-
> land Alps,—a view in the evening most wonderful in
> sunset glory . . . The nearer country, hill and dale, in the
> immediate neighborhood of La Lorraine was also charm-
> ing. The drives were of course beautiful, along narrow
> roads, smooth and even as garden walks, amid open fields,
> rich and neat with the highest degree of culture; the pass-
> ing wheel almost touching the crops, so narrow were the
> tracks.

The Wept of Wish-ton-Wish, she tells us,

> was only partly written at La Lorraine. There were too
> many excursions to the finest points of Switzerland break-
> ing in upon his writing days to allow of regular work. . . .
> The little study at La Lorraine was often vacant, the Amer-
> ican writing desk closed, the small volumes of the 32° ed-
> ition of Shakespeare, his constant traveling companions,
> lying unopened on the table, while the traveler was wan-

dering about the country, frequently in a *char-à-banc* with a portion of his family.

The first excursion from Berne—not counting such one-day trips as that to Hindelbank—took the obvious route through the Lauterbrunnen and Grindelwald valleys to the foot of the Jungfrau. Later journeys were made to Schaffhausen and Constance, and to Geneva, but Cooper's longest tour, with a guide alone for company, took him through most of the central and eastern cantons, up the Rhine to its source, and back by the Grimsel Pass to Meiringen and Thun. In leaving Switzerland by the Rhone Valley and the Simplon Pass, he saw Vevey for the first time and was so charmed that, two years later, he chose this village on the sunny shore of the Lake of Geneva for a month's residence and some rambles which are described in the final volume of his travels.

In all of these wanderings Cooper had an entirely care-free attitude with regard to his routes and his objectives. The general direction and the length of each trip seems to have been roughly settled in advance, guidebooks and histories were studied with care and diligence, but the trip itself was usually made with map in hand and no set itinerary. At several points in his journeys the enthusiasm of an acquaintance of the road determined or changed his course; at others a debate was necessary to explain the perplexing relationship of the map to the actuality. But at all times the progress was constant, and Cooper noted carefully the past history as well as the present details of each valley or town through which he passed, each evening recording in his journal a few notes on the day's experiences. The journal, one of the few which the novelist ever kept for an extended period, formed the nucleus of the letters which make up the first volume of his *Sketches in Switzerland,* the third of his *Gleanings in Europe.*

With the exception of Italy, Cooper found Switzerland more congenial than any other European country, for here, in addition to natural beauty, an abundance of romantic tradition was revealed to him at every turn. Whether or not he had read Schiller he does not say, but the legend of William Tell forms the background of his keenest enjoyment of Morgarten and other places associated with national origins. The chances are, however, that he gained his knowledge of this tale from such unromantic sources as Picot, for the modern skepticism on all such subjects had not yet prevented the acceptance of Tell's escape from the clutches of the tyrant Gessler as historical fact.

The events associated with the affiliation of the cantons of Uri, Schwyz, and Unterwalden appealed to the defender of the principle of federal union; whereas the ruins of the castle of the Hapsburg family furnished inspiration for a paragraph on that "false policy that has endeavored to raise up, in the center of Europe, an Empire of discordant materials to counteract the power of Russia and France."

On the other hand, the castles of the Erlach family at Spietz and Hindelbank aroused only sympathetic thoughts in the mind of the American landed proprietor. The power of the latter family was economic, and in this sort of dominance Cooper believed.

Thus his comments on the scenes before him were the result of a newly acquired knowledge of Switzerland's past, colored by firm political and economic convictions of his own. The struggle between France and Austria for the mastery of the mountain cantons, which commenced in 1798, aroused his sympathy wholly for the Grisons, caught between the opposing forces, and the internal developments of the years since 1815 provoked his favorable comment wherever he discovered them. By the year of his first visit, 1828, Swiss independence and unity had been finally asserted, and the government, as well as the physical character of the twenty-two cantons contained most of the features which they present today, in spite of important constitutional revisions in 1848. When, therefore, Ralph Restless (Captain Maryatt) accuses Cooper in 1838 of being secretly "disappointed with his examination into the state of the Helvetic Republic," he fails to limit his comment, as Cooper limited his criticism, to those aspects of the present and past of the nation definitely associated with tyranny and oppression. With modern confederated Switzerland, which at that time was undergoing an even more severe test of permanence than the United States, Cooper found himself in complete and hopeful sympathy.

The eager anticipation which Cooper had experienced on crossing the Swiss border was repeated with even greater intensity as he looked southward from the roof of the Milan cathedral and realized that behind the wall of the Apennines lay the "true Italy." He was prepared to find that ancient and sunny land the most desirable in all Europe, and he was not disappointed. A winter in Florence, a summer divided between the olive groves of Tuscany and the Bay of Naples, a final winter in Rome, and a brief residence in Venice, combined with leisurely journeys over most of the highroads between Paestum and the Po, left his ardor undulled. "If there is any country out of my own in which I would wish to live," he told his friend G. W. Greene several years after his return to America, "it is Italy. There is no place where mere living is such a luxury."

In spite of his accomplishment in the writing of romances, "mere living" is the best description of his activity during the next year and a half, from October 1828 to May 1830. After a pause at Milan, the journey in the family traveling carriage was continued on October 15. A loitering, sight-seeing drive of five days across plain and mountains, by way of Parma, Modena, and Bologna, brought the party, on October 20, to the door of the Hotel York in Florence.

As usual, the stay at a public inn was as short as possible. Old Caspar, their coachman, guide, and personal attendant during the journey, was dismissed, and Mr. and Mrs. Cooper, the four girls, nephew William, and young Paul sought quieter and more permanent lodgings for the winter.

The apartment upon which their choice finally settled was in the Palazzo Ricasoli on the corner of the Via del Cocomero (now the Via Ricasoli) and the Via de Biffoli (now the Via Biffi), only a step from the Duomo. Somewhat more modest than the great palaces of the Medici and Strozzi, this none-the-less imposing reminder of a treacherous and powerful Florence still retained its somber exterior, its sheltered court, and its great rooms with ceilings nearly twenty feet high. Through ten of these rooms Cooper distributed his family and their possessions, he engaged his servants, and he lighted his wood fires against the October chill. His description of his palace home is characteristic in its zest and accuracy.

> We took an apartment [he says] in one that belongs to an ancient family who still inhabit a portion of the building, and as our rooms are on the street, we may be said to occupy the fortress. The great gate is of iron, and the great stairs, of course, massive and solid. The lower floor is occupied only for the offices and stables. Then comes what is called a *mezzanino,* or a low story, with small windows, but which has some very good rooms. Above this is our apartment, with ceilings nearly twenty feet high, large rooms all *en suite,* and windows to look out of which we ascend two steps. The walls would bear considerable battering, though the position of the house protected it from any danger of such a nature . . . We have two noble bed-rooms, besides several smaller; a large drawing-room; a good cabinet for myself; an ante-chamber, and baths, offices, etc., all furnished, for the moderate sum of sixty dollars a month. We have ten good rooms in all, besides the offices.

Here they burnt in their lamps "oil which you would be happy to get on your lobsters and salads"; and the master of the establishment, who, according to his daughter, "was very critical in laying the wood," warmed a corner of his gloomy grandeur with bright flames on his hearth and with his own cheerful hospitality.

He tells Dr. De Kay that "there are so many Manhattanese who pass this way, that we are never long without gossip of the city"; and yet he adds later, "As to Americans here, I see little and know less of them." Doubtless the first reference is to his own good friends who sought him out and the second to what permanent

American colony there then was in Florence. Among
the former was George W. Greene, who turned up one
hot summer evening, at his villa outside the city walls,
together with the English engraver, George Cooke,[1]
Gouverneur Wilkins, with whom he made a trip to the
coast, and the young sculptor, Horatio Greenough, to
whom the American novelist was a timely friend. Without reputation and far from his home, Greenough accepted Cooper's suggestion that he make a marble group
of "Chanting Cherubs." The bust of the novelist which
is now in the Boston Public Library is testimony to the
beginning of a friendship which gave America her first
sculptor of importance.

Of the "swarms" of English people then in the Tuscan
capital, Cooper knew many. Lord Lansdowne, who had
entertained him in London, crossed his path at a mountain inn near the frontier on the journey south, and many
others whose names are mentioned made a part of those
cosmopolitan gatherings which also included the American. The French Minister, M. de Vitrolles, also num-
bered him among the guests at a masked ball during
carnival time; and exiles from other Italian states were
met at dinner or reception.

Chief among his new-made Florentine friends were
Marchese Gino Capponi and Marchese Giuseppe Pucci.
Both of these lovers of fine arts and free consciences were
members of old Italian families, as well as members of
that international clan of intelligent liberals who, after
the peace of 1815, devoted their principal energies to history, literature, and art, allowing their political activities, at least for the moment, to lapse.

[1] G. W. Greene, *Biographical Studies,* pp. 53–56.

A contemporary memorial[2] speaks of Pucci as the Florentine Mæcenas and bears witness to the large sums which he spent "in protecting learned men and artists whom he turned aside from foreign unappreciative curiosity." Capponi, on the other hand, played a less passive rôle. The traditional loyalty of his family to the ducal house of Tuscany had not been dimmed in him by his attendance upon the court of Napoleon or by his friendship with Lord John Russell and Francis Jeffrey in the England which he so much admired. Although complaining of the "profound melancholy of the mind condemned to inaction and restraint" by the *laissez-faire* policy of the restored ducal government, he nevertheless devoted himself to the intellectual awakening of the people of Florence by means of his review, the *Antologia,* modeled on the *Edinburgh,* and by his studies in Florentine literature and history.

Both of these men, like Cooper, could profess and live according to a liberal political philosophy without sacrificing the essential aristocracy of their natures. Both were representative of the passing order of landed proprietors whose liberalism of spirit made them sympathetic with the new but temporarily suppressed nationalist movement throughout Europe. It is not difficult to reconstruct the basis of their friendships with Cooper, nor the results of that association. It is no accident that the *Antologia* contained long and favorable reviews of the *Notions of the Americans* and of the rare Florentine edition of *The Wept of Wish-ton-Wish.*

The oppression of the Austrian domination in the

[2] H. M. Migliarini, *Alla Memoria del Marchese Cav. Giuseppe Pucci,* Firenze, 1839.

Northern Italian states and of the Papal and Sicilian governments in the South had made Florence, where the Hapsburg rule was less severe and direct, a refuge for all those of liberal opinion. Cooper naturally found the social atmosphere to his liking, and, in his two interviews with the Grand Duke spoke of many things of common interest. A son of the widowed Madame Ricasoli, who was later to take a leading part in the events of 1848, was then a page at court, and many others contributed to this curious blending of the old and the new. Grand Duke Leopold's interest in America was intelligent, although passive.

The result was that Cooper entered the social life of Florence more than that of any other Italian city. The "lords, dukes, and princes" whom, according to his wife, he almost affronted by sometimes preferring a retired life to the round of their entertainments, were, many of them, foreign *emigrés*. "At the receptions of Don Camillo Borghese," he writes, "one sees most of the strangers," and it was probably at these receptions that Cooper's own intimacy with the Bonaparte family commenced. Since his exile from the land of his choice at the downfall of Napoleon, Prince Borghese had retired to the land of his ancestors. The palace in Rome was, however, uninviting, and he was content to leave its magnificent apartments to the care of his brother, Prince Aldobrandini. In Florence he could enjoy the more congenial society of his wife's family, most of whom had by now become, in effect, peace loving Tuscan citizens, forgetful of their stormy experiments in imperial intrigue. Princess Pauline Borghese herself had died in 1825, and Caroline and Jerome spent most of their time in Trieste, but the other living members of the family were usually to be found in lazy, liberal Florence. The Prince, who seems to have formed a sort of hub for the family group, opened his doors with little distinction to those who came, with the result that the company was interesting, though, as Cooper remarks, "not of the purest water."

With Louis Bonaparte, Comte de St-Leu and ex-King of Holland, Cooper formed a more personal relationship. It was he who invited the American family to witness the fête on the Arno from the windows of his palace. Napoleon's elder brother, Joseph, Comte de Survilliers and ex-King of Naples, as well as Lucien, who bore the title of Prince of Canino, were also there with their wives and children. Cooper seems to have liked them all, but he especially admired the young Prince Napoleon Louis, son of Louis and elder brother of Napoleon III, who died only two years later at Forli in the Romagna. Doubtless the extended residence of so many of the Bonapartes in America furnished the common ground of these conversations, but there are temperamental reasons as well for Cooper's associations with ex-kings and princes of the revolutionary and post revolutionary era.

This interesting and varied life was interrupted in February by a business trip to the north. Apparently Cooper found it necessary, or convenient, to have his new novel, which he had just completed, set up and privately printed in English so that it might simultaneously reach his publishers in many lands. His first thought was to take his manuscript to Paris for the purpose, and on February 26, 1829, he set out on the initial stage of his journey, leaving his family in Florence and traveling by regular post. His letters to his wife, published in his

Correspondence tell of this journey in some detail, and the more formal record of his progress is to be found in his *Italy*.

The picturesque coast-line of the Riviera and the port-city of Genoa did not fail in their appeal to a one-time sailor whose business was the writing of romances. In Marseilles, however, on March 3, he found a printer who held out hopes of being able to do the work for him immediately. His plan was, therefore, to hurry the book through the press and return to Florence in three months' time, but within the week the printer failed him and he determined to carry a type-setter back with him and have the work done under his own supervision at the Florentine house of Molini. The fact that the only man to be found who could work in English was deaf and dumb and bore the name of Richard Heavisides with appropriate grace, does not seem to have discouraged him; for the project was only revised many months later when the type-setter revealed a dangerous and ungovernable temper. Through the kindness of the Grand Duke, the work was then completed in the government offices.

The trip back from Marseilles to Leghorn (Livorno) was made in an English brig, and upon his arrival in Florence, Cooper immediately laid his plans for the summer. He had thought of Leghorn itself, for the sea was always an attraction, but he had settled upon the Villa S. Illario instead. Until the July heat brought with it a touch of malaria, the novelist lived in a "trim and spruce rather than picturesque" villa on a hill, a few hundred yards from the Porto Romano on the road to Certosa. The narrow lane of S. Illario a Colombaia strikes off at right angles and climbs the hill between high walls and olive trees, dividing Cooper's villa and the church of his friend the priest, and finally joining numerous similar little lanes at the top. Among the other attractions of the villa, writes Cooper, "it has two covered belvederes, where one can sit in the breeze and overlook the groves of olive trees, with all the crowded objects of an Italian landscape." Both belvederes, or balconies, have gone long ago, that communicating with Cooper's room having become a tiled roof over an almost fortress-like entrance to the sunny garden; but that of the priest is still there, covered with vines.

On May 25, 1829, Cooper wrote to his friend Dr. De Kay of New York: "We intend to visit Lucca, Pisa, and Leghorn again. From the latter to Naples by water, touching at Elba; if practicable, we shall stay at Naples until October, and then for the Eternal City. In March for upper Italy and Venice." The further projects of visits to Russia and Scandinavia were abandoned in favor of a return to Paris in August 1830. The first part of the program was, however, carried out almost to the detail, and when his lease expired at the end of July, he set out once more, this time with his entire party, for the coast.

Cooper was most himself when he felt a deck, however modest, beneath his feet. It was a true sailor who wrote: "The little *Bella Genovese* got her anchor, with a light wind at north-west, about five in the afternoon, and began to turn out of the harbor. In half an hour we had made three or four stretches, which enabled us to weather the head of the mole, when we stood to the southward, with flowing sheets."

The voyage down the coast in this thirty-ton felucca, with its crew of ten, was a series of delights. Six days

of sea air restored the life which had almost been parched
out of each of them during the final month in Florence,
and, on August 10, the little boat dropped anchor in the
Bay of Naples.

Several weeks were devoted to sight-seeing in Naples,
Pompeii, and Herculaneum, and another to house-hunt-
ing, before the move was made across the bay to Sorrento, and the spacious apartments of the Casa detta del
Tasso occupied for the remainder of the summer.

This house is, in many ways, the most interesting of
those which Cooper rented during his European rambles.
Said, probably erroneously, to have been the birthplace
of Tasso, it was a shrine for many pilgrims who doubtless had read the following passage from Mrs. Mariana
Starke's then popular guide to Italy:

> But the object peculiarly interesting to strangers is the
> paternal mansion and birth-place of the amiable though
> unfortunate Torquato Tasso; . . . This mansion, delight-
> fully situated on a cliff supposed to have been the site of
> an ancient temple, displays on an outside wall, a muti-
> lated bust, in *terra-cotta,* of the immortal bard; and in the
> saloon upstairs are a marble bust, called Bernardo Tasso,
> though more probably it represents a Roman senator; a
> medallion of Alexander, finely executed; another of Julius
> Caesar when young; another of Agrippina; and another
> of Marcus Aurelius; they are ancient and were all found
> at Sorrento. Beyond the saloon is a terrace commanding
> an extensive view of the Bay of Naples; but the chamber in
> which Torquato Tasso was born is fallen into the sea.
> This mansion now belongs to the Duco di Laurito, who
> descends, in the female line, from Tasso's family.

THE VILLA S. ILLARIO, FLORENCE

THE VILLA TASSO, SORRENTO

Today, Tasso's villa is a part of the Hotel Tramontano and the wall of the adjoining convent has fallen into the sea, but the apartment which the Coopers occupied is much as they left it. The well, the grand staircase, the vista of the Bay of Naples through a sequence of rooms and the grand sala with a pseudo-classic bust and its gilded chairs have been preserved for a very good reason. The Cav. Guglielmo Tramontano not only boasts of these two illustrious names in the history of his home, but he can produce a list of former guests which includes Long-fellow, Renan, and Ibsen, as well as most of the crowned and uncrowned rulers of Europe for more than half a century. The shade of Cooper is here at least in company worthy of its society! "The terrace," says Susan Cooper, "became the quarterdeck of the author," and here, be-tween trips to Capri, Ischia, Pompeii, Vesuvius, and even Paestum, most of *The Water-Witch* was written, although the printing of it was not even attempted in a country of such strict censorship as the Kingdom of the Two Sicilies. Thus the Bay of Naples furnished the inspira-tion for a novel of far-distant waters. The mind of Cooper had not yet become thoroughly imbued with the Euro-pean scene, or surely here, as well as in Venice, in Switz-erland, and on the Rhine, he would have turned into romance the secret chambers and passages below him, and the ruins of former civilizations carved from the perpendicular rock or covered by the clear blue water a stone's throw from the shore.

Fortunately for the Coopers, the representative of their government then at Naples was one of those men who early set a high standard of hospitality and helpfulness for the United States Consular Service. Alexander Ham-

mett, Consul at Naples from about 1809 until 1856, became for the time their most constant friend, and through
his means many trips were simplified and many doors
opened. It was he also who interceded with the authorities for Greenough when the latter was suffering from
a temporary mental weakness induced by malaria. But
the record of his other deeds will never be written because the documents which could reveal them probably
no longer exist. In a nation which still had dungeons
for political prisoners, the services of such a man were
not superfluous.

But the cliff-dwelling at Sorrento was too remote to
tempt many visitors, and the life of the last three months
of the summer of 1829 was self-centered and contempla-
tive rather than adventurous or socially varied. With
the first cold rain of autumn, the *Divina Providenza*
was called upon for a final crossing, a second carriage was
hired at Naples, and the party set out for the Eternal
City.

The old post road to Rome was almost identical with
the present day rail journey, *via* Capua and Terracina,
and across the Pontine Marshes. The Hôtel de Paris,
where the Coopers rested after their journey, is not listed
by Mrs. Starke, but the Via Ripetta is mentioned as a
particularly desirable location for lodgings. Here, between the Porto di Ripetta (the site of the Ponte Cavour)
and the Porto del Popolo, a step from the Palazzo
Borghese and not far from the Spanish Steps of Keats
memory, an apartment was found. A clear view from
the back windows across the Tiber disclosed the Castle
of Sant' Angelo, and, in direct line beyond, the dome of
St. Peter's. But no mention of the number on Cooper's

door nor detailed description of his rooms survives to furnish a key to further information than this.

The Rome of 1829 had little in common with the Rome of today; perhaps no other Italian city has seen greater development within the past century. The inhabited portion had shrunk back from the old walls until it was huddled in the river bend within the inner circle of the hills. The now highly developed eastern and southern quarters were then rubbish heaps and fields. Bits of broken walls and pillars marked the sites of ancient temples and monuments, but many of them were still unidentified. Excavations had barely commenced. In the Forum an avenue of trees led diagonally from the arch of Septimius Severus almost to the arch of Titus, and the lower part of Byron's "nameless column with a buried base" had only recently been uncovered. The Coliseum, as well as numerous isolated columns, basilicas, and baths, were left crumbling and overgrown with weeds in the midst of desolate fields. The sense of a dead civilization must have been far easier for a hurried tourist to grasp than it is today, reconstructed as it must be now from the guide book and in the whirl of modern traffic; but there was far more to tantalize even the amateur archæologist in the throng of mysteries on every side.

And an archæologist Cooper now became. His interest in ancient civilization had already been aroused by the ruins of Pompeii and Herculaneum, and, with the aid of Winckelmann's letters and other authorities, he had made himself familiar with the current knowledge on the subject. He had studied the location of the various towns lying about the foot of Vesuvius at one epoch or another and of the lava streams which had brought about their destruction. The treasures which had been uncovered by the recent excavations in this region aroused his investigative mind, particularly the manuscripts of Herculaneum which were then in the process of being unrolled and deciphered. His "intense curiosity" was sufficient, therefore, to overbalance even his "reverential awe" as he entered the Porto San Giovanni.

One of his first calls was on the Baron Bunsen, archæologist and religious historian; and his daughter records, "he was much interested in the information he received from him." It is reasonable to infer that this information bore in some respects upon the revision of the *Description of Rome,* by Volkmann and Lelande, upon which the Prussian Minister expended most of his spare time and energy between 1818 and 1829.

Even more a haunt of artists and poets than of pleasure seekers, the city on the Tiber offered the American many congenial acquaintances among her *emigré* group, a society not unlike that which had accepted him at Florence. The Polish patriot-poet, Adam Mickiewicz, released at the age of thirty-one from his Russian prison, was spending the winter in Rome, and it was presumably he who accompanied the novelist on those rides on the white horse Chingi which form the topic of several of the letters of his *Italy*.

Cooper also tells of a call upon Prince Aldobrandini, then occupying the upper floors of the Palazzo Borghese in his brother's absence in Florence, as well as a picnic on Monte Mario with a Russian princess, doubtless the Princess Galitzin, and a company of Russians, Poles, French, Swiss, Germans, and Italians, but no English. His daughter notes also that he furthered his Florentine intimacy with the Bonaparte family by paying his respects to the simple but dignified Madame Mère, mother or grandmother of them all, and that, while in her salon, he met the young Prince Louis Bonaparte, later Napoleon III, who, whip in hand, presented anything but a royal appearance.

Instead of joining the general exodus of foreigners, after Easter Sunday, April 11, 1830, had come and gone, Cooper delayed a few days to pay a visit to Tivoli. There was now neither business nor pleasure to keep him in Italy. The journey north was soon undertaken. Over the mountains to Ancona and the Adriatic, their route then followed the coast to Rimini and, pausing once more in Bologna, they finally reached Venice *via* Ferrara and Padua.

The weeks spent in Venice are notable because they furnished the knowledge and background for *The Bravo,* but his record of the visit itself is not so colorful as those of the months in other Italian cities. Absence of sounds and of friends conspired to make even Venice monotonous, and before the spring was well advanced, the travelers were again on the road, this time bound for Verona and Innsbrück. At this point, for the first time since his arrival at Cowes four years before, the connected narrative of Cooper's European wanderings breaks off for more than a few weeks. We leave the American family in May 1830, in their two privately chartered carriages on the road to Dresden, to join them again in Paris in the fall. The intervening residences in Dresden and Frankfurt can scarcely be discovered in the existing records.

CHAPTER TWELVE

Lafayette and Liberty

THE journey to Dresden and the short residence in an apartment overlooking the Alt Markt was prompted by the usual combination of motives. Neapolitan censorship had prevented the earlier plan of putting *The Water-Witch* into type and issuing it privately so that sheets might be provided to English, American, German, and French publishers at the most advantageous moments. The alternatives were a return to Paris or London, or an excursion into Germany. The love of travel decided in favor of the latter.

Again the Cooper caravan moved across fertile plains and climbed through mountain passes. The route lay by way of Tyrol and Munich. They stayed in Dresden until July brought rumors of revolution in Paris. The lure was too great. An excursion into Russia was abandoned and Cooper set out for the scene of those battles for the principles of human liberty in which, for the next two years, he was to offer to his friend Lafayette a more than passive support.

He went ahead himself in August as a scout to determine whether or not it was safe for his family to follow. At Frankfurt he received more reliable news from the front. "All is quiet in France and promises to remain so." "Lafayette has yielded to necessity, and the Bourbonites have done the same thing. Charles X is nearly forgotten, and Philip I seems to be moderate and wise. . . . Perhaps I shall go no further than the frontier, for there is little to be seen now in the capital."

He proceeded, however, and reached Paris on the 20th. The streets were filled with Americans, all on quests similar to his own. "I have not seen the General," he reported, "who is all in all here. He is universally admitted to be the most powerful man in France. That he might have made himself chief of the government appears to be acknowledged all around. He is courted, flattered, feared, and respected. I have written to him, but thought it more delicate not to intrude."

He paused at the Hôtel d'Incri and set about the task of finding an apartment. Lafayette was now on the rue d'Anjou, having left his grape-vines at La Grange when the revolution was first proclaimed. Cooper wished to be near him. His choice was No. 22 rue d'Aguesseau, a fine old *hôtel* on the corner. Later he moved to an apartment in the rue Champs Elysées (now the rue Boissy d'Anglais).

Lafayette was not slow in welcoming him. Within a month he had arranged for his presentation to the pseudo-republican King. Meanwhile, Mrs. Cooper and the children had followed and were installed in their new home.

On the evening of September 19, Lafayette called for Cooper in his carriage. They continued to the Palais Royal, home of the Orléans family during their days of plain citizenship. On the way they picked up Louis Mc-Lane, then United States Envoy to Great Britain.

The ante-room of the palace was crowded with ministers and diplomats. The King was dressed in the uniform of the National Guard and the ladies in his family had affected a republican simplicity of dress. They were polite, but there was a stir of uneasiness as Lafayette entered. "The affectations and egoisms of rank," wrote Cooper in his diary, "are offended by his principles, and there is a pitiful desire manifested by the mere butterflies of society to turn his ideas and habits into ridicule." Even before the interview was over, Cooper saw that the attitude was not confined to butterflies and that it went deeper than ridicule.

Louis Philippe spoke with interest for a few moments of his recent visit to America, and then retired. As the American party left the room, a young officer remarked, *"Adieu, l'Amérique!"* The fear of losing their worthless distinctions and their tinsel, thought Cooper, gives great uneasiness to many of these simpletons. For the time, however, he believed that Lafayette had the confidence of the King, and upon that supposition he built his hope that the July monarchy might survive.

A reception to the American ladies in Paris completed the royal gesture of friendliness between the two republics. On September 23, Cooper went again to the Palace, this time for dinner. The King led Mme. de Lafayette, and Lafayette the Queen, into the dining room. The dinner, Cooper thought, might have been taking place in Washington. There was no display and much friendly conversation.

"You have visited many countries," said the Queen, "which do you prefer?"

"Italy, in which Your Majesty was born, for its nature," replied Cooper; "and France, in which Your Majesty reigns, for its society."

Monarchy and democracy had met on a happy and

neutral plane. A little display did not trouble Cooper; he had been reading Jefferson's letters. The great democrat had been somewhat unphilosophical, he thought, when he resented the forms of the old order and affected a simplicity which was too far in advance of the facts. A gradual transition, he thought, was more honest as well as more practical.

By January 19, his confidence in the republicanism of Louis Philippe was already shaking. "Here we have just got out of the *provisoire*," [1] he writes to Samuel Rogers.

The *furor* of moderation is likely enough, I think, to put us all back again. . . . The intentions of the *juste milieu* are obviously to make the revolution a mere change of dynasties, while the people have believed in a change of principles. Could the different sections of the opposition unite, the present state of things would not endure a month.

"Now France is guilty of the extreme folly of attempting to imitate a system which is just found out to be intolerable to those who have some relief for its abuses," he wrote to Silliman on June 10.

France has no countries subsidiary to her prosperity, and the sentiment of the nation is opposed to aristocracy, and yet such is the secret object of her present rulers. They do not see that England has got on in spite of her aristocracy, and not by its means, and that when the true agents of her wealth and power are beginning to fail her, that she cannot bear the inflictions of that aristocracy, and is about to get rid of it, too, along with other evils, but there is something so seductive in the social distinctions and the

[1] G. P. Fisher, *Life of Benjamin Silliman*, I, 334–36.

real superiority of the English gentlemen over their neigh-. bors, that it proves too powerful for their patriotism. It is fashionable to say that France is not good enough for free institutions. Surely this involves a fallacy. Free institutions mean the responsibility of the rulers to the ruled; and the worse the former are, the greater is the need of this responsibility. We trust the word of an honorable man; we look for bond and mortgage from a knave. If men were virtuous, government would be unnecessary. A strong police can exist in a republic; the strongest and best in Europe is in Switzerland—and that is all which is required to suppress ordinary vice; and, as to public corruption, surely the more responsibility the better.

Again, there is no better training for public virtues than publicity and freedom. You will ask me what I expect from all this. It is my opinion things cannot stand as they are. The press is virtually free in France, and five years have made a great change in its tone. The government has been guilty of the weakness of offering a premium to all the revolutionists in Europe to overturn them, since without France no other country can get on. I have little respect for the King, though I think he is rather a weak than a bad man. It is impossible to foretell what course events will take in this inflammable nation, but the movement cannot be stopped. There will be more or less freedom all over Europe fifty years hence; or even sooner. Public opinion has already secured it in most countries, despotic or not in name, and public opinion will exact pledges for its continuance. At present all the efforts of France are turned towards peace. If this were done with a good motive, it would be respectable, though it were weak. But the motive is a narrow selfishness. The powers that be, know that a war, in the present state of Europe, would inevitably throw the people uppermost; and this is a result they are determined to avoid at any hazard.

They wish to be nobles, and in that vulgar reason you have what just now forms the whole spring of English and French policy—self, self, self.

Cooper's final opinion about the July monarchy was outlined in conversation with Lafayette. He did not believe that the compromise policy of Louis Philippe would survive because the throne had been created before a republican form of government had been developed. The French people had trusted to a man rather than to institutions, and the deeper aspirations of the man they had selected were obviously monarchical. Whatever the outcome, however, he believed the French people would be benefited socially as well as politically by their brief glimpse of republican principles. He gave the new Orléans dynasty three years in which to reveal its true nature and be deposed.

"What would have been your solution to the problem of July?" asked Lafayette.

Cooper replied that he would have created a provisional government under which republican checks and balances could have been put into operation. As soon as possible, the throne would have been offered to the legitimate Bourbon pretender, Henry V, because his youth promised well for an education into the opinions which were to govern the new era, and because the French people would greatly prefer the legitimate line of their ancient dynasty to the branch of the family which, in the person of the elder Duke, had made for itself an unpalatable social reputation.

An extension of the suffrage "as much as facts would justify," would have been the first step in the transforma-

tion. A moderate property qualification, in addition to
that of intelligence, would be substituted for the absolute property representation of the older order. The House
of Peers would be converted into a Senate after the
American plan of representation, the departments acting
as states, with the important modification that the entire
electorate should vote for every senator, and the terms
of members of both houses would be restricted to not
more than five years. The ministry would be directly
responsible to these representative legislative bodies and
the King merely their organ. Cooper concludes his project with the significant remark, "I have no doubt that
our own system would be better, could we devise some
plan by which a ministry should supersede the present
executive." His observation of European ideals and forms
in government and society were already modifying his
enthusiasm for democracy as expressed in the American
experiment.

At Lafayette's home he was always welcome. "The
candor and simplicity of his opinions form beautiful features in his character," he writes; "and the *bienséance* of
his mind (if one may use such an expression) throws a
polish over his harshest strictures that is singularly adapted
to obtain credit for his judgment." His own uncritical loyalty to the opinions and the person of Lafayette furnished
the materials for a constantly deepening friendship. The
Fourth of July meetings of the Americans in Paris were
usually tributes to Lafayette, and on December 8, 1831,
a great dinner was given in his honor with Cooper in
the chair.

Meanwhile, the ground was gradually slipping away
under Lafayette's feet and he turned to Cooper for assist-

ance and sympathy on almost every occasion. As a representative from Meaux in the Chamber of Deputies, he threw himself into the vain task of constructing a republic about the mock democratic figure of Louis Philippe. He was the recognized leader of the opposition to the *juste milieu* or compromise party. Even before the end of 1830 he had resigned as Commander of the National Guard under pressure; and on March 13, 1831, the ministry of Casimir Périer came into power. The throne was a silent witness of events, as step by step the reaction asserted its power. The subtleties in the political developments of the next two years were too great for the direct methods of Lafayette and the uncompromising political principles of Cooper.

Even in the first days of his return to Paris, Cooper was approached by his friend for advice. "The 'Commission on Theatres' has asked me some questions as to the regulations controlling American theatres, which I fear I may answer incorrectly," he wrote on September 9, 1830. "You must be familiar with the regulations governing the theatre of New York, be they state laws or city ordinances."

But it was in the more serious problems of the inherited peerage and the revision of the taxes that Cooper's involvement in French internal affairs first became pronounced. The "Finance Controversy," arising from the discussion of the French budget of 1832 drew the two men closer together and had a profound and far-reaching influence, both upon the development of Cooper's opinions, and upon his subsequent reputation at home and abroad.

"Permit me to enclose and to recommend to you an

article in the *Revue Britannique*," wrote Lafayette on September 9, 1831, "a preliminary discussion of the French budget, asserting that the American Government is more expensive than that of France. . . . Be pleased, therefore, to favor me with your critical observations." The journal, although dated June 1831, had only just appeared, and the article in question, written by the editor Emile Saulnier, was obviously a bit of government propaganda intended to forestall the attacks of the Opposition when the budget bill was introduced into the Chamber early in January 1832.

Two motives prompted Cooper's careful and extended reply, which was published, both in English and in French, in December. His friendship for Lafayette would alone have been sufficient to justify a reply; but the controversy was focused upon an issue which was a never failing provocation to him. His *Notions of the Americans* had opened his long campaign in defense of American ideals and institutions against European attacks which attempted the vindication of the old order. Here again monarchy and political aristocracy were being justified by citing the failure of the American experiment. The American form of government was more expensive, and therefore less desirable than the monarchical form of France. Cooper did not care what became of France; but he did care what France thought of America. He rushed generously and enthusiastically to the defense.

Lafayette had his letter printed in French and bound up with other correspondence on the subject, including a letter from General Bernard, for circulation in the Chamber on January 6, 1832. The bill had been submitted the day before, but its discussion was postponed for a week. As on practically all other issues, the Opposition failed to make its point.

This fact, however, does not prevent Cooper from having been in the right. Saulnier's arguments were persuasive but specious; Cooper's were abrupt, direct, and in the main sound. He disclosed his opponent's method of distorting evidence to prove his points, and he proved that the American form of government was not extravagant. With that he would have dropped the matter had not Saulnier printed in his journal a letter in support of the French cause, from Leavitt Harris, attaché of the American legation and later Chargé d'Affaires. This, together with further remarks from the editor, provoked Cooper to his series of letters in the *National,* daily organ of the Opposition. For several weeks the French press of both parties was alive with comment on the controversy, and the interest was reflected in the presses of England and of the United States. Lafayette wrote to both Gallatin and Livingston, then Secretary of State, for data in support of his case. The latter sent a circular letter to the States and brought with him the resulting statistics when, the next year, he became Envoy to France. Gallatin dismissed the controversy as futile.

In his first and longest letter, Cooper had relied upon such statistical evidences as he could gather from the current issues of annuals, supplemented by his own experiences as a tax-payer in New York. He stuck close to his facts and developed his argument with his customary dogmatic enthusiasm. In his replies, his anger at the representation of his adversaries became more vehement and his style more sharp. He would not have pushed the debate beyond these rebuttals if it had not been for Livingston's effort to collect statistics. His main point had been that the fundamental differences in the institutions and principles of the two nations made a fair comparison of their resources and their taxes impossible. Livingston's action, however, implied an acceptance of the principle that a comparison of the costs of a strongly centralized government with those of a republican federation of states could be accurately accomplished. Saulnier's conclusions had not been based on the sum of the expenses of the cities, villages, arrondissements, cantons, and communes of France. It was unfair, therefore, to include in the American estimate the expenses of the states and the municipalities of the Union. Cooper made this point in his letter to the American People which appeared in the Philadelphia *National Gazette* on Wednesday, December 5, 1832. With the exception of his summary of the controversy, which appeared in the second part of his *Sketches in Switzerland* some years later, it was his final word on the subject, even though Lafayette kept the discussion active in the French press for several years.

The effects of the controversy upon Cooper's reputation did not, however, come to an end with his silence. It was almost the first evidence the American public had received that its beloved romancer was vitally concerned with the problems of the world about him and that his attitude was not wholly one of uncritical acceptance of the actions as well as of the principles of his national government. On this issue he had taken sides against the official representatives of the United States at a foreign court. William Cabell Rives, then the American Envoy to France, was one of his intimate friends and the two men saw much of each other socially. In the "Finance Controversy," however, they were not in open sympathy. Rives seems not to have disapproved either of Cooper's opinions or his actions, but his nego- tiations, then in progress, concerning the claims of Amer- ica against France, made it necessary for him to preserve a diplomatic silence. Cooper never understood his atti- tude. He was obviously not ready to eat, with Washing- ton Irving and others of his fellow citizens, the humble pie served on European tables for American consump- tion.

This was the only problem of internal French politics into which Cooper was drawn, but Lafayette's activities had never been confined to his own country, and his world liberalism involved his American friend in the general European turmoil of revolutions in the early thirties. Belgium was the first, closely followed by Po- land; and the liberal movements in Italy, England, and Greece claimed the close attention of both men.

"The news from Belgium this morning is very seri- ous," Cooper wrote in his diary on September 23, 1830. "This contest will draw on the war which, in some shape or other, must grow out of the late revolution. The Dutchmen seem very obstinate, and the Belgians very spirited. The hatred of all elevations of the lower classes, among the European aristocracy, is so intense that fight they must, to their own certain destruction."

He was interested in the actions in the field as well as in the principles involved in the contest. Lady Russell later detailed to him the account which her husband had written to her of the campaign. The armistice had halted the advance of the Prince of Orange and prevented the taking of Louvain, thereby avoiding the defeat of the French and the seizure of Brussels. "After which we would have seen Prussia, and I think, England, in the field," concludes Cooper. Later, with Mrs. Cooper, he visited the fields of battle.

The attitude of the detached observer which Cooper maintained toward this revolution was not repeated in the struggle of the Poles for freedom from Russia. His sympathies for the suppressed nation had first been aroused by Adam Mickiewicz as the two men rode about Rome on horseback during the preceding winter.

At the same time, Lafayette, in Paris, had been offering secret aid to the rebels through their emigré representatives, and was, as a result, the object of suspicious observation on the part of the Paris authorities. A police report in the French national archives [2] tells of dinners at the bookshop of J. Barbesat, in the rue des Beaux Arts No. 6, over which Chodzko presided and which Lafayette, Benjamin Constant, Jullien, and other French sympathizers attended. By July 1830, affairs in Poland had begun to approach a crisis. The new French revolution stimulated the hopes of the liberal party, but it also caused Tzar Nicholas to assume increasingly aggressive measures in order to anticipate the incipient revolt. Recognizing his true enemy, he planned a war against France, but the conspirators were one step ahead of him. Aware of the direction which events were taking, they communicated with Lafayette and apparently received encouragement. Only the letter itself, which apparently no longer exists, could determine the exact nature or extent of this encouragement, but there seems little doubt that he conveyed to the Polish leaders a fairly definite expression

[2] MSS. *Police Générale, Affaires Politiques,* F7; 6988; dos. 73703.

of hope that the liberal party in France would be strong enough, not only to prevent the Polish army from being forced into war on the Russian side against France, but that it would even be able to furnish open support to a revolt against the oppressors. The revolution broke out on November 29, 1830, and Warsaw fell to the rebels on December 1.

When, finally, Lafayette felt that his sympathy for the Poles could become open, he urged French intervention in the Chamber of Deputies. Again he showed his wisdom in turning chiefly to Cooper for American aid. With this support he succeeded in accomplishing much informally, which he was at the same time fighting for unsuccessfully on the floor of the Chamber. From the secret meetings at the bookshop of M. Barbesat there developed, after the overthrow of Charles X, an organization known as the French Polish Committee, with Lafayette as its chairman, the function of which was to arouse French interest and to enlist French aid in the cause of the Polish insurgents in order to encourage the revolution while it was in progress, to aid Polish exiles in Paris and elsewhere, and to bring pressure to bear upon the French and other governments to encourage legislation or action favorable to the insurgents and opposed to Russian dominance. As an adjunct to this work a committee of the American residents of Paris was also formed with similar aims and agenda. Cooper was its chairman. These committees, working in harmony chiefly because of the close personal association of their heads, did much for the cause of Polish freedom.

Among those on the American committee was W. B. Habersham, who had come to Paris to study.

The kindness of Messrs. Morse and Cooper [he writes] [3] introduced me to Lafayette during the summer of 1832, and induced him to invite me to join the three as a fourth in a committee appointed for the purpose of disposing of a large sum of money sent from America to aid the Poles in their struggle with Russia. Poland having fallen, our duty became to aid, with the connivance of the French government, the escape of Polish refugees, and to do this we met, at the house of Mr. Cooper once a week, in the rue St-Dominique, the leaders who had escaped and were qualified to advise us. The association gave me a certain position among the leaders of the political clubs and some considerations with Frenchmen of note, and through them acquaintances elsewhere who furnished me with ideas to which I shall refer hereafter.

Cooper's interest in the question became active soon after the outbreak of open hostilities, toward the close of 1830. His letters to his friends in America at this time contain long and sympathetic accounts of, and comments upon, the revolutionary movements then general in Europe, but none of his early discussions of the Polish question have been preserved. His complete sympathy with the position of Lafayette may, however, be deduced from the reply of Charles Wilkes, on March 9, 1831, to an expression of his friend's opinion. "It is impossible," says Wilkes, "not to feel a deep sympathy for the Poles, and yet mine does not extend so far as to induce me to wish that France should interfere to prevent Russia from suppressing, what Russia will call at any rate, a downright insurrection—which would inevitably bring on, it appears to me, a general war."

[3] Morse MSS., Library of Congress.

Cooper's sympathy, on the other hand, apparently did extend this far, and his aid soon took a more effective form than the mere expression of his views. When young Alvan Stewart, later a New York lawyer, arrived in Paris in July of this year, he found the Polish propaganda in full swing, with Cooper and Lafayette at its head. Inquiring at the home of Rives, he learned that the anniversary of American independence was to be celebrated at No. 104 rue Richelieu, a "splendid apartment." The dinner was presided over by Cooper, with Lafayette on his right and Rives on his left. Both guests of honor were cheered individually, and a subscription taken up in favor of the Poles.[4] On this occasion the American envoy apparently did not feel it necessary to exercise the caution which later characterized his attitude toward this question.

The immediate result of this meeting was an appeal to the American people for further aid. There appeared in Paris shortly thereafter a small folio, of three pages, containing the resolution drawn up at the Fourth of July meeting, with Cooper's letter to Lafayette and Lafayette's answer, as well as an address "To the American People," signed by Cooper as Chairman and by J. A. Washington as Secretary. This last document, which was copied in the American papers of the day, seems, undoubtedly, to have been of Cooper's authorship also. "I have received your address about Poland," writes William Dunlap from Burlington, Vt., on September 20. "Heaven help the brave fellows! I can only pray for them. Your effort is not without its effects in this country."

Neither was it without effect in Poland, although it

[4] MS. Journal in the library of the N. Y. Historical Society.

took a more practical turn than that of printed persua-
sion. How far Cooper put his hand into his own pocket
in aid of the cause will probably never be known, but
it may be guessed from Lafayette's reference to the subject in his last letter to Cooper. "I would have written
you sooner," he explains in 1834, "had I not every day
expected to recover your hundred dollars. The Pole
French Committee, who are penniless, have not yet returned that borrowed sum, originally appropriated by
us to poor Chodzko [of the earlier gatherings] who has
been obliged to leave France and is now languishing
in a corner of England."

With the increasing stress in Warsaw throughout the
summer, culminating in the complete failure of the revolution in October, the activities of these French and
American friends of Poland became more rather than
less pronounced. The first anniversary of the insurrection
celebrated in Paris on November 29, 1832, was not a
particularly happy occasion. Lafayette once more demon-
stated his keen feeling for the dramatic, the weapon with
which he had won most of his victories over the mob
throughout his career, when he appeared before a tense
and mingled audience in the costume of a grenadier of
the Polish National Guard. It was the open espousal of
a lost cause. But the friends of liberty before him had
not given up their hopes for the ultimate success of their
principles. There is something pathetic in Lafayette's
eloquence:

> It is in the name of the Central Committee and of all
> the Polish committees of France; in the name of the Amer-
> ican Committee, interpreter of the Polish associations of

LAFAYETTE AS COOPER KNEW HIM

From the portrait in the Hôtel des Invalides, Paris,
painted in the park of his château, La Grange, in
1834 by Mme. Joubert. Photograph by Giraudon,
through the courtesy of The State Street Trust
Company of Boston.

the other hemisphere, that a former comrade-in-arms of Kosciusko, honored at the end of his career by the title—so precious to him—of the Polish national guard, comes today to receive the first of our prescribed brothers to arrive in this capital.[5]

Determination and loyalty did not fail as success became more and more of a mirage.

Further efforts along the same lines are reflected in a letter of Elizabeth Marlay, an Englishwoman then in Paris, to Cooper early in 1832. "It has been suggested to me," she writes and the suggestion may well have come from Lafayette,

that you might again lend a helping hand to the Poles, were you to ask Mr. Morse to contribute any sketches, or drawings which he would make, or spare, as prizes in the lottery set on foot at this moment by the friends of these poor refugees. Many of the French artists, with Gerard at their head, are doing so, giving paintings, more or less finished, as they can afford time,—and I, who am commissioned to sell tickets and have chiefly to deal with those who care little for Poles, or paupers of any kind *here,* know how valuable anything from the pencil of an artist is as an inducement to such persons to try their luck.

There need be little fear that this request or its accompaniment, the request that Cooper himself purchase one of Miss Marlay's lottery tickets, was refused. Samuel F. B. Morse, the American artist and inventor, was then too intimate and too sympathetic with Cooper to have had any great difference of opinion with him on such a matter as this.

[5] *Memoirs,* VI, 627–29.

Throughout the winter of 1831-32, the work of Cooper and of Lafayette persisted in the Polish cause, which, by this time had become mere charity without further hope of political consequence. "I have seen more of him this winter than last," writes Cooper of his friend in February, "owing to the circumstance of a committee of Americans, that have been appointed to administer succor to the exiled Poles, meeting weekly at my house, and it is rare, indeed, that he is not present on these benevolent occasions." In the collection and distribution of these funds in aid of stricken liberals, the arbiter of many revolutions found solace, and in his American friends he found sympathy. Meanwhile, the conditions of the Polish refugees in France became worse and worse. The ministry even went so far as to evoke an old law against foreign political exiles, by which means it banished some of the more troublesome agitators. Upon the career of reaction in the Chamber, Lafayette found his influence vanishing. Protocols and ratifications of which he did not approve passed in a steady and morose succession, unaffected even by the death of Périer, who had been stricken by the now rampant cholera.

So bad had the situation become that even the distribution of financial aid to the Poles was not easy. In his reabsorption of the conquered people into his empire, the Tzar had discarded all masks and had set to work in earnest. "The emperor of Russia continues his horrors in Poland," writes Lafayette in April. [6]

> Our envoy, Dr. Howe, has done marvels in the cantonments of Elbing; the American money distributed by him, in counteracting the lies of the Prussians who said that no

[6] *Memoirs,* VI, 658.

one was concerned about the Poles either in France or elsewhere, has revived the courage of these brave people, separated from their officers and sub-officers. Howe was arrested, contrary to the rights of peoples, secretly retained for four weeks, and released at the demand of Mr. Rives, but with an escort to the French frontier.

One further appeal to the American people by Cooper, published in June 1832, concludes the record of this aspect of his friendship with Lafayette. The Fourth of July dinner of that year was not a success, but the reasons for its failure can only be conjectured.

As for this dinner, [wrote Cooper afterward,] I have only to say that one of its incidents went to prove how completely a body of Americans are subject to common and inconsiderate impulses, let the motive be right or wrong, —of how low estimate character is getting to be among us,—and to determine me never to be present at another.

The list of toasts on this occasion is the only clue we have to the exact nature of this incident. This list had been submitted to General Bernard, a true friend of America and the personal advisor of Louis Philippe, for approval. The two-day revolution of June 5-6 was still too fresh in the public mind to allow for great safety in a gathering of republican sentiment. General Bernard, in his reply to Cooper, warns against any allusions to the "varying opinions which divide France at this time." "So," he concludes, "my dear and honored friend, if Mr. Rives attends the dinner and if you think that it will go off without party feeling as regards the affairs of France, I will accept an invitation if it be sent me; if you think otherwise, you will render me a true service by not inviting me."

This was a heavy responsibility for Cooper, and as Lafayette, who so recently had been borne in enforced triumph by a rowdy Paris mob, was present as guest of honor, the inconsiderate impulses of the American guests do not seem much of a mystery. A word for Lafayette might be interpreted as a word against Louis Philippe, and, although the toasts seem harmless enough, the situation was so charged that a very little flame would ignite it.

The conspicuous absence of the name of Poland from the list of toasts to the revolting nations of Europe—a list which includes Greece and "our southern neighbors" —may or may not be taken as significant. Doubtless the Polish issue, as an issue, was dead in so far as France was concerned, but it must also be borne in mind that Lafayette himself had not abandoned the cause, and that peace with Russia had become even more necessary now that she had triumphed. A reference to this topic would have been ample instigation for the result which General Bernard feared, and impromptu toasts, as the General himself warns in the letter, are difficult to control. Exactly what happened we may only infer.

Cooper, however, seems to have had no further active part in the Polish movement. Once more he had proven himself, as much as Lafayette, the champion of liberal principles in other nations, fearless and determined in the face of hostile opinion.

Meanwhile Paris itself had been far from peaceful. "I returned to Paris on the 20th instant," wrote Envoy Rives to Secretary Livingston on September 29, 1831,[7]

[7] W. C. Rives, Despatch #79, Paris, September 29, 1831, to Edward Livingston, Secretary of State, Washington, D. C., in Despatches to the Dept. of State, Vol. 25, France.

and found it the seat of considerable agitation produced by the news, which had been received some days before, of the fall of Warsaw. The charges made against the ministry, on this occasion, of feeble and even treacherous conduct toward the Poles, provoked a discussion in the Chamber of Deputies, which extended into a general examination of their whole system of policy, both foreign and interior. The debate continued for several days, and was marked in its progress by great violence and even bitter personal recriminations. It resulted, however, as you will perceive by the journals which accompany this dispatch, in a vote of the Chamber, which, by a majority of 221 to 136, declared in strong terms its confidence in [the] ministers. This vote manifests more unequivocally than anything which has yet occurred, the spirit of the present Chamber of Deputies, and in the promise of decided parliamentary support it holds out to the system of the present ministry, must be considered as adding very much to the chances of preserving the general peace of Europe.

Such was the temper of these times. Rapidly Lafayette was becoming the forlorn leader of a lost cause about whom all elements of discontent, those most hostile as well as those most sacred to his principles, had gathered.

By the following June the city was stricken with cholera. The funerals of the two leaders of opposing factions, Casimir Périer and General Lamarque, provided a sharp contrast. That of Périer was dignified, solemn, and controlled by the soldiers of the King. The effort to arrange a popular demonstration in favor of the government had proven a failure. The people were sullen; but there was fear that their emotions might take an unexpected and dangerous turn.

The party of Lafayette wished the funeral of the liberal

leader to be equally dignified and controlled; but there were two alternatives for the King on this occasion. He might order his *gendarmes* to hold the mob in suppressed control, or he might allow an uprising which could easily be put down and which would discredit his enemies. Lafayette feared the latter possibility, and subsequent events proved that his fears were not without grounds.

The plans for the occasion were carefully laid by both parties. The troops forming the garrisons of Paris were ordered to be in readiness for a popular uprising if such should occur. Students at the Ecole Polytechnique, seat of the radical extremists, were forbidden to leave the walls of their institution. The friends and political sympathizers of the former deputy, together with prominent citizens and foreign refugees, were to march in solemn procession behind his funeral carriage down the boulevards from the Madeleine to the Place de la Bastille. There speeches were to be made and final honors done. Lafayette was to be one of the speakers and, arm in arm with Marshal Clausen, he led the procession. Only minor disturbances occurred along the route, but, upon arrival at the Place de la Bastille, the smouldering embers burst into flame. The cortège had been drawn up beside the tribune and speeches had been made. Lafayette, old and saddened, perplexed by the threatening mob which he had so often faced and controlled, mounted the platform, and even the cries of *"Vive Lafayette," "Vive la Liberté,"* were for the moment silenced.

This was no time for revolution. Bloodshed and riot had always failed to establish liberty and peace. He was too old now to rescue his people from their own brutality again.

Just what happened when his plea not to spoil the solemn spirit of that day was finished remains obscure. Some contemporary accounts state that from the crowd a red flag bearing the *bonnet rouge* was hoisted. Others that a man in the crowd mounted the platform and tried to put a revolutionary cap on the head of Lafayette. Cries against the King and his government mingled with cries of honor to the dead Lamarque and the living Marquis. Suddenly shots were fired and the crowd melted from the Place to the narrow streets which had already witnessed so many hours of slaughter. Barricades were erected in the rue St-Merry; fighting continued in the drizzling rain through the night. By morning the insurrection had been virtually suppressed.

Meanwhile, Lafayette and his son had hurried away and, finding a deserted fiacre, had started for their home in the rue d'Anjou near the Madeleine. But the mob was upon them. Once more the hero of two revolutions was to be taken to the Hôtel de Ville and a republic proclaimed. The horses were removed from his carriage and on a long rope the frantic insurgents dragged him through the streets in triumph—mock triumph this time, for these were not his people. He was weary and old. At seventy-five his enthusiasm for such methods had waned, and he suspected a plot. There were those in the mob who wished to throw him into the Seine, others to make him president of the republic. For a time his destiny hung in the balance. Shots were heard in the neighboring streets. Finally, no one seems to know how, he reached the Place de la Madeleine once more and was home. The *porte cochère* in the rue d'Anjou was closed; the street fighting was far away.

At five o'clock that afternoon Cooper had crossed the Seine to the Tuileries. The streets were deserted, rumors were rife. Later, at dinner, a drum outside was heard to beat the *rappel,* a soldier of the National Guards was carried past, bleeding. Once more Cooper crossed to the scenes of the disturbance. A profound calm reigned about the Palais Royal. Suddenly a body of mounted *gendarmes* went up the street at full gallop, the single report of a rifle interrupted the unnatural calm; the metal screens before the shops were hastily pulled down; the air was filled with distant shouts and shots. There was little sleep, even for neutral American visitors, that night. According to his own account, Cooper spent most of it about the bridges in the heart of the city hoping to learn news with which he could quiet the fears of his family.

Two days later, when order had been reëstablished, he visited Lafayette. Rumors had been circulated that the Marquis had been arrested, that he had escaped to La Grange, that he was still in his apartment on the rue d'Anjou.

In the latter place Cooper sought him at dusk on July 7. The city was once more calm; the rue d'Anjou was silent. The gate of No. 6 was now open, and entering without knocking, Cooper was stopped by the porter. Being recognized as a frequent visitor, he was allowed to pass. His knock was answered by the faithful Bastien, who had accompanied Lafayette to America, and was led through the long series of high-ceilinged rooms, with their Empire furniture, their gilded mouldings and rich draperies, to the bedroom where he found the General seated with his back to the door. By the mantel stood

François de Corcelles, the husband of his grand-daughter. No one else was in the apartment.

Lafayette greeted his friend without rising. There was a change in his manner. It was none the less self-assured than usual, but it had about it more of the air of the grand old man. It was serious, almost sad.

The two friends discussed the revolution of the past days and Lafayette asserted his belief that the whole of it was a plot on the part of the Government to discredit the Opposition. He was waiting to be arrested. If his enemies did not proceed to these extreme measures, he would retire to La Grange and contest the old order no longer. Although he did not admit it aloud, he knew that his life was ended and that it had closed in defeat, almost in disgrace. When Cooper asked him whether there was now any possibility of a reconciliation with Louis Philippe, he replied, "Now we are separated by a river of blood." They talked of the July days of 1830, of the principles which had caused that momentary overthrow of the *ancien régime,* of the dark future of France.

"I hope we may have our usual Fourth of July dinner at La Grange," he said as Cooper rose to leave at ten.

"But we would all be shot for sedition if we drank our usual liberal toasts now," replied his friend with a smile. The disillusionment was complete.

Lafayette's last letter to his American friend, written shortly before his death, was dated from La Grange, April 14, 1834. He tells Cooper that the finance controversy is still active. "I am happy you took up early this matter," he adds, "and shall ever rejoice to find Americans assuming the existence of a political civilization far superior to European institutions and civic habits. It is fit that what I call the 'American Era,' the American school, should be the polar star of nations pretending to freedom."

CHAPTER THIRTEEN

Pictures of the Past

MEANWHILE, Cooper had returned to his old haunts on the south bank of the Seine. During the winter of 1831–32 his daughters were once more in a French school, Paul was continuing his education in many languages under the direction of his mother and his tutors, and the head of the household was working daily on the novels in which he translated into fiction his impressions of Europe, *The Bravo,* and *The Heidenmauer.*

During the previous March he had moved to a new home in the rue St-Dominique, but again the march of progress, this time exemplified by city planning, has destroyed a landmark of considerable literary and historical interest. When the Boulevard St-Germain was carved through the Latin Quarter, according to the plans of Baron Haussmann, it followed the bend in the rue St-Dominique on its way to the Pont de la Concorde. Here, at about the present location of the rue St-Simon, was No. 59, the Hôtel St-Susanne, which was the Coopers' home during the two-day revolt and the cholera terror. They were busy and exciting years, and Cooper's lodgings, as never before, became the scene of meetings between people of importance.

189

"In some respects," he writes at this time,

we are better lodged than ever, though compelled to occupy three floors. Here the *salon* is near thirty feet in
length, and seventeen high. It is panelled in wood, and
above all the doors, of which, real or false, there are six,
are allegories painted on canvas, and enclosed in wrought
gilt frames. Four large windows are fixtures, and the windows are vast and descend to the floor. The dining-room,
which opens on a garden, is of the same size, but even
loftier. This *hôtel* had formerly much interior gilding, but
it has chiefly been painted over. It was built by the physician of the Duc d'Orleans, who married Madame de Mon-
tesson, and from this fact you may form some idea of the
style maintained by the nobles of the period.

Once again, in the somewhat tarnished halls of a past
nobility, the American democrat settled down to the
comforts which he too knew how to enjoy; and again
the spacious chairs in the great *salon* were occupied by
Lafayette and his friends, by Polish refugees who sought
counsel and aid from the chairman of their American
relief committee, by American tourists who gathered here
to celebrate the Fourth of July far from their homes, and
by liberals of many other nationalities. The establishment of Fenimore Cooper was the home of a gentleman
of means and taste, and its door was open to all who
had sufficient culture to appreciate true hospitality.

During this winter the cholera reached Paris, but many
Americans—the Coopers among them—believed that, as
the epidemic was virtually world-wide, they were as
safe there as anywhere. None of them seems to have
contracted the disease, although Cooper notes that each
day, as he took little Paul down the rue du Bac and

across the Pont Royal for his lessons, the apple women became fewer and fewer until there was none left. The lower classes seem to have been the most seriously affected, although many among the notables were also taken. Gradually the disease settled in the neighborhood of the rue St-Dominique and the Coopers had their trunks packed and their horses harnessed for a departure when Mrs. Cooper became seriously ill. It turned out not to be cholera, but now one place appeared to be as bad as another, and they gave up any idea of escape. There were two cases in the *hôtel* and hundreds about it. William died in September of tuberculosis which he seems to have contracted during the sojourn in Switzerland and Italy. He had long been ailing, and now, in addition to the personal loss which he felt deeply, Cooper was left without copyist or currier. He wrote to Caroline De Lancey, suggesting that she come over in this capacity, but the invitation does not seem to have been accepted, and he turned instead to his daughter Susan, who held the post until Cooper's death and became his literary executor.

Principal among his American friends in Paris during this winter were Horatio Greenough, R. W. Habersham, and Samuel F. B. Morse. The relationship between the young sculptor Greenough and elder novelist had commenced in Italy and Cooper's purchase of the Chanting Cherubs had done much to bring the *emigré* American artist to the attention of his countrymen. Greenough's bust of Cooper is a good, although not his best, likeness.

Nathaniel Parker Willis, the foreign correspondent of the New York Mirror, met Cooper one day in March in the garden of the Tuileries. "And here come two of our countrymen," he wrote in his *Pencillings,* who are to be seen constantly together, Cooper and Morse. That is Cooper with the blue surtout buttoned up to his throat, and his hat over his eyes. What a contrast between the faces of the two men! Morse, with his kind, open, gentle countenance, the very picture of goodness and sincerity; and Cooper, dark and corsair-looking, with his brows down over his eyes, and his strongly lined mouth fixed in an expression of moodiness and reserve.

Alvan Stewart, in his manuscript diary, gives a somewhat different picture. "After I left the Minister," he wrote in July 9, 1831,

I went to my friend Mr. James Fenimore Cooper and found his family at breakfast. I stayed two hours and listened to Mr. Cooper, who has traveled and kept house in London, Paris, Geneva, Bavaria, Florence, Venice, and Rome. He has spent five years in Europe by which he has gained much information which will supply him with never failing sources for book making. For he tells me that each new book he publishes appears and is printed the same day in New York, London, Paris, Vienna, and Rome, in the English, French, German, and Italian languages. He showed me some of his manuscripts. He has invited and agreed to take me next Wednesday to Versailles and St-Cloud, which I consider very kind in Mr. Cooper. As I was coming away, I was most affectionately requested to come and spend Monday evening with them. This is the man whom the Americans in Paris call haughty, distant, proud, and with whom they cannot get acquainted. His youngest daughter is a little older than I am, about say three years. She, under the care of her instructress, played me two delightful tunes. I then came away.

Morse was, however, Cooper's most intimate American friend in Paris. Absolutely at one in their political opinions, the painter and the novelist had also much to discuss concerning the cultural and political hopes of their country. "I am diligently occupied every moment of my time at the Louvre," writes Morse on July 18, 1832,[1] "finishing the great labor which I have there undertaken. I say 'finishing,' I mean that part of it which can only be completed there, namely, the copies of the pictures." Cooper took the two or three hours of his daily relaxation from his own work at the gallery with his friend, and Morse spent almost every evening with him at his home. The two were inseparable. "Cooper is very little understood, I believe, by our good people," concludes the artist.

He loves his country and her principles most ardently; he knows the hollowness of all despotic systems of Europe, and especially is he thoroughly conversant with the heartless, false, selfish system of Great Britain; the perfect antipodes of our own. He fearlessly supports American principles in the face of all Europe, and braves the obloquy and intrigues against him of all the European powers. . . . He is courted by the greatest and the most aristocratic, yet he never compromises the dignity of an American citizen, which he contends is the highest distinction a man can have in Europe, and there is not a doubt but he commands the respect of the exclusives here in a ten-fold degree more than those who truckle and cringe to European opinions and customs.

The vehemence of this opinion may perhaps reflect more of Morse's feelings than of Cooper's, but it at least recalls the topics and the tones of those long afternoon and evening conversations of 1832.

[1] S. F. B. Morse, *Letters and Journals,* I, 426–27.

"Tell Morse," Cooper wrote to William Dunlap on November 14, 1832, [2] "to pursue his fortunes where he can. We were both born thirty years too soon." He had reference, of course, to the fact that the American public was not yet ready to support art, whether it take the form of painting or of the novel, in any practical way. But the feeling that six years of absence from his own country had given him the advantage of perspective was already becoming a fixed idea in his mind.

During the summer of 1832, this feeling was emphasized by a trip over parts of Europe which he had visited between 1826 and 1830. On July 18, he again set out on a family expedition, destination unknown, objects, health, particularly for Mrs. Cooper, and pleasure for all.

The old *calèche* had been repaired and fitted with a rumble outside for the Saxon Jetty, hired in Germany, and François. Sacks were stowed and passports signed. A few minutes before ten, the click-clack of post-horses was heard in the street, the *porte cochère* opened, and the carriage, with its four horses and two post boys, driven into the court. The Cooper family was soon loaded in and good-byes were waved to those left behind in the *hôtel*.

"*Par quelle route, Monsieur? A St-Denis?*"

Cooper nodded. The first problem was solved.

"They are running away from the cholera," men and women called after them from the street as they passed.

The party reached Senlis in time for dinner and there spent the night. Cambrai required another day, and by seven that evening the frontier was reached. Once more the cholera menaced them, the carriage windows were

[2] *Diary*, III, 646.

closed, and Belgium entered. At Brussels, there was a *fête* in honor of the first anniversary of the reign of Leopold.

> The King appears to be personally popular, [Cooper writes,] even those who have no faith in the duration of the present order of things, and who politically are his opponents, speaking well of him. The town has but few strangers, though the presence of a court renders it a little more gay than it was last year. The aspect of everything is gloomy, for the country may be again engaged in a war of existence in a week.

Processions of peasants passed from church to church next day to pray for help against the cholera.

Sight-seeing occupied much of the time during the short pauses in many towns. The road was taken again and the first extended stop made at Spa. Here the healthful waters and the climate conspired with a quarantine to arrest the party for two weeks and her health was restored to Mrs. Cooper. The old world resort was full of paradoxes. "Some intrigued, some played, and some passed the time at prayer. I witnessed trouble in one *ménage,* saw a parson drunk, and heard much pious discourse from a captain in the navy!" A few days later they had reached the Rhine and the towers of Coblenz appeared in the distance.

In spite of his preference for the scenic grandeur and variety of the Hudson, this classic river always awakened in Cooper more of his own *toozy-moozy* than any other sight of Europe. The previous summer he had gone over this same route and had paused long at Duerckheim. *The Heidenmauer* had been the result of this experience.

The ruins of an ancient castle had awakened in him all the glamor and all the horror of the feudal past.

Now as he followed the winding valley, the succession of castles and convents that crowned the hills awakened the same conflicting impressions. As he passed Godisberg and approached the Drachenfels, the road for the first time took the bank of the river.

> Opposite to us [he writes] were the Seven mountains, topped by the ruins of the Drachenfels, crag and monastery alike wearing the appearance of having mouldered together under the slow action of centuries; and, a little in advance, the castle of Rolandseck peered above the wooded rocks on our own side of the river. The low islands divided the stream and on one of them stood the capacious buildings of a convent. Anyone at all familiar with the traditions of the Rhine has heard the story of the crusader who, returning from the wars, found his betrothed a nun in this asylum. It would seem that lies were as rife before the art of printing had been pressed into their service, or newspapers known, as they are today, for she had been taught to think him dead or inconstant; it was much the same to her. The castle which overlooked the island was built for his abode, and here the legend is prudently silent.

"You will remember," Cooper warns his reader, "that I am not now dealing in fiction, but truth, and that, unlike those who 'read when they sing, and sing when they read,' I endeavor to be imaginative in poetry and literal in my facts." Nevertheless, the romance of these antique scenes moved him deeply at the same time that his sense of practical and moral values checked his enthusiasm.

Both qualities are to be found in his literal record, and both in his romances.

"Here we are," he wrote to Morse on August 15,

> on an island of the Rhine, about half-way between Cologne and Coblenz, in a deserted convent of Benedictine nuns. I am writing to you, you rogue, in the ancient refectory, which is now the *salle-à-manger* of half a dozen Fenimore Coopers, with the Rhine rippling beneath my windows, the Drachenfels in full view by pale moonlight, a dozen feet sounding distant and hollow in the cloisters, and with a bottle of Liebfrauenmilch at my elbow.

After the family had been safely stowed away in their various cells, "where girls ought never to be put," the head of the household "sallied forth alone in quest of sensation."

He found it in the cloister. A thunder storm lighted the pitchy darkness with an occasional flash of lightning which revealed an outline of the rocks and the broken tower on the shore. In an upper gallery of the cloisters a door gave to his hand and he entered a dark chamber. The air was filled with the rattle of broken glass as the wind swept into the upper windows, and the lightning revealed the somber outlines of carved images and the upholstered chair of the Lady Abbess. Half in tune with the mood of the gloomy mystery, half in derision, Cooper, alone, shouted as loud as the wind. The withered face of an old woman appeared at the door, and he groaned. Next morning the poor old crone of the abbey-inn had a tale to tell of ghosts and spectral voices. But Cooper himself slept that night like a midshipman in the middle watch. "Strange thoughts come uppermost in such a place, and at such a time, Master Samuel. The rustling of the wind seems as the murmuring of uneasy sisters, the pattering of the rain like floods of tears, and the thunder sounds as many *gémissements* at the sins of man." Poetry—or irony—had truly become confused with facts.

Again the route was debated and Cooper's own desire to turn east to Vienna was overweighed by his wish that the children, now that the youngest had reached an impressionable age, should carry home with them a lasting memory of Swtizerland. They proceeded therefore to Zurich and Zug, and from there westward once more to the Bernese Oberland. At Zurich he just missed comparing notes on Indians with Chateaubriand, who was leaving the inn as the Cooper family arrived.

The Lake of Lucerne seemed even more beautiful to Cooper now than it had exactly four years before, and he was moved to comment on how relative to the person and the circumstance such impressions are. He did not pause long, however, but proceeded to Berne and on to Vevey. The remembered beauty of the Lake of Geneva caused him no disappointment when it was once more spread out far below him.

There lay the Leman, broad, blue, and tranquil; with its surface dotted by sails, or shadowed by grand mountains; its shores varying from the impending precipice to the sloping and verdant lawn; the solemn, mysterious, and glen-like valley of the Rhone; the castles, towns, villages, hamlets, and towers, with all the smiling acclivities loaded with vines, villas, and churches; the remoter pastures, out of which the brown chalets rose like subdued bas reliefs, and the background of the Dents, peaks, and glaciers. Taking it all together, it is one of the most ravishing views of an earth that is only too lovely for its evil-minded tenants.

The disappointment came in choosing a home for the month of September. The first choice, from a distance, had been a small *château* "on a little grassy knoll that was washed by the lake," but, upon finding this relic of the middle ages entirely uninhabitable, they turned to the Château de Piel, lying just beyond Vevey, a picturesque and delightful ruin which would have rivaled the spacious but tarnished magnificance of the Palazzo Ricasoli, the Casa Tasso, or the Hôtel de Jumilhac. Once more disappointed, this time because their term of lease was too short, they compromised on a furnished villa in a quiet section of the town and but a stone's throw from the water. "Our house," writes Cooper, "was sufficiently large, perfectly clean, and though without carpets or mats, things but little used in Switzerland, quite as comfortable as was necessary for a travelling bivouac. The price was sixty dollars a month, including plate and linen." This house, which still bears the name of *"Mon Repos,"* has been identified by M. Eugene Gonoreau, Syndic of the Commune of Vevey, as No. 7 rue de la Madeleine. Perhaps the least imposing of Cooper's European homes, it was entirely suitable to an American democrat, with a substantial income, a large family, and a desire for that sort of society which puts worth and culture before family tradition in the estimation of human character. Thus Cooper passed a quiet month at Vevey, occupied chiefly by a small boat on the lake, and interrupted only by some slight sociability with several Americans who were also summering on the shores of the lake.

Idle evenings were spent on the water with the experienced oarsman Jean Descloux (Cooper gave the spelling at hazard). Besides being a good boatman, Jean was a philosopher in his way, Cooper tells us in the introduction to *The Headsman*. At least he knew that America was a continent which lay to the westward, and that the white inhabitants of this mythical land were not all black. He even had plausible hopes that someday it might become civilized. "In short," concludes Cooper,

> honest Jean Descloux was a fair sample of that home-bred, upright commonsense which seems to form the instinct of the mass, and which it is greatly the fashion to deride in those circles in which mystification passes for profound thinking, bold assumption for evidence, a simper for wit, particular personal advantages for liberty, and in which it is deemed a moral offense against good manners to hint that Adam and Eve were the common parents of mankind.

They talked of the fathomless depth of the lake, of good and bad fishing, and of the government of Switzerland. "If one man rule, he will rule for his own benefit and that of his parasites," was the political philosophy of the Vaudois; "if a minority rule, we have many masters instead of one, all of whom must be fed and served; and if the majority rule, and rule wrongfully, why, the minimum of harm is done." On these points the American was of the same mind. As he lay in the boat and watched the evening shadows creep across the mountains, he meditated upon good and evil, the past and the future; and from the confusion of misty images the story for *The Headsman* gradually shaped itself in his mind.

The principal scenes of this novel are laid in Vevey and in the monastery on the Saint Bernard pass. With William Cox, an experienced traveler, Cooper took a trip over the pass. "My weary mule," he tells us,

> seemed at times to be tottering beneath my weight or hanging in suspense, undecided whether or not to yield to the downward pressure. It was quite dark, and I thought it wisest to trust to his instinct and his recollections. This unpleasant struggle between animal force and the attraction of gravitation, in which the part I played was merely to contribute to the latter, lasted nearly a quarter of an hour longer, when the mules seemed to be suddenly relieved. They moved more briskly for a minute and then stopped before a pile of rock that a second look in the dark enabled us to see was made of stone thrown into the form of a large, rude edifice. This was the celebrated convent of the great St. Bernard!

Even a mule, it would seem, was privileged to have recollections at such a place, and Cooper's mind carried him back to the Romans, to the marauders of the middle ages, and to Napoleon. The hospice itself, however, did not impress him. "Before we fell asleep," he concludes, "Cox and myself agreed that, taking the convent all together, it was a *rum* place, and that it required more imagination than either of us possessed to throw about it the poetry of monastic seclusion and the beautiful and simple hospitality of the patriarchs." Even seen through the prism of romance in *The Headsman* the hospice fails to take on an appearance of glamorous warmth.

The castle of the Blonay family, on the hillside behind Vevey, furnished an objective for another excursion after his return from the St. Bernard. Again the lack of comfort was as impressive to Cooper as the antiquity of the baronial hold, even *"Mon Repos"* being superior in this respect, but from the balcony the view caught and held his fascinated attention. "I know nothing of M. de Blonay beyond the favorable opinion of the observant Jean, the boatman," he notes, "but he must be made of flint if he can daily, hourly, gaze at the works of the Deity as they are seen from this window without their producing a sensible and lasting effect on the character of his mind."

On all of these excursions Cooper carried in his pocket his Ebel and his Picot, gleaning his tourist information from the former and his statistics from the latter. Leisure gave him opportunity to meditate upon the government and the character of the people. The canton of Vaud had previously been subject to Berne and had been admitted to the confederation only in 1803. Problems of aristocracy and popular government were, therefore, as vital to Cooper's Swiss neighbors as they were to himself. A recently attempted uprising at Berne against the power of the aristocracy had aroused much interest in her former dependency. "The reaction," says Cooper, "of a political dependency which lasted more than two centuries and a half had brought about, even previously to the late changes, a much more popular form of government than was usual in Switzerland, and the people here really manifest some concern on the subject of this effort of aristocracy." He then protests against even the democratic government of Vaud because the electorate is primarily based upon a land or militia qualification.

This system [he concludes] though far better than that of France, which establishes a certain *amount* of direct taxation, is radically vicious, as it makes property, and that of a particular species, the test of power. It is, in truth, the old English plan a little modified, and the recent revolution that has lately taken place in England, under the name of reform, goes to prove that it is a system which contains in itself the seeds of vital changes.

As the season advanced, the reputation of Vevey for fevers warned Cooper that his vacation was over, and Lac Leman was left with regret. The route taken was the familiar one by way of Geneva and Dijon and the family was soon back once more in their European home, Paris.

A stop was made, however, at La Grange.

"Le Général," announced Bastien, *"sera charmé de vous voir, Monsieur";* and so he was. The family of Lafayette was assembled in the drawing room, and a typically cordial French welcome awaited the much-traveled Americans. American newspapers were on the table, and soon the two old friends adjourned to the tower study to discuss nullifications in South Carolina and the advancing reaction at the Tuileries. At noon the *calèche* struck into the post road once more and by night the *porte cochère* in the rue St-Dominique swung open to welcome the Cooper family.

From October to June they remained in Paris and Cooper wrote his recent experiences into the third and last of his European novels.

When summer came, plans for the return to America were carefully laid and Cooper went to London on June 15 to arrange passage and to conduct his business with Bentley. During this time he took rooms at No. 264 Regent Street. *The Bravo* had brought £1300 for English rights alone, but *The Heidenmauer* had not proved so successful, and the best that Cooper could do on *The Headsman* was £700. Already he was feeling the effect of his announced shift from the pure romance to the novel of purpose, and of the controversy which his expressed opinions in his two novels of the latter class and in the finance pamphlet had aroused. Even though this falling off in his revenue was serious, more drastic reductions were still to come. For a number of years Bentley paid him between £350 and £500 for each work, then dropped it to £250 and finally to £100.

Morse had sailed for home in October and Greenough was still in Florence. Cooper renewed some of his old associations in London, but the McAdams were in Scotland, and few English lords and ladies remain in the city during the summer months.

Besides, Europe had fulfilled its tasks. The situation with regard to the publication of further novels could not apparently be improved, the girls were educated in the ways of the world of refinement and culture, and Cooper himself had seen and studied the old order. At home, the problem of nullification in South Carolina was threatening, and his friends Jay, Morse, and Dunlap were becoming importunate in their demands that he return. A new nation—the land of Andrew Jackson—awaited him. Reluctantly, and in a mood for criticism, he returned to Paris on the first of August for his family and sailed with them from London in September.

III
1833–1851

CHAPTER FOURTEEN

Home as Found

THE James Fenimore Cooper who landed in New York on November 5, 1833, was a very different man from the novelist who had sailed from the same harbor with his family more than seven years before. To be sure, he was still the father of a large family, and still the rival of Scott (now dead only a year) as a teller of romantic tales. But Cooper knew, and his reading public knew, that both the man and the world behind him had changed. Carlyle had already started to throw his thunderbolts at the *Edinburgh Review* and *Frasers'* from his retreat at Dunscore, where Emerson had visited him in August of 1833. In England the Whigs were in power and the Reform Bill was law; in America the "reign" of Andrew Jackson had met and passed its mid-point triumphantly; in the heart of Cooper there was reflected the deep interest in the principles of human conduct which was finding expression in the reviews, the pulpits, and the senates of the day. The revolutionaries of the early 1830's seem to have sounded a sort of call to social order. England's romantic poets were dying like candles being snuffed out after service. Her social thinkers and historians—Mill, Macaulay, Carlyle, Tennyson—were already stepping into their places. In three years Dickens would start issuing his *Pickwick Papers*. The day for tales of adventure had passed; the day of searching analysis and realistic presentation of society was coming.

Cooper himself was not aware of these changes. He did not follow current literature nor seek new models. He held to his Shakespeare and his Scott, and he thought deeply on the social and political problems which were influencing the more serious of his literary contemporaries. He issued his dictum on human liberty almost in the words of Mill two decades before the appearance of the latter's famous essay; he attempted the social problem novel with an historical setting thirty years before George Eliot developed that type. In literature he was always the pioneer and he always suffered from the crudities of the experimenter.

His experience in Europe had aged him in mind and body. His springy step seemed firmer, slower but more determined. He looked at the world with less wonder and more dismay. He had not been well; but he had recovered his strength, if not his full health. Financial success sufficient to meet his wants had brought with it an increase in worldly assurance.

America was glad enough to see him. For the winter, a house was taken on Bleecker Street, near Thompson, and his household gods erected. "French gods these," writes Dr. Wolfe, "for the house throughout was equipped with furniture from France, and ministered solely by French servitors."

"There is nothing new in New York," Morse had written the previous February, "everybody is driving after money, as usual, and there is an alarm of fire every half hour, as usual, and the pigs have the freedom of the city, as usual, so that in these respects at least, you will find

New York as you left it, except that they are not the same people that are driving after money, nor the same houses burnt down, nor the same pigs at large in the streets." Cooper was a Rip Van Winkle; the old places were familiar to him, but many of the people in them had changed.

A year earlier Irving had been given a testimonial dinner on his return after an absence of seventeen years in Europe. Now the citizens of New York addressed Cooper, some of them like Peter Jay, Dr. Francis, Jeremiah Van Rensselaer, and Bryant his old friends of Bread and Cheese days, some like General George Morris and Mordecai Noah later to become his opponents in print. "A number of your former friends," they wrote Cooper, "pleased with your return among them, are desirous of testifying to you the continuance of their friendship, of the respect in which they hold your talents, and of their approbation of your manly defence, while abroad, of the institutions of our country. They therefore beg your acceptance of a dinner at such time as shall be agreeable to you." Cooper's answer to this invitation has not survived, but he was off within the month for Washington, and the dinner never took place. It may have been accident, but it seems more like deliberate intention, that made him turn from the proferred conviviality to an interview with the President. The criticism of his part in the finance controversy, which had been appearing in the American press, had already cut into his sensibilities. "I never expected, my dear Sir," he wrote William Skinner, of Baltimore on November 15, "to be thanked for upholding American principles in the face of the enemy. . . . I have seen enough to be satisfied that, with the majority of those who affect to have opinions, anti-American sentiments are in more favor than American."

Like Carlyle, Cooper early formed the habit of emphasizing his favorite ideas by repetition. No one of these is more frequently stated, with all the enthusiasm of novelty, than the distinction between opinion and facts. By the word "opinion" he meant the entire social philosophy of a nation or of a man; by "facts" he meant the actual degree of attainment. The demagogue, to him, was abhorrent because his opinions became subservient to his facts. That man alone was free who based his opinions firmly upon facts but who held to them in the face of any amount of opposition or conflicting circumstances. His own opinion of America had been constructed from the materials of his youth, shaped by the liberalism of Lafayette, and crystallized finally in his mind when American facts were all of three thousand miles away. Meanwhile, American democracy had fallen under the pragmatic spell of Jacksonianism, and was in the process of forming new opinions less absolute but more useful in a world of industries and wealth. William Cooper would have been less a stranger in the America of 1833 than was his son.

It is not to be inferred, however, that Fenimore Cooper lived in a world of remote idealism as respects his native country while he was abroad. He read American newspapers closely whenever they came to hand; his correspondence with friends at home is full of the discussion of national problems; and he engaged traveling countrymen in home talk at every opportunity. But he related all the developments in his country to the background of European opinion which was forming in his mind. The process is easily understood if we follow his writings and his correspondence during his travel years. His attitude toward England did not change as she underwent the transformations leading to the Whig reform of the suffrage. "Wonderful changes have occurred since I had the pleasure of seeing you," he wrote to Samuel Rogers in 1831,

> but I think greater still are in store. Is not the tendency of the present spirit obvious? and ought not your aristocracy to throw themselves into the stream and go with the current? . . . To me at this distance it seems an inevitable consequence of your actual social condition that both your church establishment and your peerage must give way. America might furnish a useful example to warn the English aristocracy if they would consent to study it. Our gentry put themselves in opposition to the mass, after the revolution, simply because, being in the habit of receiving their ideas from the most aristocratic nation of our time, they fancied there were irreconcilable interests to separate the rich man from the poor man, and that they had nothing to expect from the latter class should it get into the ascendant. They consequently supported theories adverse to the amalgamation, and as a matter of course, the instinct of the multitude warned them against trusting men opposed to their rights. The error has been discovered and although individuals among those who were prominent in supporting exclusive doctrines are necessarily proscribed by opinion, the nation shows all proper deference to education and character; when these are united to money and discreetly used they are of necessity still more certain of notice. Jefferson was the man to whom we owe the high lesson that the *natural* privileges of a social aristocracy are in truth no more than their *natural privileges*. With us,

all questions of personal rights, except in the case of the
poor slaves, are effectually settled, and yet every really valuable interest is as secure as it is anywhere else.

It is curious to note the effect of the present condition
of England. When the prerogative was in the ascendant,
Charles made six dukes of his illegitimate sons (Mon-
mouth included), and George IV scarce dared own his
progeny. Even the first of the Hanoverian princes presumed to make a duchess of his mistress, but all that power disappeared before the increasing ascendency of the
nobles. Now the many and the few are in opposition, the
King comes into the account, and we hear of lords and
ladies among his offspring. A bold and able monarch would
in such a crisis regain his authority, and we should again
hear the phrase, *Le roi y pensera.* The experiment would be
delicate, but it might succeed by acting on the fears of
the middle classes, the fundholders, and the timid. With
the cast of character that has actually been made by
Providence, I think, however, there is little probability that
the drama will receive this *dénouement.*

There is an inferred opinion of the American social
order in this statement. In effect, it is that aristocracy must
be present in every stable society, but that privilege must
be reserved for those who have a natural right to it. In
short, he is preaching the gospel of aristocracy of worth.
The idea seems so obvious to him that he seldom troubles
to expand it. The change in the government of England, which took place in 1832, seemed to him a mere
readjustment of privilege in accord with this principle.
It was not in any sense a step toward equalitarianism.

He watched with similar interest the political development at home. His attitude toward Jeffersonian
democracy had always been skeptical, and for Jackson per-

sonally he had but modified enthusiasm. Apparently he had praised him in a letter to Wilkes, for the latter replied, July 29, 1830: "I cannot quite agree with you about General Jackson, although I am quite ready to believe he is as good as Adams was." In his *Notions of the Americans* Cooper had praised the General highly for his military skill, his modesty, his honesty, and his good-sportsmanship in accepting defeat at the hands of Adams. As he watched his actions as President, however, his enthusiasm waned. In a letter to Shubrick on May 1, 1831, he criticizes him for his lack of an aggressive foreign policy.

> As to ourselves in Europe; [he writes,] it is a thousand pities that the Government at home did not know their people better. When General Jackson came into power it was with a formidable character for decision and an inclination to make the flag respected. Now, to us in Europe, it seems that he or his friends for him, have done all they can do to strip him of his reputation, which was precisely the reputation we wanted. I do not say he should have blustered, but I do say, they might have left the man a character for the only quality by which he was at all honored on this side of the water. So far from France fearing him now, or his presupposed resolution doing us any good, the French Government considers him as only anxious to secure his re-election, by keeping at peace. So much for his supererogatory professions. I much fear that Mr. Van Buren is not suited to his vocation.
>
> I tell *you* but it is to go no further, that I think our claims on France are at a crisis. I lean to the opinion that they will be satisfied, but it is far from sure. Will King Andrew fight, think you?—There may be occasion.

The news of the debate on nullification and the threatened secession of South Carolina reached him in Vevey. "Our government," he tells us that he assured an inquiring foreign friend, "was mild in principle, and did not wish to oppress even minorities; but I made no doubt of the attachment of a vast majority to the Union, and, when matters really came to a crisis, if national compromise could not effect the object, I thought nine men in ten would rally to its defence." And when Lafayette asked his opinion on the future of the Union in the light of this crisis, he replied that a large confederation seemed to him more secure than a small one, for the very diversity of interests would tend to hold in check special movements toward separation as at this time the new states of the southwest served as a brake upon the older southern states.

To Morse, he wrote from Vevey on September 21:[1]

> I see the French papers are for breaking up the Union but that gives me little concern. The madmen of South Carolina may break their own heads, but the Union is much beyond their strength. If the people of the United States thought for themselves about themselves, they would laugh at all such fears, but Europe gives them qualms. How miserable is this! However, things are stronger than men, and this result will have scope. In ten years Messrs. Hamilton and Co. will be names universally deprecated or universally pitied at home, as slander may occur in court. For any set of men to presume to direct the fates in America is like the thunder of a theatre, good to amuse children and frighten the nervous. But they who look at

[1] From the Collection of W. F. Gable, Esq., American Art Assoc., Feb. 13–14, 1924.

their own little horizons can not see this. Let it go. I hope the end will be to set up another tribunal in place of the Supreme Court which is an English theory engrafted on American necessities, and like everything else that has come from our doctrinaires must crumble. How many absurd theories have I outlived, and how many more are fated soon to fall?

All of this reveals in Cooper a close and active concern for developments at home. It was obviously in some such tone as this that he wrote to Henry Cruger of South Carolina in 1830, for Cruger answered on September 24,

Permit me to request you to suspend your opinion until we have had a fair hearing. . . . You say you will go with us if we will confine ourselves to constitutional remedies. What else do we propose? Your great error lies in not considering the states as sovereign, and independent, and coördinate parties to a compact, to which the Federal Government was no party because it existed but as a consequence. Consolidation is your fallacy.

Although not a Federalist of the old school, consolidation was Cooper's fundamental political conviction, and it proved not to be a fallacy. Throughout his defense of American institutions abroad, he assumed this premise. A belief in the integrity of the country and of the mind of its people underlay all his predictions and conclusions.

His faith in the American people was, however, beginning to show signs of weakness in 1832. "I know no country that has retrograded in opinion," he wrote, "so much as our own within the last five years. It appears to me to go back as others advance." The cause of his skepticism was, of course, the reception by the American press of his part in the finance controversy. Dunlap and his other friends tried to soften his disappointment by praise and by assurance that he would receive his due in the future. "As to what you say of my pen belonging to mankind," he replied to one such gesture on March 16, [2]

> it is very flattering coming from an honest man and an able man, but I am greatly afraid the opinion is pretty nearly limited to two or three of us. I know not why it is so, but all that I see and hear gives me reason to believe that there is a great falling off in popular favor at home. I rarely see my name mentioned even with respect in any American publication, and in some I see it coupled with impertinences that I cannot think the writers would indulge in were I at home, though their insignificance would in truth be their shield were I at their elbow. There may be better writers than I in the country, but there is certainly no one treated with so little deference. It is no crime not to be the best, in or out of the country, and as I commonly support sound political doctrines, and always good, I can claim to be alluded to as not disgracing the attic excellence of American Literature. I ask no puffs—they disgust me, but for God's sake let me not have deprecatory praise and pealing censure. But I sicken of the subject and sometime of—I will not finish the sentence. If I had seen one frank manly gentlemanly allusion to myself as a writer in a single American publication in five years, I would not have thought of it. One fact is beyond dispute—I am not with my own country—the void between us is immense—which is in advance, time will show.

The first issue between Cooper and the American

[2] *Diary of William Dunlap*, II, 606–07.

people after his return from Europe centered upon his Venetian novel *The Bravo*.

His defense of American ideals, as he conceived them while abroad had received an earlier statement in his *Notions*. This work was followed by his attack upon Basil Hall in Colburn's *New Monthly* for October 1831, by his defense in the *Revue Encyclopédique* of slavery in America as a necessary evil, and by his contributions to the finance controversy. The opinions, or principles, underlying this defense were formulated and illustrated by his European trilogy, *The Bravo, The Heidenmauer,* and *The Headsman*. It is in the consideration of these novels that most students of Cooper's thought run upon their first real snag. The problem novel has always been considered, if not the highest, as least an admissible art form. Cooper, as usual, stumbled upon it without reference to the experience of others. His motive was simple: He appreciated Scott as a writer of romance, he differed with him as a social thinker. He had written *The Pilot* after the appearance of *The Pirate,* not to improve upon art, but to correct seamanship. He now invaded Scott's favorite preserve, medieval Europe, not to improve upon *Quentin Durward,* but to dispel the glamor with which Scott had endowed the institutions of fuedalism. He chose for his topic the decline of the old order before the growing liberalism of the new. His Venice is a city in the decay of waning powers; his monastery of the Palatinate has already felt the power of the Lutheran movement; in *The Headsman,* the corruptions of the old social order are resolved in the purifying atmosphere of the Bernese Alps.

Cooper does not hesitate to affirm his purpose at the start:

A history of the progress of political liberty, written purely in the interests of humanity, is still a desideratum in literature. In nations which have made a false commencement, it would be found that the citizen, or rather the subject, has extorted immunity after immunity as his growing intelligence and importance have both instructed and required him to defend those particular rights which were necessary to his well-being. A certain accumulation of these immunities constitutes, with a solitary and recent exception in Switzerland, the essence of European liberty, even at this hour. It is scarcely necessary to tell the reader that this freedom, be it more or less, depends on a principle entirely different from our own. Here the immunities do not proceed from, but they are granted to, the government, being, in other words, concessions of natural rights made by the people to the state, for the benefits of social protection.

Such a statement of the doctrine of popular sovereignty is hardly an auspicious opening for a novel of adventure; and, as more than one critic held, Cooper was implicitly pledged to give his public only the diet upon which he had brought it up. But *The Bravo* is, nevertheless, one of the best of Cooper's romances. The plot is involved, the action constant, the characters believable types, and the setting as glamorous as any of Scott's.

The moral which Cooper wishes to draw from his story is merely that the good in human nature will triumph over the evil in government. His bravo, a spy in the pay of the Council of Three, is finally executed by the powers whom he unwillingly serves, but the fundamental integrity of his character brings happiness to many. "Thus men too much practised in the interests of life constantly overreach themselves when brought in contact with the simple and intelligent; and the experience of every day proves that, as there is no fame permanent which is not founded on virtue, so there is no policy secure which is not bottomed on the good of the whole." Personal morality and the principles of just government are, to Cooper, identical.

In *The Heidenmauer,* the element of action or adventure gives way even further to that of social purpose. He lays his scene in the Palatinate in the early 16th century because at that time and place the group mind of man was undergoing a transition from medieval to modern social and religious ideas. Although he does not say so, he is interested in this change because he sees in it a parallel to the changes in the group mind of his own day. In the middle ages the social mind was dominated by the church through the agency of superstition. This agency is personified in the Benedictine Abbot of Limburg, the crafty Bonifacius, and his monks of different temperaments and different degrees of conviction, notably Father Johan, the fanatic, and Father Arnolph, the self-effacing humanitarian. The agency of change is the religion of Luther which has reached this remote region in the valley of the Rhine only by rumor, but which acts on the minds of the mass of the people and prepares them for overthrowing the Benedictine dominance and sacking the Abbey. This is accomplished by the concerted efforts of Count Emich of Leningen, representing the physical power of the nobles, and of Heinrich Frey, the burgomaster of Durckheim. Their actions are prompted by a rebellion against the evils of the old order and a desire (on the part of Emich) to gain power, rather than by any

conviction of the new order. Bonifacius probably under-
stands the nature and power of Lutheranism better than
any one else in the story, and yet others are the agents
in his defeat.

In thus showing the effect of Lutheranism in liberating
the mind of man from superstition, and the social order
from corruption and hypocrisy, Cooper draws an obvious
parallel to his own time in the effect of the American
ideal in liberating the modern mind from the corruption of a world controlled by the ancient régime. He does
not state this in so many words, however, and there is
small reason to suppose that anyone in his own day
understood the point of his conclusion.

In his final paragraph, Cooper states what may be taken
as his guiding motive throughout his later writing:

> To this tradition—true or false—we attach no impor-
> tance. Our object has been to show, by a rapidly-traced
> picture of life, the reluctant manner in which the mind of
> man abandons old to receive new impressions—the in-
> consistencies between profession and practice—the error in
> confounding the good with the bad, in any sect or per-
> suasion—the common and governing principles that con-
> trol the selfish, under every shade and degree of existence—
> and the high and immutable qualities of the good, the
> virtuous, and of the really noble.

The problem motivation had triumphed, and the novel
fell dead from his pen. It does not deserve such an extreme
fate. Judged as a romance of adventure, it is too slow; but
as an examination into the reasons for the decay of
feudalism in Europe and into the social inheritance of
America, it is worthy of serious study.

The third novel in the trilogy is more of a story and less of a social document than the second. The scene of *The Headsman* is laid at Vevey during the *fête des Vignerons,* or harvest festival, and the St. Bernard Pass. The story is built upon the Bernese law that the son of a headsman must succeed to the profession, and upon the social stigma which attends its practice. Again the deep good of human nature triumphs over the sophistications and prejudices of a decadent society, this time of the early 18th century. The moral is insisted upon with less vehemence than in the other two novels, but it is the same. In his little boat on Lac Leman, Cooper had bethought him

of the analogies that exist between inanimate nature and our own wayward inequalities; of the fearful admixture of good and evil of which we are composed; of the manner in which the best betray their submission to the devils, and in which the worst have gleams of that eternal principle of right, by which they have been endowed by God; of those tempests which sometimes lie dormant in our systems, like the slumbering lake in the calm, but which, excited, equal its fury when lashed by the winds; of the strength of prejudices, of the worthlessness and changeable character of the most cherished of our opinions, and of that strange, incomprehensible, and yet winning *mélange* of contradictions, of fallacies, of truths, and of wrongs, which make up the sum of our existence.

There is a mellowness in this—and in the book itself— which inevitably springs from the rich soil of Europe even in the mind of the transplanted American. Cooper's conclusion is that his country has a priceless heritage which she must guard and a brilliant future toward which she must work. The heritage is twofold: European tradition grants to her the culture and the sanity which comes from long living; American resources grant exemption from the evils and prejudices attendant upon that culture. "Society," Carlyle was declaiming at this time, "Society, long pining, diabetic, consumptive, can be regarded as defunct. . . . Call ye that a Society where there is no longer any Social Idea extant?" To Cooper too, European society was defunct, but to him the social idea existed in his own land.

To *Le Livre des Cent-et-Un* in 1832 he contributed an allegory entitled "No Steamboats—a Vision," in which the three dominant social ideas of Europe, represented by Mm. de Portefeuille, de l'Hérédité, and Blouse, visit him in his Paris apartment to protest against American civilization. All the familiar European prejudices against the new world are condensed in this brief sketch, one of the most successful pieces of irony Cooper ever attempted.

. Naturally, his shift from action to inquiry was not popular with the American public. The complaint was twofold: first, that he had no business to write problem novels of any sort; second, that any sort of criticism of America, even though of new world institutions and ideals, was indefensible. To this point his fiction had concerned itself with the consideration of human action only, at least as far as America was concerned. Now the principles underlying that action were being submitted to analysis.

It was some time before the complaint of his public reached Cooper's ears. When it did, however, it came as a torrent, and it was met with the spirit which one might expect of Natty Bumppo if he had been greeted unexpectedly by an onrushing mob of painted Indians. The *New York American,* the journal which had earlier opened its columns to Cooper himself, now printed, on June 7, 1832, a long article on *The Bravo* signed "Cassio." Its author was Edward Sherman Gould, a writer of some local renown whose pen was dipped in the journalistic gall so prevalent in the period. On a visit to Paris, Gould had picked up the Baudry edition of the novel for incidental reading during his travels. The typical traveler, however intelligent, is not accustomed to carry Burton's *Anatomy of Melancholy* or Mill's *On Liberty* in his hip-pocket. Detective stories or romantic love tales are his more usual literary fare.

Evidently, it was this sort of diet that Gould expected. Naturally, he was outraged when he learned that the adventure recounted in these pages was only a cloak for a serious analysis of the social man. The moral itself missed him entirely, but its effect on the action pained his sensibilities.

His complaint is that Cooper is "written out" and suffers from "barrenness." The plot seems redundant and vague, the "hero" of the quality of a supernumerary, the conclusion unsatisfactory. Cooper, he decides, is obviously writing solely for money, and playing false with his obligations to his public. The editor of the paper adds a half-hearted apology for "Cassio's" rage, and on June 9, there appeared in the same columns a spirited defense of Cooper, signed "U." This anonymous author points out that Cooper had a "higher aim" than mere story-telling, namely, "under the cover of an interesting story to paint in colors not to be mistaken, the Venetian Republic, and to show that though in name a free government, there existed a most wide difference between appearance and reality."

Here the debate might well have ended, and would have if Cooper had been a different sort of man. The copy of the *American* containing "Cassio's" article came to Cooper's hand in Paris, and he dispatched to the *Albany Daily Advertiser* the following letter, on April 2, 1833:

Dear Sir—Since my arrival from Switzerland, I have taken no particular pains to investigate the affair of the critique on *The Bravo,* that appeared in the *New York American,* though one or two circumstances have occurred to corroborate, what I never doubted, that it was the translation of one of the attacks of *juste milieu,* a little altered to adapt it to the American reader, for as you may remember, it professes to come from an American. The *Journal des Debats,* the oracle of the party of the Doctrinaires, published, some time before, the original, allowing for the translation and the necessary alterations, as I understand. This fact alone would put the question of its origin at rest, were there not sufficient internal evidence to prove it, without referring to the stupid blunder of quoting the Paris edition of the work! I take the report you mention, of this critique having been written by an obscure clerk in a counting house to be a subterfuge. It might have been forwarded to the American through such a channel, or it might have been translated by such a pen, for the work is done in so bungling a manner, that, as you will recollect, I detected its French origin before twenty lines were read. I am not disposed to deny the obscurity of the translator. When work of this description is done, it is usually committed to understrappers. Depend on it, however, that it was translated at Paris, clerk, or no clerk.

The Bravo is certainly no very flattering picture for the upstart aristocrats of the new *régimes,* and nothing is more natural than their desire to undervalue the book; but the facility betrayed by our own journals, in an affair of this nature, is a source of deep mortification to every American of right feeling. I ought to have said, there is a gentleman now at Paris, who (I am told) says he was present when one of the editors of the American wrote the article. You may make this statement as the companion to the report of the agency of the "obscure clerk"; both stories cannot be true, since they contradict each other. I have no doubt that Mr. — discovered the truth, and that — is the true author of the article, with, perhaps, the exception of the alterations which exist in the translation. This — is a common hack writer—was then in the employment of the *Journal des Debats,* and would have written an eulogium on *The Bravo* or anything else, the next day, for a hundred francs. It is unnecessary to say anything to you touching the venality of the French and English reviews. As a general rule, nothing appears in either without favor or malice.

This letter is an excellent example of the conversationalist Cooper at his worst. He is entirely justified in his anger at the obvious bias of the offending criticism; he is perhaps tactless in paying any attention to it; his identification of the American with a French review, and his resulting imputation of the political motivation to the writer, is extravagant even though not without grounds. It may, too, have been Morse who first put him off the track. Both the French and the American daily presses were wholly motivated at this time by politics, and there was no reason for not suspecting collusion. Gould, however, vigorously denied any foreign inspiration for his attack, and his own failure to grasp the political significance of the novel is testimony in his behalf. The whole thing is cheap, and might be dismissed if it were not a brick in a larger edifice. The New York *Courier and Enquirer* and other American dailies, took up the battle cry. The fight was on.

The effect upon Cooper was what anyone who knew the man might easily have predicted. He had never accepted the praise of his earlier novels personally. They had depicted his native land and its people; there was a just national pride in this acclaim. He was little more than the spokesman of America. Like Milton, he had always identified himself wholly with the cause he served. Any comment, whether praise or blame, upon his writing was a comment upon the principles to which he held. "Cassio" was Cooper's Salmasius, and he rushed to do battle with this puny Goliath in much the same spirit that impelled Washington to take command of the rebel colonists.

The *Letter to His Countrymen* was the result, published by John Wiley in 1834. Hurt personal pride contended with the righteous wrath of the injured prophet in its pages. He must defend himself in order to defend his country from herself. The enemies were now within the body politic. Small minds were gnawing at the heart of the American ideal.

So many pages of this tract are devoted to self-vindication that no critic of Cooper has as yet done justice to its purpose. "Cooper's temperament had always been precariously balanced," says the most recent of them.[3] "Now it trembled from the center, and never firmly regained its

[3] H. W. Boynton, *James Fenimore Cooper*, pp. 254–55.

seat." That the letter "should have been a jewel of polished and reticent prose," is beside the point. Cooper was
not an Emerson or an Addison. His temperament was
fundamentally romantic and his mind always received
its impetus from his emotional responses to stimuli. Sid-
ney's *Apologie* would have been more intelligible had
he adopted Aristotle's classic calm as well as his ideas;
Shakespeare would have written better history if Falstaff
had not run away with his imagination.

In a consideration of Cooper's *Letter,* its purposes should
come first; its method and its success as controversial
prose should come second. Its purpose is clearly stated:

> The practice of quoting the opinions of foreign nations,
> by way of helping to make up its own estimate of the
> degree of merit that belongs to its public men, is, I believe,
> a custom peculiar to America. That our colonial origin
> and provincial habits should have given rise to such a usage
> is sufficiently natural; that journals which have a poverty
> of original matter should have recourse to that which
> can be obtained not only gratuitously but, by an extraor-
> dinary convention, without loss of reputation, and with-
> out even the necessity of a translation, need be no mystery;
> but the readiness which the practice can be accounted for
> will not, I think, prove its justification, if it can be shown
> that it is destructive of those sentiments of self-respect, and
> of that manliness and independence of thought, that are
> necessary to render a people great, or a nation respectable.

The fifty-four pages which Cooper then devotes to
proving that he comes to the discussion "with clean
hands," but that his opponents do not, may be dismissed
in a word. Any reader of the journals of that period will

have sufficient proof of their provocation; their wisdom
does not affect the issue at this late day. In France, in
England, and in America, the press was dominated by
political motives, and the American press was admittedly
subservient in opinion to that of Europe. Cooper's sus-
picions carried him in some instances to absurd length,
but in his primary assumption he was correct: there
was a direct connection between the anti-governmental
part he had taken in the French finance controversy and
the hostility with which his novels of purpose were
greeted in America. A personal justification was necessary
as a clearing of the ground.

The constructive part of the *Letter* occupies only thirty-
seven pages. It is based upon evidence which Cooper
had assembled from his own experience, during his foreign residence, that the principles of the Constitution
were being gradually undermined by the habit of imitat-
ing European practices both in internal and in foreign
affairs. It is a call to order: clear, concise, well reasoned,
and adequately supported by example. It probes to the
foundations of the American system, compares them with
those of Europe, emphasizes their greater value, and issues a firm warning against the short-sightedness which
was undermining them. Cooper wrote no better controversial prose than this and, at his best, there were and
are few who could equal his blunt and searching style.

His entire attack is founded upon his belief in the
principle of popular sovereignty as the distinguishing
feature of the American system. "The action of this government," he says, "is obtained by a system of representation which, while it is compound and complicated
in its elements, possesses, in fact, the redeeming and essen-

tial quality of simplicity by providing that none but the common interests shall be subject to control." Danger threatens this individual liberty when the limits of the compact are over-stepped. The Union, to be strong, must be a compromise between aristocracies and democracies, and must maintain approximately homogeneous forms in its society. But it is obviously impossible to reduce Virginia and Vermont to exactly the same social status. A strong central government, rigidly restricted in its powers, is the only safeguard. This was created by the Constitution and only a severe interpretation of that document can hold the nation together.

Further, the limits upon the powers of the various branches of the central government, as defined by the Constitution, must be rigidly enforced, as any over-stepping of the authority granted by the will of the people constitutes a dangerous aggression. The highest powers are granted to the legislative branch, but the judiciary and executive branches have powers of their own, as clearly defined and as subject to popular sovereignty. Again the authority of the Constitution must be absolute.

From his own experience, Cooper then cites examples where the following of European precedent had led to practices dangerous to this view. The appointment of foreign representatives of the United States, especially in emergencies, had often led to the exercise of arbitrary powers on the part of the President or of his appointees. On the other hand, Congress had no power to interfere with the President in his withdrawal of the government funds from the Bank of the United States, because the public moneys are under the control of the Secretary of the Treasury, an executive appointee. The example of monarchies had suggested the arbitrary appointment of a foreign representative, and that of the British parliament the usurping of executive powers by congress.

> If this Union shall ever be destroyed by any error or faults of an internal origin [Cooper concludes] it will not be by executive, but by legislative usurpation. The former is easily enough restrained, while the latter, cloaked under the appearance of legality and representation, is but too apt to carry the public sentiment with it.

Cooper was never a party man, in the ordinary sense, but he believed in constitutional government of a firm and uncompromising sort. Authority, he held, must be delegated by the intelligent to the intelligent. He mistrusted the looser conceptions of democracy which had more of the sound and less of the fact of popular sovereignty about them. His theory of the ideal democracy was becoming more and more clearly defined, more and more a matter of conviction.

CHAPTER FIFTEEN

The American Gentleman

I N 1834 the old debate between the De Lancey and the
Cooper backgrounds was settled once for all, at least
as far as a place of residence was concerned. Otsego
Hall was renovated according to plans drawn up by
Morse and became the home of the American gentleman
for the remainder of his life. Later winters were spent in
New York, on St. Mark's Place near Third Avenue, but
the family seat now became and remained the "Wigwam" of *Home as Found*. "I may be induced to take
the old house," Cooper had written Richard from Vevey
in 1832, "fix it up, and spend six months of each year
in it. My habits and pursuits require town for the rest
of the year."

The alterations never fully met with the owner's approval. Cousin Jack, of the novel, was made responsible
for "transmogrifying" the old house, and the philosophical Edward Effingham accepts with some skepticism the
composite of Greek and Gothic which resulted. "It is
not your taste that I call in question," he remarks, "but
your provision against the seasons. In the way of mere
outward show, I really think you deserve high praise;
for you have transformed a very ugly dwelling into one
that is almost handsome." It was the castellated roof on

231

the mansion which gave its fictional owner his qualms; and when the actual snows of Otsego collected on the shingles, there were leaks to be repaired.

The interior had likewise been enlarged to conform with the standards of Parisian *hôtels*. "My hall," writes Cooper, "is the admiration of all the mountaineers— nearly fifty feet long, twenty-four wide, and fifteen feet high. I have raised the ceiling three feet, and regret it had not been ten. I have aversion to a room under jurymasts."

"The library," wrote G. Pomeroy Keese, [1]

> the room in which Cooper invariably wrote, was a well proportioned apartment of about twenty by twenty-four feet and twelve in height, situated in the most retired part of the house, and having a southern and western exposure. Its deep recessed windows, dark oak wainscoting, and the thick shade of the numerous trees in the vicinity, shutting out the glare of the sun's rays, combined to give it an appearance of quiet and repose so eminently befitting a room of its character; while the sides were well lined with books of a miscellaneous description—which was in a measure owing to an agreement at one time in force with his publisher, by which he received a copy of every book issued by the firm. There were, however, many works of much interest and value, although it is believed a complete set of his own works was not among the number.

Upstairs, the large north bedrooms were nicknamed "Siberia" and "Greenland"; the southern rooms "Florida" and "Italy." The grounds were laid out with the formality of an English garden. The town boys were told to play their newly discovered game of baseball on the village

[1] S. M. Shaw, *A Centennial Offering*, p. 208.

square and the Cooper garden was surrounded by a wall with great gates opening only to favored guests.

During the summer Cooper took an intense interest in his garden, and Susan's own knowledge of nature is a reflection of this hobby of her father's. "It was his delight," she tells us, "to watch the growth of different plants day by day. His hot-beds were of the earliest, and he was the first to grow egg-plant, Brussels sprouts, and other unusual vegetables and fruits."

An action portrait of Cooper at forty-five will serve for the entire last decade and a half of his life. His activities did not materially change. He was frequently absent from Cooperstown, but he never again thought of any home other than Otsego Hall.

"He was habitually industrious," writes Keese,[2] "not alone as an author, but in all the business of life. He rose early, and a considerable portion of his writing was accomplished before breakfast, which did not usually take place until about nine o'clock."

Later he bought a small farm on the Vision hillside, and there did some of his writing.

In the summer [Keese continues] hardly a day passed that he did not visit his farm, known as the Chalet, situated about a mile from the village on the eastern shore of the lake, and from its heights commanding an extensive view of the village, and valley of the Susquehanna at the south, and bounded at the north by the hills which girt that extremity of the lake. It was this view, one of the most beautiful in the vicinity, that was the occasion of the purchase of the farm by Mr. Cooper. Its attractions to the agriculturist are not commensurate with the beauty

[2] S. M. Shaw, *A Centennial Offering*, pp. 207-208.

of the situation. Indeed, a more forbidding spot could not well be chosen, as far as a mere return for the labors of the husbandman is considered. The whole farm, of about two hundred acres, is in fact a mountain abruptly rising from the shore of the lake to the height of about four hundred feet, and with the exception of two or three level terraces of a few acres each, is an unbroken hillside, dotted with stumps in the clearings, but a large part still covered with the primitive forest. It was on this farm that Cooper sought relaxation from his mental labors, and he visited it almost daily in the summer.

The varied duties of the day being accomplished, the gathering shades of twilight frequently found Cooper promenading the large hall; his hands crossed behind his back, his brow carrying the impression of deep thought, his head also doing duty, as far as possible in the way of gesticulation, by frequent and decisive nods of approval or otherwise of his thoughts, to which he often gave utterance in audible sounds—no doubt to be committed to paper the following morning, as he rarely wrote much in the evening. These perambulations were often continued after tea; although usually in the evening he was to be found in the midst of his family, either reading the papers, or indulging in his favorite game of chess with Mrs. Cooper.

The *Letter to His Countrymen* had concluded with an eloquent farewell to the public:

I came before you as a writer when the habit of looking to others for mental aliment most disqualified the public to receive a native author with favor. It has been said lately that I owe the little success I met with at home, to foreign approbation. This assertion is unjust to you. Accident first made me a writer, and the same accident gave a

direction to the subject of my pen. Ashamed to have
fallen into the track of imitation, I endeavored to repair
the wrong done to my own views, by producing a work
that should be purely American, and of which love of
country should be the theme. This work most of you received with a generous welcome that might have satisfied
anyone that the heart of this great community is sound. It
was only at a later day, when I was willing more obviously
to substitute American *principles* for American *things*,
that I was first made to feel how far opinion, according
to my poor judgment, still lags in the rear of facts. The
American who wishes to illustrate and enforce the peculiar principles of his own country by the agency of polite
literature, will for a long time to come, I fear, find that
his constituency, as to all purposes of distinctive thought,
is still too much under the influence of foreign theories
to receive him with favor.

It is under this conviction that I lay aside the pen. I
am told that this step will be attributed to the language
of the journals, and some of my friends are disposed to
flatter me with the belief that the journals misrepresent
the public sentiment. On this head I can only say that,
like others similarly situated, I must submit to any false
inferences of this nature to which accident shall give
birth. I am quite unconscious of giving any undue weight
to the crudities of the daily press, and as to the press of
this country in particular, a good portion of the hostility
it has manifested to myself is so plainly stamped with its
origin that it never gave me any other uneasiness than
that which belongs to the certainty that it must be backed
by a strong public opinion, or men of this description
would never have presumed to utter what they have. The
information on which I act is derived from sources entitled to more respect than the declamations of the press.

I confess I have come to this decision with reluctance,

for I had hoped to be useful in my generation, and to have yet done something which might have identified my name with those who are to come after me. But it has been ordered differently. I have never been very sanguine as to the immortality of what I have written, a very short period having always sufficed for my ambition; but I am not ashamed to avow that I have felt a severe mortification that I am to break down on the question of distinctive American thought. Were it a matter of more than feeling, I trust I should be among the last to desert my post. But the democracy of this country is in every sense strong enough to protect itself. Here the democrat is the conservative and, thank God, he has something worth preserving. I believe he knows it, and that he will prove true to himself. I confess I have no great fears of our modern aristocracy, which is wanting in more of chivalry than the *accolade.*

Had I not been dragged before you rudely, through the persevering hostility of one or two of the journals, this duty to myself would have been silently performed. With the exception of the extract of the letter published by Mr. Morse, this is the only instance, during the many years that we have stood to each other in the relations of author and reader, in which I have ever had occasion to trouble you, either directly or indirectly, with anything personal to myself, and I trust to your kindness to excuse the step I have now taken. What has been here said has been said frankly, and I hope with a suitable simplicity. So far as you have been indulgent to me, and no one feels its extent more than myself, I thank you with deep sincerity; so far as I stand opposed to that class among you which forms the public of a writer, on points that, however much in error, I honestly believe to be of vital importance to the well-being and dignity of the human race, I can only lament that we are separated by so wide a barrier as to render further communion, under our old relations, mutually unsatisfactory.

Cooper undoubtedly believed that he would write no more novels when he penned this farewell. His sensibilities would not allow it. But the habit of writing was now firmly rooted and the need of income from this source was pressing. His inheritance had been loaded with debts, his savings had been small. The six years which intervened between the appearance of the *Letter* and the return to pure romance in *The Pathfinder* were devoted entirely to experiments in social criticism and historical investigation. Allegorical satire, travel letters, two attempts at the novel of manners, an elementary textbook in democracy, and a history of the navy were the literary products of the period.

The *Monikins* was Cooper's only attempt at sustained satire. From the literary point of view it was not a success in its own day and has stirred no enthusiasm in anyone but a single erudite German who took the pains to study it. Lounsbury boasts that he was the only member of his generation to get through it, and recent Cooper scholars do not offer much evidence of having qualified for the select society of its readers.

It is, however, far from impossible reading and contains the germ of almost all of Cooper's ideas. "There are pages," says Susan, "full of wit, fun, the most clever satire, and strong truth." There are also pages full of ponderous prose and obscure allegory. The effort to string the idea out to the conventional two-volume limit was its undoing. The long story of the sad ends of the elder Goldencalf and his wife, of the formalities of passing his wealth on to his son, of the purchase by the latter of the Hall and village of Householder, and of his meeting with the Connecticut Captain Noah Poke could be compressed into a single chapter.

The book is in the mock-realistic tradition of Swift and Defoe and, like Robinson or Gulliver, Sir John Goldencalf gives all the details of his birth, education, and inheritance, before he embarks upon his adventure. It is, however, less factual and more wordy than these classic models.

The story really begins when the newly-created nobleman meets, in the Champs Elysées, a party of monikins, or manikin-monkeys, being put through stunts by their captors. They are dressed in ridiculous organ-grinder clothes, and the pained expression on the cultivated face of one elder male arouses the humanitarian impulses of the young Baronet. As a result, the whole party is purchased and taken back to the hotel where Goldencalf and Noah Poke are staying.

Perhaps this discussion of the novel should have been prefaced by a note on the social-stake theory of society, as this theory motivates Goldencalf in all his actions. Cooper is attempting to examine the theory of a property qualification for suffrage, in its broadest and most humanitarian form, and to prove it unsatisfactory as a foundation principle for social government.

The older Goldencalf had devoted his life to the accumulation of wealth; the younger devotes his to the wise use of these savings. He determines to invest in as many and as various activities as he can in order to broaden his social views. "No sooner does any one interest grow painful by excess," he tells us, than a new claim arises to divert the thoughts, a new demand is made on the sensibilities; and by lowering our affections from the intensity of selfishness to the more bland and equable feeling of impartiality, forms that just and generous condition of the mind at which the political economists aim when they dilate on the glories and advantages of their favorite theory of the social stake.

A plantation in the West Indies (where the crop was destroyed by a hurricane), a cotton factory (seriously handicapped by import duties and foreign competition), an English estate (on which rents were in arrears and difficult to collect), and a plantation in Louisiana (where smallpox had invaded the slave quarters) helped the social theorist to work out his humanitarian-utilitarian scheme. Not at all discouraged, he employed his Yankee captain and set out for the South Pole and the steam atmosphere of the monikin-lands.

The monikins themselves are Swift's Yahoos given the intelligence of his Houyhnhnms. They are a breed of monkeys in which the reasoning qualities of man are developed and the bestial nature subdued. The seat of reason is the tail, which, as Dr. Reasono explains, can be longer, straighter, and more flexible than the cramped quarter of the human skull. These qualities, the philosopher boasts (and what social allegory is complete without a philosopher guide?) are reflected in the ideas of the people.

Leaphigh is but an allegorical England, a land in which society is founded on a rigid caste and social-stake system. Some of the satire is exquisite, as when the throne is maintained although the monarch himself is dispensed with and his eldest male cousin is retained as his spokesman. The use of colors to denote the various social gradations is an admirable device, but no less practical than that of branding a number within the class upon the hind quarters of every citizen. Thus, by a definite and rigid system, everyone is fitted into his permanent social niche.

It is left to the American Monikin, Brigadier Downright, to point out the error in the theory.

> Your social-stake system [he argues] supposes that he who has what is termed a distinct and prominent interest in society will be the most likely to conduct its affairs wisely, justly, and disinterestedly. This would be true, if those great principles which lie at the root of all happiness were respected; but unluckily, the stake in question, instead of being a stake in justice and virtue, is usually reduced to be merely a stake in property. Now, all experience shows that the great property-incentives are to increase property, protect property, and to buy with property those advantages which ought to be independent of property, *viz*: honors, dignities, power, and immunities. I cannot say how it is with men, but our histories are eloquent on this head. We have had the property-principle carried out thoroughly in our practice, and the result has shown that its chief operation is to render property as intact as possible, and the bones, and sinews, and marrow of all who possess it, its slaves.

The unsophisticated Anna later offers the preferred substitute for this social theory. "I know little of these things, Sir John," she admits, "but to one ignorant as myself the most certain security for the righteous exercises of power is to be found in just principles." Much of the social criticism of the nineteenth century can be referred, like this, to the Golden Rule.

Thus Cooper disposes of the social government of England. That of America fares even worse, not because the underlying ideas are false, as in the former case, but because selfishness and shortsightedness have led to bad practices. As the *Walrus* approaches the land of Leaplow, it is beset by ships bearing nominating committees of the two great and the one minor party. The party system is to America what the caste system is to England. "Our social arrangement," explains Judge People's Friend, "is founded on a hint from nature; a base, as you will concede, that is broad enough to sustain a universe. As a people, we are a hive that formerly swarmed from Leapshigh; and finding ourselves free and independent, we set about forthwith building the social system on not only a sure foundation, but on sure principles. Observing that nature dealt in duplicates, we pursued the hint." Thus was the two-party system discovered— a monikin has two eyes, two ears, two feet, why not two parties?

The scholar who attempts to tie Cooper down to party affiliation after reading this scathing satire of division for the sake of division would classify moths as birds. The Horizontals and the Perpendiculars are thorough-going burlesques of the present-day Republicans and Democrats. The tangents could well be Farmer-Laborites, Socialists, Communists or any minority group. These things do not seem to change, and Cooper's criticism of his national government is as pertinent and as shrewd now as it was when it was written. Similarly his comment on the claims controversy with France (Leapthrough) is so nearly ap-

plicable to the German war-debt debate as to make the
present-day patriot wince. "It was stoutly maintained,"
he says, "by certain ingenious logicians, that the only true
way to settle a bargain to pay money was to make a new
one for a less sum whenever the amount fell due; a plan
that, with a proper moderation and patience, would be
certain, in time, to extinguish the whole debt."

But Cooper's criticism of America in this book, however acid, has beneath it his underlying conviction that
the heart of the nation is sound. The concern for dollar
diplomacy and money interests in politics was merely
a moral eclipse, easily predictable by the sagacious monikins. "The shadow cast its malign influence," Goldencalf tells us, "on every interest connected with monikin
life. Temples were raised to God on speculation; the
government was perverted to a money-investment, in
which profit, and not justice and security, was the object; holy wedlock fast took the aspect of buying and
selling, and few prayed who did not identify spiritual
benefits with gold and silver." The American form of
political economy reduced itself to a selfish and natural-
istic basis, as did the English. Caste or party, human nature remained the same.

The Monikins contains one of Cooper's earliest and
most effective denunciations of the theory of democracy
as a leveler of social inequalities. The monikin seat of
wisdom, the tail, was, in Leaplow, bobbed to a standard
length, and the residue of all was boiled up and served
to the press as the material of public opinion from which
to construct its articles and news. The burlesque process
is so true a description of the actual that the idea hurts
now almost as much as it must have in Cooper's time.

CHILDREN OF JAMES FENIMORE COOPER

From a drawing by Susan Fenimore Cooper.
Courtesy of James Fenimore Cooper, Esq.

In conclusion, Goldencalf sums up a few of his lessons in axiomatic form:

> That every man loves liberty for his own sake and very few for the sake of other people.
> That moral saltation is very necessary to political success at Leaplow, and quite probably in many other places.
> That of all the 'ocracies (aristocracy and democracy included) hypocrisy is the most flourishing.
> That what men affirm for their own particular interests they will swear to in the end.

And many others, but finally,

"That men have more of the habits, propensities, dispositions, cravings, antics, gratitude, flapjacks, and honesty of monikins than is generally known."

Like all good satirists, Cooper found himself ultimately confronted with the fundamental inconsistencies, the selfishness, and the bestiality of human nature, rather than with the particular inconsistencies and the variant practices of different political and social systems. His wit had probed deeper than his wisdom had contemplated. From social institutions he reached moral law or moral anarchy.

The Monikins appeared in 1835 and contained the freshest and most concise statement of what its author had learned during his years in Europe. He now set to work on a revision of his travel journals and letters, which appeared under various titles during the next three years. First came the *Sketches in Switzerland* (1836), the record of his first visit to that country in 1828; the second part concerned itself more with the later journey down the Rhine and the residence in Paris in 1832. The three volumes of *Gleanings in Europe, (France, England,* and *Italy)* followed during the next two years. The order of the journeys was not maintained; the books were issued as seemed to suit best the demands of the publishers. None of them was financially successful in America or abroad. The first part of *Switzerland* had some use as an informal guide to that country; the *France* and the *England* both gained circulation in the countries which they criticized, chiefly because of the indignation which they aroused. The *Italy* passed almost unnoticed.

The chief value of these works is that they reveal Cooper in an informal mood and contain some of his most pungent social criticism and his most brilliant natural description. The pompousness of his formal style is almost entirely absent; in its place is a vital intimacy which brings the author very close to the reader.

Commentary on America continued, chiefly by way of comparison and illustration throughout all his discussions of European scenes, institutions, and ideals. Some of it was favorable, some unfavorable. "The first great change that I could wish to make in America," he says characteristically in *France,*

> would be to see a juster appreciation of the substance, and less importance attached to outward forms, in moral things. The second would be to create a standard of greatness and distinction, that should be independent, or nearly independent, of money. The next, a more reasoning and original tone of thought, as respects our own distinctive principles and *distinctive situation,* with a total indifference to the theories that have been broached to sustain an alien and an antagonist system, in England; and the last (the climax), a total reform in the kitchen.

Although informal, these books were definitely prepared for press. Cooper had made his notes with the intention of writing a comprehensive work on the state of society in Europe, but the reception of *The Bravo* had discouraged him. His comments are given a sharper edge by reference to his own hurt feelings, or they are dulled by a hammering upon his favorite ideas. The result is repetitious, informal, brilliant, shrewd, and irritating, all in one. They are books for incidental and adventurous reading, not for the soothing of troubled spirits or the whiling away of idle time.

The last of these came from the press in 1838, the year in which *The American Democrat* was issued by the Phinneys in Cooperstown. Both the book and its edition were small, but its appearance marks a high point in the development of Cooper's criticism. It is his most direct and his fullest statement of his social theory and his ideal for his country, considerably modified in the decade since *The Notions*.

The thesis of this textbook on democracy is simple. It is merely the American principle of liberty for the individual within a society in which common rights are adequately protected by constitutional checks and balances. It is a frontal attack upon that conception of democracy which would reduce all human values to a dead level, however high that level might be. Further, it is an attempt to prove that a gentleman might exist in a democracy without the aid of an arbitrary caste system. To Cooper, such a gentleman was the highest type of the human species.

The book was an effort to aid America in her recovery from the moral eclipse described in *The Monikins,* from her blindness to values, from her dollar worship, from her mass humility. "Power," he states, "has most to apprehend from its own illusions. Monarchs have incurred more hazards from the follies of their own that have grown up under the adulation of parasites than from the machinations of their enemies; and in a democracy the delusion that would elsewhere be poured into the ears of the prince is poured into those of the people." The American mass, he was convinced, was its own most dangerous enemy.

Cooper's first purpose is to distinguish republics from monarchies and despotisms, and aristocracies from democracies. He then proceeds to an explanation of the unique character of the United States, a federated republic with democratic social organization. "The government of the United States was formed," he explains,

by the several states of the Union, as they existed at the period when the Constitution was adopted, and one of its leading principles is that all power which is not granted to the federal authority remains in the states themselves, or what is virtually the same thing, in the people of the states. This principle follows as a necessary consequence from the nature of the grants to the federal government, but it has been clearly expressed in a clause of the instrument, that was introduced by way of an amendment in 1801. This feature distinguishes this federal government from all the federal governments that have gone before it as it was the general and ancient rule that liberty existed as a concession from authority; whereas here we find authority existing as a concession from the ruled. . . . It follows that the Constitution of the United States was formed by the states and not by the people of the entire country, as contended; the term used in the preamble being used in contradistinction to the old divine right of sovereigns, and as a mode of expressing the general republican character of the government.

Representation is a natural consequence of this principle, as the constituencies in the various states must have their voices in federal policy. The novel machinery of the American republic was thus constructed to conform to its novel principles. Cooper then treats once more of the executive, the legislative, and the judiciary branches of the government and reëmphasizes the need for enforcing the distinction between the special prerogatives of each of these departments.

These political principles are rather obvious to anyone who has given any thought to the Constitution, but their social corollaries are not so obvious. It was in these that Cooper came to an issue with his times and his public. He now proceeds to an explanation of the word "equality" as applied to American theory and practice. No equality of any kind or anywhere, he asserts, can be absolute. There are, however, different kinds of equality which may admit differing degrees of attainment. In America, civil equality, or the right to administer the laws, is almost absolute, and far more nearly so than in any previous civilization. Political equality, or the right to make the laws is almost absolute, and far more nearly perfect in America than elsewhere, but is limited by conditions of age, sex, and freedom.

With social equality America should, Cooper believes, be sparing, and physical and moral equality are obviously conditions contrary to fact. Men are "created free

and equal" only in so far as civil and political rights
are concerned, and even here good government requires
in practice a generous modification of the ideal. "The
very existence of government at all," Cooper concludes,
"infers inequality. The citizen who is preferred to office
becomes the superior of those who are not, so long as
he is the repository of power, and the child inherits the
wealth of the parent as a controlling law of society."

After reading Cooper's attack upon the social-stake
theory in *The Monikins,* it may be somewhat surprising to find him insisting upon the rights of property as
the unequal principle most justified in any form of social organization. "If we would have civilization and the
exertion indispensable to its success, we must have property; if we have property we must have its rights; if
we have the rights of property, we must take those consequences of the rights of property which are inseparable
from the rights themselves." In *The Monikins* Cooper
protested against making any material possession of interests the governing principle of a moral order; in the
anti-rent trilogy, *Satanstoe, The Chainbearer,* and *The
Redskins,* he was to defend the rights of inheritance in
property as a fundamental principle of a stable society.
The two positions are supplementary rather than contradictory. It is not necessary to make a fetish of a working principle. But his contemporaries did not understand
this distinction.

The American conception of liberty is also unique,
Cooper believes, in the history of the world. "Perfect
and absolute liberty," he premises, "is as incompatible
with the existence of society as equality of condition."
Even in a natural state liberty is impossible; in organized

society it may be defined as "such a state of the social compact as permits the members of a community to lay no more restraints on themselves than are required by their real necessities and obvious interests." Although admitting the superiority of government by majorities to any form of government by minorities, however enlightened, Cooper lays great stress upon the need for checks upon the mass will. "Liberty, therefore, may be defined," he concludes, "to be the controlling authority that resides in the body of the nation, but so restrained as only to be exercised on certain general principles that shall do as little violence to natural justice as is compatible with the peace and security of society."

These are the fundamental principles of the American state as Cooper conceives them. The remainder of his book concerns itself with their application and the dangers attending their practice.

> It is a besetting vice of democracies [he says] to substitute public opinion for law. This is the usual form in which masses of men exhibit their tyranny. When the majority of the entire community commits this fault it is a sore grievance, but when local bodies, influenced by local interests, pretend to style themselves the public, they are assuming powers that properly belong to the whole body of the people, and to them only under constitutional limitations. No tyranny of one, nor any tyranny of the few, is worse than this.

Having granted both political and social inequality, as well as a just basis for the curtailment of individual liberty, Cooper is now ready to define his American gentleman. Society demands that some shall be in high, some in low station, as dictated by their abilities and the circumstances of their lives. A public trust brings with it the duties of political or public station; the relationships of man and man, of parent and child, of master and servant, bring with them the duties of private station. The American gentleman is he to whom society has entrusted those factors in civilization which rise above the level of natural wants.

> The social duties of a gentleman [says Cooper] are of a high order. The class to which he belongs is the natural repository of the manners, tastes, tone, and, to a certain extent, of the principles of a country. They who imagine this portion of the community useless drones who consume without producing, have not studied society, or they have listened to the suggestions of personal envy instead of consulting history and facts. If the laborer is indispensable to civilization, so is also the gentleman. While the one produces, the other directs his skill to those arts which raise the polished man above the barbarian.

There only remained to distinguish this new world gentleman from him of the old world of feudal tradition.

> The democratic gentleman must differ in many essential particulars from the aristocratical gentleman, though in their ordinary habits and tastes they may be virtually identical. Their principles vary; and, to a slight degree, their deportment accordingly. The democrat, recognizing the right of all to participate in power, will be more liberal in his general sentiments, a quality of superiority in itself; but, in conceding this much to his fellow man, he will proudly maintain his own independence of vulgar domination as indispensable to his personal habits. The

same principles and manliness that would induce him to depose a royal despot would induce him to resist a vulgar tyrant.

The stern personal pride of Judge William Cooper, the belief in social ascendency inherited with the De Lancey and Heathcote lands, and the ideal of a liberal aristocracy so perfectly represented in Lafayette, are all in this statement. Cooper was an American gentleman— a democratic gentleman—but his countrymen were not in the mood for gentlemen of any sort.

CHAPTER SIXTEEN

War With Press and People

MEANWHILE, the American gentleman and the American people had descended from the level of pure theory in their dispute. They were already at grips in the courts, Cooper represented by his nephew Richard, the American people represented by the American press. The last phases of Cooper's life are intensely dramatic, but their drama lies in the realm of ideas rather than of physical actions.

The so-called "Three Mile Point Controversy" was the issue which brought matters to a head. But the argument as to the property rights of the heir of William Cooper to a favorite picnic ground on Lake Otsego was merely the match which touched off the dynamite. Cooper himself stresses at every possible opportunity the principles which underlie his position. His opponents, with the possible exception of Greeley, rarely meet him on these grounds. To them, he was a dangerous enemy or a misguided fool. Personalities absorb their attention most of the time, and, as a result, the issues for which Cooper battled are frequently lost from sight.

These principles may be stated briefly. Cooper was fighting for:

(a) A class consciousness in America founded on a flexible principle of moral worth and individual ability, but controlling social life, as in Europe, through education, wealth, and property.

(b) An American press, freed from imitative servility to foreign presses and foreign political interests, and guided by high moral and patriotic ideals.

(c) An American literary criticism, freed from personal abuse, and consciously fostering a national literature.

The Three Mile Point Controversy opened on the issue as it involved property rights. It very soon, however, proceeded to the second point, the degrading influence of a leveling democracy upon the quality of the press. With the publication of *Home as Found,* it became centered upon the law of libel in the State of New York, and it was upon this point that the issue was fought most vigorously in the courts. With his successful arguing of case after case, Cooper established the right of the individual in a democracy to certain immunities. His character could not be publicly attacked without evidence of the truth of the charges. Upon this basis of individual immunity, a social structure which recognizes differences in the individuals who compose it, could be built. American democracy today takes such differences for granted, in its social if not its political composition. In Cooper's day it did not.

A detailed review of the court proceedings and a quotation of the decisions and the newspaper comments on the trials would here be profitless and boring. The documents in the case have been reprinted and discussed too often already, usually with the result that the investigator himself gets lost in the jungle of contradictory facts, personalities, and opinions. It will be sufficient to outline the course of events as they influenced Cooper's own ideas and actions.[1]

Four stages in the proceedings may be noted. From July 22, 1837, until November 1, 1838, the debate was local in its interest and involved only the people and the press of northern New York State. With the publication of *Home as Found,* the press of New York City became interested, and the issue focused upon the ethics of journalism and the law of libel. By June of 1839, reviews of the *Naval History* had begun to appear, and, without losing its bearing upon the law of libel, the debate then touched upon matters of patriotic interest, namely the truth or falsity of Cooper's account of Elliott's part in the Battle of Lake Erie. This broadened its scope and greatly increased public interest. The final stage is the most significant because, with the entrance of Horace Greeley to the lists, in November, 1841, Cooper at last gained an opponent who understood the larger issues involved, and who, with his articles on "The Press and the Law of Libel" crystallized public opinion. Cooper won almost all of his cases and established his position in the courts and in the law; he almost completely failed in winning public favor for his cause; posterity has profited by the practices resulting in part, at least, from his efforts, without being clear as to the rights and wrongs of the issues involved.

It is unfortunate perhaps that personal and petty interests sometimes are the means of arousing indignation on matters where a larger and more philosophic view

---

[1] *Cf.:* Lounsbury, pp. 143–230; Boynton, pp. 265–329; and E. R. Outland, *The "Effingham" Libels on Cooper,* Madison, Wisconsin, 1929.

might be more effective. Cooper is doubtless recording an actual circumstance of his own return to Otsego Hall when he tells of Mr. Effingham's first day in his reconstructed "Wigwam" in *Home as Found.* "As they came in front of the hall windows," he says, "a party of apprentice-boys were seen coolly making their arrangements to amuse themselves with a game of ball on the lawn directly in front of the house."

Mr. Effingham turned to his agent Aristabulus Bragg, a well-meaning individual and worthy in every respect except in his devout reverence for the will of the majority.

"Surely, Mr. Bragg," said the owner of the Wigwam, with more displeasure in his voice than was usual for one of his regulated mind, "you do not countenance this liberty?"

"Liberty, sir!—I am an advocate for liberty wherever I can find it. Do you refer to the young men on the lawn, Mr. Effingham?"

"Certainly to them, sir; and permit me to say, I think they might have chosen a more suitable spot for their sports. They are mistaking liberties for liberty, I fear."

"Why, sir, I believe they have always played ball in that precise locality."

"Always!—I can assure you this is a great mistake. What private family, placed as we are in the center of a village, would allow of an invasion of its privacy in this rude manner? Well may the house be termed a Wigwam, if this whooping is to be tolerated before its door."

"You forget, Ned," said John Effingham, with a sneer, "that an American always means just eighteen months. Antiquity is reached in five lustra, and the dark ages at the end of a human life. I dare say these amiable young gentlemen, who enliven their sports with so many agreeable oaths, would think you very unreasonable and encroaching to presume to tell them they are unwelcome."

"To own the truth, Mr. John, it would be downright unpopular."

"As I cannot permit the ears of the ladies to be offended with these rude brawls, and shall never consent to have grounds that are so limited, and which so properly belong to the very privacy of my dwelling, invaded in this coarse manner, I beg, Mr. Bragg, that you will at once desire these young men to pursue their sports somewhere else."

All of the factors in the Three Mile Point Controversy are suggested by this incident: the short memory of the changing population of Cooperstown, the immunities implicit in property rights, the ideals and feelings of a gentleman in a democracy, and the low level of American opinion on matters of personal liberties and responsibilities in the social compact.

Three Mile Point was a popular picnic ground a short distance down the lake from the village of Cooperstown. In the days of William Cooper it had been more or less private, but between 1809 and 1834 the Cooper family had paid little attention to it, and the public, composed almost entirely of newcomers, had learned to regard it as communal property. When Cooper reasserted the exclusive right of the family to it, there was an immediate protest. On July 22, 1837, there appeared in the Cooperstown *Freeman's Journal* the following curt notice:

The public is warned against trespassing on the Three Mile Point, it being the intention of the subscriber rigidly to enforce the title of the estate of which he is the representative, to the same. The public has not, nor has ever had, any right to the same, beyond what has been conceded by the liberality of the owners.

J. FENIMORE COOPER,
Executor for the estate of the late Wm. Cooper.

The clause in William Cooper's will upon which this notice was based read:

> I give and bequeath my place called Myrtle Grove [Three Mile Point], on west side of Lake Otsego, to all my descendants in common until the year 1850; then to be inherited by the youngest thereof bearing my name.

On the evening of the day upon which Cooper's notice appeared, certain of the citizens of Cooperstown met and passed a set of resolutions declaring, without evidence, that William Cooper upon his death had willed the Point to the community, that his son had taken actions and used language which rendered him odious to his fellow citizens, and that the said citizens should disregard the said Cooper, remove his works from the public library, and publish their sentiments in all the village papers.

Andrew Barber, editor of the *Otsego Republican* of Cooperstown, Elius Pellet of the *Chenango Telegraph* of Norwich, and Theodore S. Gold of the *Oneida Whig* of Utica published hostile commentaries upon the proceedings. There is no doubt that Cooper, in spite of his strong aversion to all party alignment, was considered to be a leading Democrat, and that these attacks savored strongly of political motivation. A party system was therefore responsible for carrying a local dispute into the

national limelight and for falsely maligning a prominent
citizen of the republic.

It was not in Cooper's disposition to let such circumstances pass unnoticed. The suit of Cooper *vs*. Barber was
announced almost immediately and the war was on. A
suit against Pellet quickly followed. The republication
of an article from the *Chenango Telegraph* in the *Albany
Journal* in August 1837 involved Thurlow Weed, the first
of Cooper's major antagonists. Pellet soon dropped from
the picture, but Barber was for long a pathetic exhibit
and Weed an insistent antagonist.

Homeward Bound appeared on August 16, 1837, and
its sequel *Home as Found* the following November. The
intimate bearing which these two books have upon the
detailed circumstances of the controversy have obscured
their significance in the history of Cooper's thought and
work. They are almost always treated as little more than
documents in a legal process. Self-justification was, of
course, one of Cooper's motives in writing them, but as
always it was self-justification because of the social and
literary principles involved.

Cooper had attempted a chronicle of manners in his
first novel *Precaution,* but the experiment is without significance because of its purely imitative nature. He had
immediately turned to romance and developed a type
of novel with a gradually increasing moral purpose. In
the earlier works this purpose was manifest in little more
than the portrayal of heroes of unusually pure motives,
but in *The Bravo* and its successors it had been responsible for the pattern of the plot structure and the entire
motivation of the story. When this literary type proved
unacceptable to his public, Cooper determined to lay

aside his pen. But the need for pointing his moral to his times tempted him to try to adorn another tale. The romance of purpose had proved ineffective. A more nearly sound literary impulse directed him to experiment once more with the novel of manners. In *The Monikins,* he had already experimented with social satire; the novel of manners is a kindred literary type.

Cooper has stated these purposes explicitly in his prefaces and, in addition, the novels speak for themselves. In introducing *Homeward Bound,* he says,

> It was commenced with the sole view to exhibit the present state of society in the United States, through the agency, in part, of a set of characters with different peculiarities, who had freshly arrived from Europe, and to whom the distinctive features of the country would be apt to present themselves with greater force than to those who had never lived beyond the influence of the things portrayed.

Cooper had said that he was thirty years ahead of his time. The purposes which he here outlines were converted into fiction, from thirty to fifty years later, by Mark Twain, William Dean Howells and Henry James. The international novel of manners did not mature in America until after the Civil War when the seeds of native literature at last produced a healthy crop of homegrown realism. Cooper was once more the literary pioneer, sound in his impulses, uncertain and far from perfect in his methods.

Even if he had had the ability to write such a novel, the habits of twenty years and the absence of a model were practically insurmountable obstacles. Nevertheless,

his approach was essentially the right one. He chose, as
did Goldsmith, Fielding, and Jane Austen, materials of
which he had an intimate personal knowledge and he
shaped his story about people whom he knew in life.
He planned to motivate his plot entirely in terms of
man's relationships, in the social state, and to deal ex-
clusively with problems of manners and etiquette. He
had learned while abroad to think of etiquette as the
language of a national mind in dealing with moral and
ethical problems. The unwritten laws by which men and
women govern their actions in their relatively formal
social life seemed to him the distinguishing features of
a civilized society. His emphasis upon forms sometimes
led him to lose sight of the purpose for which forms are
adopted, but his realization that etiquette and ethics bear
a word-and-meaning relationship to each other was
sound.

The chronicle of manners intention scarcely survives
the first page of *Homeward Bound*. As Cooper himself
puts it, the cry was for "more ship," until the work was
"all ship." His public was not to blame; the tang of salt
water was irresistible to the former midshipman. Before
he realized the direction of his story, the *Montauk* was
under full sail with the British frigate *Foam* after her.
Disablement, a lost course, fights with Arabs on the
African coast, mistaken identities and concealed relationships—all the old materials of deep-sea romance came
into play and *Homeward Bound* had become another *Red
Rover*.

Cooper smiled at his failure and started again in the
sequel, this time with more success in holding to his purpose, less in awaking the sympathies of his readers. But

the author of *Home as Found* wrote under the impulsion of no deluding hopes.

> We believe that no attempt to delineate ordinary American life, either on the stage or in the pages of a novel, has been rewarded with success. Even those works in which the desire to illustrate a principle has been the aim, when the picture has been brought within this homely frame, have had to contend with disadvantages that have been commonly found insurmountable. The latter being the intention of this book, the task has been undertaken with a perfect consciousness of all its difficulties and with scarcely a hope of success. It would be indeed a desperate undertaking to think of making anything interesting in the way of a *roman de société* in this country.

The virtual impossibility of any such literary mode in America Cooper attributed to the constantly shifting basis of its society and its lack of a capital, in the European sense. "I expected to see a capital in New York," he makes his English Baronet remark, "and in this I have been grievously disappointed. Instead of finding the tastes, tone, conveniences, architecture, streets, churches, shops, and society of a capital, I found a huge expansion of commonplace things, a commercial town, and the most mixed and least regulated society that I have ever met with."

The reason for these conditions Cooper puts into the mouth of the brusque John Effingham. "Look about you, Ned," he says to his milder but less appealing cousin,

> and you will see adventurers uppermost everywhere; in the government, in the town, in your villages, in the country

even. We are a nation of changes. Much of this, I admit, is the fair consequence of legitimate causes, as an immense region, in forest, cannot be peopled on any other conditions. But this necessity has infected the entire national character, and men get to be impatient of any sameness, even though it be useful.

To Cooper's mind, America had reached a degree of civilization at which the national character should begin to take shape and to find expression in arts, institutions, and manners. The difficulties were two:

> On the one hand, the arts of life, like Minerva, who was struck out of the intellectual being of her father at a blow, have started full-grown into existence, as the legitimate inheritance of the colonists, while on the other, everything tends toward settling down into a medium, as regards quality, a consequence of the community-character of the institutions.

The story of *Home as Found* is simple. Edward Effingham, a descendant of the family of the same name in *The Pioneers,* has just returned with his daughter Eve from a residence abroad during which the father had been uniformly accepted in the best social circles of the continental capitals, and the daughter had received an education similar to that of the Cooper girls and like them learned the languages and knew how to appreciate the amenities of the life of the Europeans. With them is "Cousin Jack" Effingham, a bachelor whose experiences had added an element of harsh irony to his frank character and broad though dogmatic views of life.

Cooper himself has often been compared to his Edward Effingham, whom he describes as a singularly just-minded man, and having succeeded at an early age to his estate, he had lived many years in that intellectual retirement which, by withdrawing him from the strifes of the world, had left a cultivated sagacity to act freely on a natural disposition. At a period when the entire republic was, in substance, exhibiting the disgraceful picture of a nation torn by adverse factions, that had their origin in interest alien to its own; when most were either Englishmen or Frenchmen, he had remained what nature, the laws, and reason intended him to be, an American.

No one could possibly doubt that he meant in this character to personify those dominant traits in his own character which best spoke his ideal. The inference that he intended a faithful and realistic self-portrait, which was made by his contemporaries, is unfair. As a matter of fact, he managed unintentionally to put more of himself into John than into Edward. He describes the former as a "man of strong feelings, which is often but another word for a man of strong prejudices." After living with these two men for almost a thousand pages, Cooper still finds John Effingham to be

a strong-minded and proud man, his governing fault being the self-reliance that indisposed him to throw himself on a greater power for the support, guidance, and counsel that all need. . . . He felt how much more just, intuitive, conscientious even, were his own views than those of mankind in general; and he seldom deigned to consult with any as to the opinions he ought to entertain, or as to the conduct he ought to pursue.

The result is that John Effingham comes to life in these pages, whereas Edward and his daughter Eve remain waxen images, symbols of the ideals which their creator held for himself, his daughters, and his country.

The American democrat is represented in two of his leading types in the persons of Aristabulus Bragg and Steadfast Dodge. Bragg was like Dodge in that

> he considered everything that presented itself in the name of the public, as sacred and paramount, and that so general and positive was his deference for majorities, that it was the bias of his mind to think half-a-dozen always in the right, as opposed to one, although that one, agreeably to the great decision of the real majority of the entire community, had not only the law on his side, but all the abstract merits of the disputed question. In short, to such a pass of freedom had Mr. Bragg, in common with a large class of his country-men, carried his notions, that he had really begun to imagine liberty was all means and no end.

Bragg is vulgar, lacking in the finer sensibilities, and servile to what he believed the immediate public opinion to be; but he is also vigorous, downright, materialistic, and ambitious. In many respects he was exactly what European critics still imagine the characteristic American type to be.

Dodge, on the other hand, had all of Bragg's weaknesses, but none of his stronger qualities. He is fundamentally a hypocrite. It is in him that Cooper launches his direct attack upon the press. "Our friend Dodge of the *Active Inquirer*," he quotes a burlesque clipping from the *People's Advocate*,

> is instructing his readers and edifying mankind in general with some very excellent and pungent remarks on the state

of Europe, which part of the world he is now exploring with some such enterprise and perseverance as Columbus discovered when he entered on the unknown waste of the Atlantic. His opinions meet with our unqualified approbation, being sound, American, and discriminating.

A specimen of Mr. Dodge's accuracy and verve is given:

> Reached Bruxelles (Mr. Dodge pronounced this word Bruckselles) at seven in the evening, and put up at the best house in the place, called the Silver Lamb, which is quite near the celebrated town house, and, of course, in the very center of the *beau* quarter. As we did not leave until after breakfast next morning, the reader may expect a description of this ancient capital.

John Effingham sums the matter up with his usual point: "The government is a press-ocracy, and its ministers, self-chosen and usurpers, composed of those who have the least at stake, even as to character."

The story has virtually no plot apart from the events leading up to the satisfactory mating of Eve. In the process, however, the various groups of New York society are satirized (that of the literati being burlesqued in a most thorough fashion), the society of the commercial city compared with that of the more stable but provincial life of Albany, the center of agriculture, and the problems confronting the property owner in a democracy examined in all their ramifications. Cooper threw into the book all he knew and thought about the social life of the State. It is an honest and a thorough piece of work and an invaluable social document, if not a successful example of literary art.

One may imagine the state of mind of James Watson Webb, then editor of the New York *Courier and Enquirer,* when he read this book. In illustration of Cooper's point that journalists at that time felt they had nothing to lose by stating their frank opinion on any subject, he sat down on November 22, 1838, and put his entire mind into a review which concluded:

And now we take our leave of these volumes, which, were they not intended to traduce our country, and more particularly our *countrywomen,* and hold them up as objects of public scorn to the intelligent and refined of Europe, would never have received a notice at our hands. As a novel, *Home as Found* is absolutely beneath criticism. It is void of plot, and was written for the vile purposes we have named, and to enable Mr. Cooper to pamper his insatiable vanity. After leaving this city, he conducts the reader to Cooperstown, where he would have the uninitiated suppose that he has a baronial castle, with a park of unlimited extent. This, however, is a mere harmless vanity, with which we have no disposition to quarrel; but here again, every body but the members of his own family are described as *fools,* whose *vulgarity* is only equalled by their ignorance; and yet we have good reason to believe that in the society of Cooperstown there is more intellect and knowledge of the world, than in any town of the same size in the Union. Another object of this selfish book is to enable Mr. Cooper to abuse the public for having laughed at his political address to the people in behalf of General *Jackson,* when he hoped to be appointed Secretary of the Navy; and also to explain the nature of his recent quarrel with the villagers in regard to a certain Point of Land in Lake Otsego, and to villify and traduce *Lockhart,* whom he declares to be *"inherently a knave,"* for having reviewed as he did, Mr. C's work on England. If our readers have any curiosity on the subject, they will be fully gratified; but we much question whether the gratification is worth the vexation every American must experience on reading Mr. C's wholesale slanders upon our countrywomen. We are aware that Mr. C. once said that there were not *three* Ladies in America, and that he was peremptorily made to retract the slander; but we did not believe it possible, until we read *Home as Found,* that he would dare to give publicity to sentiments which go to sustain such an insulting accusation. He is, however, small game; and we hope that our ladies will show their self-respect by treating him and his volumes with the silent contempt he so richly merits.

This review opened the second stage of the debate, and was quickly supported by Webb's colleagues in New York City, Park Benjamin of *The New-Yorker* and the *Evening Signal,* and W. L. Stone of the *Commercial Advertiser*. The tone of all these comments is similar and trial followed trial in rapid succession.

In his own defense before the bar of public opinion, Cooper published a series of letters in *Brother Jonathan*. The issue of February 12, 1843, contains his answer to Webb in particular and shows that he has been misquoted and misrepresented intentionally. He again affirms the positive purpose of his novels:

Now beyond a question, [he writes,] the prevalent opinion of Europe is that America has little or none of this permanent respectability. It is supposed we are a republic from a want of the materials to form a monarchy. It has long struck me that something is gained in behalf of just principles in showing that this is not true; but that our government is as much one of choice as of necessity. It has also struck me that the pages of a novel are a proper medium for removing this old European notion by presenting such pictures of society as exist. With this view, from the very first I have endeavored to show my foreign readers—and they are not absolutely insignificant as to character or numbers—that we have substantially the same social elements here as are to be found in all civilized countries.

Horace Greeley first became interested in the controversy when his former associate Park Benjamin entered the lists. He became actively involved by publishing in his New York *Tribune* in November 1841 a letter on the Weed trial at Fonda, as well as much subsequent editorial comment. His position is summed up in his statement long after the dust of battle had subsided.[2] "What I claim and insist on is just this: That the editor shall be protected by the nature and exigencies of his calling to the same extent, and in the same degree, that other men are protected by the exigencies, the requirements of *their* callings or positions respectively."

A liberal interpretation of this position would allow an editor to say anything he wished. This Cooper protested, and this neither the law nor the ethics of journalism will now allow. How much Cooper's "War with the Press" had to do with correcting current practices and raising journalistic ethics can never be accurately determined. He undoubtedly injured his own popularity seriously; but he stated and he proved by law the justice of a limitation upon the press to protect personal reputations from printed slander, and he distinguished between the literary criticism which concerns itself with writings and that which probes into the private lives of writers.

[2] Parton, *Life of Horace Greeley*, p. 203.

Whatever its other effects, the controversy had a profound influence upon his writing. His stories for the next decade, with a few notable exceptions like *The Pathfinder* and *The Deerslayer,* were consistent attempts at various forms of the social problem novel, the most successful of which was *Satanstoe.* His daughter has expressed his new purpose in introducing *Homeward Bound.*

Under influences of this character, [she writes,[3]] the first works of a long series were written. It required but brief reflection to show that in behalf of a young nation there was much especial mental work to be done. There was fresh seed to be sown in the new soil. The infusion of old and eternal principles into new forms was to be carried out. The cultivation of a healthful national tone, blending the self-respect of a firm position with that spirit of mental growth, of moral amelioration, becoming the period of early youth —the cherishing of clear moral truth, of sound reasoning, of strong common sense, of pure feeling, of good taste— all this needed to be carried out into detail, amid institutions partially novel in form. To be one among those who should aid in this onward progress, this upward growth, of a high, free Christian civilization, became his object as a writer; and he threw himself into the task with that ardor, that untiring spirit, and that buoyancy of a hopeful nature, which so strongly marked his course through life.

[3] *Pages and Pictures,* pp. 286–87.

CHAPTER SEVENTEEN

National Pride and the Navy

THE building up of national self-respect in terms of a firm position was, however, something more than a mere matter of words to Cooper. His novels might serve to point out defects in national manners and social ideals, but pride in institutions must be the result of a sense of power. The pride and the resentment of patronizing criticism which had become so dominant a motive in his personal actions was easily transferred to the national mind. If America was to be roused from her humiliating lethargy, she must assert her national indignation at the patronizing attitudes of foreign powers.

The War of 1812 had helped. Cooper's resentment at the British imprisonment of American seamen had been stimulated by his own experiences on the *Sterling*. The war had settled that particular issue, but it had not put an end to British and French disregard for American commercial rights on the sea. Dissension in Congress was impeding the development of a navy adequate for the protection of American rights abroad. Courtesies from foreign powers could hardly be expected until there was self-respect at home. Preparations for another naval war—and perhaps the war itself—was the only answer.

Cooper had hinted at the need for a naval war while he was still abroad. When the claims controversy was at its height he had written; "Think you King Andrew will fight? There may be occasion." And he had, as early as 1828, made something of a sensation at a London dinner by remarking, "There is the island of Bermuda. You hold it solely as a hostile port to be used against us. I think for the peaceable possession of that island our government would make some sacrifice, and, by way of inducement to make the arrangement, you ought to remember that twenty years hence England will not be able to hold it."

Now, upon his return from Europe, he had discovered to his own satisfaction that not only Europe but America herself needed some vigorous demonstration of American power in order to cement internal factions and arouse foreign respect. The effect of this line of thought was to stimulate him in his determination to write a history of the navy of the United States, not so much to record past achievement as to stimulate future growth.

There were already several so-called naval histories of the War of 1812 and of the United States available. The war had succeeded in arousing enough controversy to find a reflection in the book as well as in the stock market. In 1813 there had appeared the first of them, *The Naval History of the United States from the Commencement of the Revolutionary War to the Present Time,* by Thomas Clark. The author was a respectable classical scholar who had been engaged, with the rank of an army captain, in constructing the defences on the Delaware River. He had for some time been planning an American history, but those same friends who have indirectly written so many books urged him to concentrate on that aspect of the task for which there was an obvious public interest. One slim volume sufficed to hold the anecdotal and miscellaneous facts he had gathered, another for some documentary support. Jefferson and Adams praised the work, the *Port Folio* acclaimed it, and for a number of years it remained the standard American work on the subject.

A veterinary surgeon, by name William James, who had spent some time in America as a prisoner during the war, attempted soon to present the other side of the case. The result was his *Naval Occurrences of the Late War,* in 1817, and a naval history a few years later. The impartiality of the author was revealed by his reversal of all the prejudiced facts and opinions in Clark's pro-American view of events. This book was accepted by the British as the standard work on the War of 1812, even though there were some doubts as to whether James had not perhaps gone just a little too far. His facts, however, were many and impressive.

Cooper's first published comment on the subject, apart from his sea romances, seems to have been his two articles contributed to the *Naval Magazine* in January and March 1836. Jackson had, on October 5, 1834, ordered the navy to prepare for active service in an enforcement of the claims treaty with France. Only British intervention prevented war, for Jackson, like Cooper, did not believe in apologizing "for the statement of truth and the performance of duty." Nevertheless, France paid.

I shall begin [writes Cooper] by remarking that too many (in regarding the present controversy with France) appear to have lost sight altogether of the great object which the nation has in view. They seem to think that the preservation of peace is all that can be desired. To this end they direct their reasoning, their influence, and their hopes. Peace is not the object we seek. Peace we have; and in order to maintain it, no great ingenuity is necessary. To effect this abstract purpose, we have only to abandon all claim to our rights, all pretensions to character, and to lose sight entirely of one of the greatest objects for which this Union was formed and for which we have become a nation; *viz*. the security of the citizen when removed beyond the protection of his own municipal laws. The preservation of peace, in our present situation, is but a secondary or collateral consideration. True humanity, like true policy, is just as much interested in our not mistaking the accessary for the principal, in this matter, as it would be in refusing the use of bullets in warfare, that we might go back to the condition of society in which men are beaten to death with clubs.

There follows an estimate of expenses and of the means of manning vessels for a war with France.

The *History of the Navy* appeared on May 10, 1839. Into it Cooper had thrown his best thought and the most accurate research of which he was capable. Even the first edition made a bid to become the standard treatment of the subject, and, in many respects, it still retains this position. It was at least three times as long as Clark's narrative and as detailed as James's. Cooper claimed for it the accuracy of objective historical perspective in his treatment of past events, but he was open in his statement of hopes as to its effect upon American naval policy.

The resulting controversy on the Battle of Lake Erie has tended to divert critical attention from the scope and value of this work as a whole. Cooper ultimately vindicated his position on that well-fought issue, but he never succeeded in getting his readers back on the main track. Contemporary reviewers were very quickly shunted down the desired siding by the efforts of the Perry family, whither Cooper and all his later critics have followed them. A few gracious and somewhat patronizing remarks about how really good the work is after all, usually serve to introduce the inescapable analysis of the tortuous course of the controversy. But the book *is* good—certainly the most straightforward narrative prose that Cooper ever wrote. The tang of the sea is in it without the fictional absurdities of *The Red Rover* and *The Water-Witch*. Arguments are presented with the sledgehammer blows of dogmatic conviction; facts and statistics are recorded with mathematical care and completeness; its drive of enthusiasm and its general readability suggest Macaulay's and Froude's histories. There are not enough people today reading Cooper's *History of the Navy*.

Early returns from its sale were extremely encouraging. On July 21, 1839, its author reported from Philadelphia, "About 2,000 copies of the *History* have been sold, and new orders are beginning to come in. . . . Some opinions are strongly in its favor, though a few cavil at it." Even after Burges and Mackenzie had published their comments, his confidence was maintained.

> Tristam Burges has come out with his monody on Lake Erie—likewise Mackenzie-Slidell, in the *North American*. The first is bombastical, silly, and absurd . . . . Mackenzie is superficial and jesuitical . . . . The *History*, notwithstanding, will carry all before it. It is well spoken of in England, I hear, and will maintain its ground. When

abridged, it will be worth $500 a year to me, for the next twenty-eight years; and of course for my life. Nothing can drive me but new occurrences.

During the next two years he was diverted from his plan for the third volume by the preparation of the abridgment, but throughout his battle with Stone his confidence in his work was maintained. The complete history went to the third American edition during its author's lifetime and the abridgement to a second. After his death both versions were continued and republished frequently until the time of the Civil War. Almost all of these editions were issued abroad and several of them translated into French and German. All in all, its contemporary popularity compared favorably with that of any of his novels. By 1860, when the novels were illustrated by Darley and handsomely republished, the *History of the Navy,* together with Cooper's other critical prose, had been virtually discarded by the public.

Cooper's purpose is clearly stated and fully elaborated in his introduction which, together with other passages dealing with opinion rather than fact, he omitted from the abridgment. It must be remembered that he had served his own term in the navy during a period when the post-Revolutionary curtailment was still operative and when, in spite of frequent threats of another war, Congress was taking no steps toward adequate increases in ships or men. These facts undoubtedly had supplemented the desires of his wife in converting him from a midshipman into a country gentleman. Even after 1815, the increases, though encouraging, were insufficient to meet with his ideas.

While those who have reflected have clearly foreseen [he writes] that the republic must assert its place in the scale of nations, defend its territory, and maintain its rights, principally by means of a powerful marine, all are compelled to acknowledge that the growth of this branch of the public service has been slow, uncertain, and marked by a policy as timid as it has been fluctuating . . . . It has long been confessed that America possessed every qualification for the creation of a powerful navy, but men and money. The necessary skill, the required aptitude for sea-service, and the other requisites have always been admitted; but it has been asserted that neither the finances, nor the population would allow of the drain on their resources that is unavoidably connected with a strong marine. The two deficiencies, if they actually existed, would certainly be fatal.

The levelling influences of the pseudo-democratic theory, and its result in party politics, seemed to Cooper the primary cause of the difficulty. "The new government of the Union," he writes, in discussing the early engagements with the Dey of Algiers,

was now to experience evils of this nature that are perhaps inseparable from popular power, and to contend with the cry of extravagance, as extravagance is usually viewed by those who have not sufficient information to understand that, as in ordinary transactions the highest pay commands the best services, so in public things the expenditures made in a time of peace are the surest means of obtaining economy in a time of war.

It was Cooper's purpose to prove that:
(1) A large, powerful, and well trained naval force

in times of peace is essential to the maintenance of national honor abroad and self-respect at home.

(2) Appropriation by Congress of sufficient funds to maintain this force and to build adequate vessels would be a justifiable expenditure.

(3) Increase in the number of ranks in the naval service would foster ambition and thus stimulate enlistment and promote morale.

These are, of course, the arguments of the "big navy" men of today, but their statement in Cooper's day was something of a novelty. American naval successes in time of war met with public acclaim; the desirability of a powerful peace establishment in a country which had but recently promulgated the Monroe Doctrine was not so obvious. In pointing to the phenomenal successes of Paul Jones, Cooper hoped to impress his readers with the inadequacy of the *Ranger* and the *Bon Homme Richard,* and with the inferior arms, powder, and shot in their equipment, as well as with the romantic pride in the hero's intrepidity and his amazing achievement. Cooper's accounts contained the kind of impartiality which is still excluding sound histories of our country from certain city high schools.

But it is as a narrative that the *History* has its principal appeal for the modern reader. Cooper introduces his account by a brief record of the part which ships played in the early settlement. His first war episode is characteristic of his style and of his treatment of material:

The first engagement that probably ever occurred between inhabitants of the American colonies, and enemies afloat, was a conflict between John Gallop, who was engaged in a trade of this nature, in a sloop of twenty tons, and some Narragansett Indians, who had seized upon a small vessel belonging to a person of the name of Oldham, known to have been similarly occupied. As this, in a certain sense, may be deemed the earliest sea-fight of the nation, we consider it worthy to be related.

Some time in May, 1636, Gallop, in his little sloop, manned by two men and two boys, himself included, was standing along the Sound near Plum Island, when he was compelled to bear up by stress of the weather, for a refuge to leeward among the islands that form a chain between Long Island and Connecticut. On nearing the land, he discovered a vessel very similar to his own, in size and equipments, which was immediately recognized as the pinnace of Mr. Oldham, who had sailed with a crew of two white boys and two Narragansett Indians. Gallop hailed on nearing the other craft, but got no answer, and, on running still nearer, no less than fourteen Indians were discovered lying on her deck. A canoe, conveying goods and manned by Indians, had also just started for the shore. Gallop now began to suspect that Oldham had been overpowered by the savages; a suspicion that was confirmed by the Indians slipping their cable and running off before the wind, or in the direction of Narragansett Bay. Satisfied that a robbery had been committed, Gallop made sail in chase, and running alongside of the pinnace, in a spirited manner, he fired a volley of duck-shot at the savages. The latter had swords, spears, and some fire-arms, and they attempted a resistance, but Gallop soon drove them below to a man. Afraid to board in the face of such odds, Gallop now had recourse to a novel expedient to dislodge his enemies. As the pinnace was drifting with no one to manage her, she soon fell to leeward, while the sloop hauled by the wind. As soon as the two vessels were far enough asunder, Gallop put his helm up, and ran directly down on the weather quarter of the pinnace, striking her with so much violence as to come near forcing her over on her side. The shock so much alarmed the Indians, who were on an element and in a craft they did not understand, that six of them rushed frantically on deck, and leaped into the sea where they were all drowned. The sloop again hauled off, when Gallop lashed an anchor to her bows in such a manner that by running down on the pinnace a second time, he forced the flukes through the sides of the latter, which are represented as having been made of boards. The two vessels were now fast to each other, and the crew of the sloop began to fire through the sides of the pinnace, into her hold. Finding it impossible, however, to drive his enemies up, Gallop loosened his fasts, and hauled up to windward a third time, when four or five more of the Indians jumped overboard and shared the fate of those who had preceded them. One Indian now appeared on deck and offered to submit. Gallop ran alongside and received this man in the sloop, when he was bound hands and feet, and put into the hold. Another soon followed this example, and he was also received on board the sloop and bound, but fearful that if two of his wily foes were permitted to commune together, they would liberate themselves, the second prisoner was thrown into the sea. But two Indians now remained in the pinnace. They had got into a small apartment below, and being armed, they showed a disposition to defend themselves, when Gallop removed all the goods that remained into his own sloop, stripped the pinnace of her sails, took her in tow, and hauled up for the islands again. But the wind increasing, the pinnace was cut adrift, and she disappeared in the direction of Narragansett Bay, where it is probable she was stranded in the course of a few hours.

On board the pinnace, Gallop found the body of Mr. Oldham. The head had been cleft, the hands and legs were

much mangled, and the flesh was still warm. The corpse
was thrown into the sea.

Thus terminated this extraordinary conflict, in which
Gallop appears to have shown as much conduct as courage,
and which in itself illustrates the vast superiority that professional skill gives on an element that requires practice
to be rendered successfully available.

The simplicity and the gusto of this narrative are
maintained in all Cooper's accounts of naval engagements, whether the story be of Captain Kidd and the
burial of his treasure in Gardiner's Bay, the loss of the
Philadelphia in the Tripolitan War, or the engagement
between the *Constitution* and the *Guerrière*. The main
action centers upon the three naval wars in which the
United States had been engaged, the Revolution, that
with the Barbary States, and that of 1812. Some of the
best action pictures take place in the Mediterranean. The
periods between the wars are reserved for further discussion of the purposes and hopes of the navy.

A history of battles and campaigns is in its very nature
controversial, and yet Cooper's treatment of his subject
was studiously objective. He tells us that he had deliberately omitted documentation because his footnotes would
have occupied as much space as his text. His research is
original according to the strictest standards, and in the
writing he tells us that he strove for a middle course
between the severe style of factual narrative and the personalities that embellish "light labors."

The *History* was, in the main, successful in avoiding
the pitfalls of prejudice. There was no escaping the issue
of the battle of Lake Erie, however; the factions were
already too deeply entrenched. Cooper had been especial-

ly careful to verify his facts and to maintain his even tone of impartiality in this case because he was fully aware of the difference of opinion between the Elliott and Perry forces, as to whom credit was due for the American victory. Besides, M. C. Perry, the brother of O. H. Perry, had tried to influence his judgment even before the *History* went to press.

Like all such controversies, this war of words looks petty now in the perspective of time. It seems that in this inland water engagement between the British and American forces, Perry commanded the entire American squadron and was also in personal command of the *Lawrence*. Elliott, the second in command, directed the *Niagara,* in size the equal of the *Lawrence*. There were also a number of smaller boats.

The principal fire of the British was directed against Perry, and the *Lawrence* was finally forced to strike her colors. The *Niagara* drew up a few moments before the end and Perry transferred to her, reopened the battle, and brought it to a victorious conclusion.

There was never any question as to Perry's right to the principal credit for the victory. The only question was how much of this credit Elliott justly shared or whether there were any grounds for criticism of his conduct. Perry, in his dispatch after the battle, praised Elliott highly and mentioned no criticism. Several years later he completely reversed his position and drew up charges against Elliott. At the time Cooper wrote, it looked as though the issue might come before a naval court for trial.

Cooper examined his facts and told his story without taking sides. He justified Perry's generalship and praised his bravery; but he also gave Elliot his due, and he preferred to accept Perry's first impressions of the conduct of his subordinate rather than his later opinions.

The objections to his position were not that he had failed to do justice to Perry, but that he had recognized merit in others as well. Articles by several members of the Perry family appeared immediately, and speeches were made in the Rhode Island Historical Society in defence of this favorite son. Cooper chose to direct his counter attack upon William L. Stone, editor of the *Commercial Advertiser,* for articles by William A. Duer published in that journal during June 1839. The suit was a part of his campaign against the press in his effort to define libel, and it was perhaps his most brilliant success in that effort.

Cooper was not fighting for Elliott. He had little more than toleration for the man, and he later paid no attention to the fulsome gratitude that was showered upon him. He was fighting for his right as an historian to present the truth as he honestly believed it to be, and against the policy of the press in attacking his character as well as his ideas.

Stone objected that such a case could not be settled by a judge, and, by agreement, it was heard in a New York City court room on the afternoon of May 16, 1842, by three referees. Cooper chose to argue his own case, and he raised eight questions. All of the referees agreed that the account of the battle had been written in a spirit of impartiality and justice, and the majority that it was true in its essential facts and that Cooper had faithfully fulfilled his obligations as an historian. On the other hand, the referees unanimously agreed that the reviewer had not been faithful to his trust, that he had deliberately misquoted, that he had indulged in personal imputations, that his review was untrue in essential facts, and that it had not been written in a spirit of impartiality and justice. The case had been admitted as an ordinary suit for libel, the plaintiff was awarded the verdict, and the defendant was required to publish the full text of the decision in the newspapers of New York, Washington, and Albany.

Henry T. Tuckerman, who was present at the trial, has left a revealing picture of Cooper's conduct of the case.

The portrait which he paints has in it the sense of power in isolation. The clash between the man and his times becomes for the moment intensely dramatic. There is something not far from heroic in Cooper's devotion to the principles for which he was fighting, and there is a poetic justice in his victory.

A more unpopular cause [he writes] never fell to the lot of a practiced advocate; for the hero of Lake Erie was and had long been one of the most cherished of American victors. We could not but admire the self-possession, coolness, and vigor with which the author, on this occasion, played the lawyer. Almost alone in his opinion—the tide of public sentiment against his theory of the battle, and the popular sympathy wholly with the received traditions of that memorable day—he stood collected, dignified, uncompromising; examined witnesses, quoted authorities, argued nautical and naval precedents with a force and facility which would have done credit to an experienced barrister. On the one hand, his speech was a remarkable exhibition of self-esteem, and, on the other, a most interesting professional argument; for when he de-

scribed the battle, and illustrated his views by diagrams, it
was like a chapter in one of his own sea-stories, so minute,
graphic, and spirited was the picture he drew. The dogmatism was more than compensated for by the picturesque-
ness of the scene; his self-complacency was exceeded by
his wonderful ability. He quoted Cooper's "Naval History" as if it were "Blackstone"; he indulged in reminiscences; he made digressions and told anecdotes; he spoke
of the maneuvers of the vessels, of the shifting of the wind,
of the course of the fight, like one whose life had been
passed on the quarter-deck. No greater evidence of self-reliance, of indifference to the opinion of the world, and
to that of his countrymen in particular, of the rarest descriptive talent, of pertinacity, of loyalty to personal conviction, and a manly, firm, yet not unkindly spirit, could
be imagined than the position thus assumed, and the manner in which he met the exigency. As we gazed and listened, we understood clearly why, as a man, Cooper had
been viewed from such extremes of prejudice and parti-
ality; we recognized at once the generosity and courage,
and the wilfulness and pride of his character: but the effect was to inspire a respect for the man, such as authors
whose errors are moral weaknesses never excite.

Cooper followed up his victory by a pamphlet in which
he set the case before the public and proclaimed his
moral as well as his legal victory.

The charge against my history [he writes] was that it
was written—meaning the part connected with Lake Erie
—to glorifying Captain Elliott and to lessen Captain Perry
in the public estimation. The answer was that the points
I have here discussed were controversial, and not necessary
to, or fit for, history. I chose, then, to follow the facts
which belonged properly to such a narrative, and which I

conceived to be sufficiently established. The arbitrators justified this course.

Later, when Mackenzie was submitted to a court martial for having executed at sea three members of his crew for suspected mutiny, Cooper prepared an elaborate review which was annexed to the printed report of the proceedings. He analyzed with studied composure the part which Mackenzie had played and completely undermined his position. "Captain Mackenzie was bound to show," he concludes his summary,

> That such a case was presented to him, as JUSTIFIED him in BELIEVING in all the facts mentioned in the first of the two cases given, and then to show that he allowed the accused every opportunity of defense that he was *justified* in *believing* could be granted to them, with safety to his vessel. The reader will see that our issue does not turn on the literal facts of the case, but on the manner in which these facts, real or supposed, were presented to Captain Mackenzie.

In the preface to a late edition of *The Red Rover,* he paid his respects in a similar fashion to the Rhode Island Historical Society.

Cooper's audacity is further illustrated by the fact that his life of Perry, which appeared in *Graham's Magazine* exactly a year after the decision of the Lake Erie Case in his favor, abandoned the impartial narrative point of view of the *History* and reviewed in detail not only the circumstances of the battle but the merits of Perry's actions both during the fighting and in his subsequent attacks on Elliott. He concludes his biography with one of the most fiery paragraphs he ever set on paper.

The name of Perry [he writes] will ever remain associated with American naval annals. His victory was the first obtained, in squadron, by the regular and permanent marine of the country, and its reputation precedes all others in the order of time. The peculiar character of his personal exertions associated him more closely with his success, too, than is usual even for a commanding officer, securing to his renown a perpetuity of lustre that no one can envy who justly views his exertions. All attempts to rob Perry of a commander's credit for the Battle of Lake Erie must fail; for to this he is fairly entitled and this the good sense and natural justice of men must award him; but too much is exacted when his admirers ask the world to disregard the known laws that regulate physical force; to forget the points of the compass; to overlook testimony, when it is direct, unimpeached, and the best a case will admit of, in favor of rumors that can be traced to no responsible source; to believe all that even Perry says today, and to forget all that he said yesterday; in short, to place judgment, knowledge, evidence, the truth, and even the laws of nature, at the mercy of embittered disputants, who have fancied that the ephemeral influence of political clamor is to outlast the eternal principles of right, and even to supplant the mandates of God.

The *Lives of Naval Officers* continued to appear serially in *Graham's* until 1845 and were collected into a volume the following year. They are in many cases a mere reworking and elaboration of material already used in the *History,* but their personal tone adds to them a certain spice which is not always present in the longer work. Those of Bainbridge, Paul Jones, and Perry are perhaps the most colorful; that of Woolsey is interesting because of its bearing upon Cooper's own experience on Lake Ontario.

A side-light on Cooper's naval war grew out of a review which appeared in the *Edinburgh Review* in April 1840, and which compared his work with that of James. Cooper answered in the *Democratic Review* for May and June 1842. In his first article he exposed the lack of nautical knowledge possessed by the "horse-doctor"; in the second, he attempted to answer the criticism of his own work. Once more the personal issue became identified with the national. The old hostility to England was awakened, the old chafing under the patronizing criticism of the elder nation.

> As to England [he writes] and the peculiar relation in which she now stands to this country, we have a word to say. It is a fact not to be concealed that the national hostility that has so long prevailed in England toward this country is fast being transferred to America. The hold which England has on our *feelings* has got to be slight indeed, and it is now confined principally to a few bookworms, devotees of monarchy, and the remains of the old school of doctrinaires in politics. We should say, notwithstanding the great increase of population, that where England had two men with her in feeling at the declaration of the war in 1812, she would not have one today. Setting aside the direct interests of trade, we believe a war with that country might, at any hour, be made extremely popular in this. Nor can we conceal from ourselves that America is much more likely to rush into a conflict in the present deranged condition of her material interests than when all her pecuniary resources are prosperous. Then, change would be deprecated by the multitude; now, it is sought. In the actual state of the country, many sources of wealth would

be immediately benefited by a war. Such would be the
fact with railroads, canals, manufactories of all sorts, and
even with banks. These are considerations that ought to
render all men cautious who really wish to see justice
done by means of reason and friendly dealing rather than
by a resort to force.

We are not the advocates of war except in cases in which
the nation is clearly right. We do not believe that commu-
nities, any more than individuals, are justifiable in making
the last appeal unless fully sustained by moral principles;
and we reject the plea of mere policy as altogether un-
tenable. Still, we firmly believe that the dignity of a nation is inseparable from its policy, and we see an intimate
connection between the maintenance of this dignity and
the maintenance of its rights.

He then returns to his old theme of the attitudes of
strutting superiority on the part of England and of
groveling mental dependence on the part of America,
concluding,

We most sincerely hope that the difficulties which now
exist between this country and England may be, fairly and
creditably to both parties, amicably disposed of. If war
should come, however, we will know what to expect in a
naval point of view. We shall by no means be annihilated.
England cannot, in 1842, do with America what she was
unable to effect in either 1776 or 1812. Still we shall have
a brave and stubborn enemy to contend with. Battles, by
sea and land, will be both won and lost, and the result
will be to satisfy each party that neither is to be despised
as an enemy, while each ought to be prized as a friend.

The articles had appeared anonymously, according to
the custom of the day, but the editor did not feel that he

could subscribe to these opinions and added a note in which he revealed their authorship. Whatever vindication Cooper finally won for his opinions and actions, he usually found that, in the end, he stood alone. His crusade for a large peace navy, whether right or wrong, was fought with consistency and sincerity. It was but a part of his whole program for his country, one of many means open to the new America for making her power felt abroad and for developing her pride and sense of unity at home. But because of his great love for the sea, and of the intimate knowledge he had gained from his own naval experience, he threw more of himself into these books than into almost any others he ever wrote.

Four romances at this time carried Cooper's reawakened interest in the sea into fiction, *The Two Admirals, Wing-and-Wing, Afloat and Ashore,* and *Miles Wallingford,* but the first alone reflects his belief in the naval destiny of the United States. A part of his program was the substitution of well-organized fleet movement for the somewhat miscellaneous character of the American naval engagements of the past. "It is a strong proof of the diffusive tendency of everything in this country," he writes, in the preface to *The Two Admirals,*

that America never yet collected a fleet. Nothing is wanting to this display of power but the will. But a fleet requires only one commander, and a feeling is fast spreading in the country that we ought to be all commanders; unless the spirit of unconstitutional innovation and usurpation, that is now so prevalent at Washington, be controlled, we may expect to hear of proposals to send a committee of Congress to sea in command of a squadron.

The choice of "the old French war," rather than any conflicts in which the young American navy had been engaged was demanded by the requirements of his plan. The novel was written to illustrate the movements of fleets, and America as yet had no fleet.

One of the few manuscripts left by Cooper at his death was *Old Ironsides,* an account of the adventures of the frigate *Constitution,* originally intended for inclusion in the *Lives of Naval Officers.* It was published in *Putnam's Magazine* in May and June 1853. This vessel was to Cooper the symbol of his ideal for the new navy, a strong ship manned by courageous and able men. Reconstructed, it has become a memorial of this early American navy.

CHAPTER EIGHTEEN

The Complete Critic

THE gradual strengthening of Cooper's social and religious convictions does not seem to have embittered his personal relationships. The final decade of his life presents a curious paradox. In his lawsuits he hammered his opponents to the wall with uncompromising thoroughness; in his writings he reduced his ideas to a few fundamental principles and insisted upon these with reiterated earnestness; but his love for his family and his home grew with the mellowness of a happily advancing age, and those of his friends who were not alienated by his ideas became firmer in their attachment to him as their admiration for his character increased. Like many another social critic, Cooper had come to have little respect for man in the mass, but a great warmth of affectionate feeling for the individual man.

He has been described at this time in his life as "a fine looking man, with a large manly figure, rather tall and stout, with a full broad forehead, strong features, lips full, firm and determined, with large, clear, gray eyes."[1] The portraits which have survived indicate a certain flabbiness of person and a carelessness in attire which written reminiscences do not substantiate. One wonders whether the artists who sketched the two portraits which are perhaps the most familiar to Cooper's readers were not them-

[1] S. M. Shaw, *A Centennial Offering*, p. 205.

selves somewhat influenced by the hostile public attitude
toward him. Certainly the results are not flattering.

Life in Cooperstown during this period was the
typically uneventful round of the small inland town
which had ceased to develop. An ovation to President
Martin Van Buren in September 1839 when he passed
through the village, the Cooper trials in the local Court,
and the two incendiary fires in 1849 which caused the
Phinneys to move their printing business to Buffalo,
seem to have been the most exciting occurrences. Cooper
kept pretty much to himself when he was at home. In
1839, he presided at a meeting of the County Educational
Society, the purpose of which was to improve the local
public school system, and on March 4, 1847, he delivered
an address at a public meeting to organize relief for the
suffering people of Ireland.

The residents of the town, in spite of memories of
Three Mile Point, do not seem to have been markedly
hostile to him. The Rev. Ralph Birdsall tells us that [2]

> the general sentiment toward Fenimore Cooper in his
> home town was not altogether created by his success as
> a writer. It may be that the aged Miss Nancy Williams,
> who lived in a house which still stands on Main Street next
> east of the Second National Bank, was not alone in her
> estimate of this kind of success. Her favorite seat was at
> the front window where she was daily occupied in knitting,
> and watching all passersby. Whenever Fenimore Cooper
> passed, whom she had known as a boy, Miss Williams
> called out to him: "James, why don't you stop wasting
> your time writing those silly novels, and try to make some-
> thing of yourself!"

[2] *Story of Cooperstown*, pp. 245–247.

Whatever may have been the village estimate of his fame as a novelist [continues Mr. Birdsall] there were certain personal traits in Cooper that went farther than anything he ever wrote to fix the esteem of his fellow citizens. Among acquaintances whom he admitted as his social equals he was universally beloved; to these he showed all the charm and fascination of a gracious personality and a brilliant mind. The more intimately Cooper was approached the more unreservedly he was admired, and within his own family he was almost adored. In the humbler walks of life those who habitually recognized Cooper as a superior had nothing to complain of. But there were many in Cooperstown who had no warmth of feeling toward Fenimore Cooper. They were quick to detect in him an attitude of contemptuous superiority towards the villagers. Some of the neighbors felt that he willingly remained a stranger to them. When he passed along the street without seeing people who expected a greeting from him, his friends averred that it was because his mind, abstracted from present scenes and passersby, was engaged in the dramatic development of some tale of sea or forest. But those who felt snubbed by his indifference were less charitable in their interpretation of his bearing toward them. . . . Cooper himself was entirely unconscious of any arrogance in his attitude, and when, in connection with the later controversies, it came to his knowledge that some villagers accused him of posing as an aristocrat in Cooperstown, he resented the imputation with some bitterness.

Nevertheless, when the small boys and girls of the village stole into the Hall garden for roses or berries, they were likely to find its owner descending upon them with stick in hand; and if he caught them, he would not let them go until he had lectured them on the crime of theft.

To his children's friends, he took a very different attitude, and his neighbor, later to be Mrs. Synnott but then a small girl, by name Alice Trumbull Worthington, tells us that,

> To meet Fenimore Cooper on the street in the village was always a pleasure, his eye twinkled, his face beamed, and his cane pointed at you with a smile and a greeting of some forthcoming humor. When I happened to be passing the gates of the old Hall, and he and Mrs. Cooper were driving home from his farm, I often ran to open the gate for him, which trifling act he acknowledged with old-time courtesy. His fine garden joined my father's, and once, being in the vicinity of the fence, he tossed me several muskmelons to catch, which at that time were quite rare in the village gardens.

Cooper later wrote a letter to this neighbor which revealed anything but a boorish attitude toward children.

> I am so much accustomed to newspapers [he says] that their censure and their praise pass but for little, but the attentions of a young lady of your tender years to an old man who is old enough to be her grandfather are not so easily overlooked. . . . I hope that you and I and John will have an opportunity of visiting the blackberry bushes, next summer, in company. I now invite you to select your party, to be composed of as many little girls, and little boys, too, if you can find those you like, to go to my farm next summer, and spend an hour or two in finding berries. It shall be your party, and the invitations must go out in your name, and you must speak to me about it, in order that I may not forget it, and you can have your school if you like, or anyone else. I shall ask

only one guest myself, and that will be John, who knows the road, having been there once already.

On another occasion, when Caroline A. Foote, afterwards Mrs. G. Pomeroy Keese, brought her young friend Julia Bryant, daughter of William Cullen Bryant, to the study of the novelist with an autograph album, Cooper sat at his old desk and laughingly dashed off these lines:

> Charming young lady, Miss Julia by name,
> Your friend, little Cally, your wishes proclaim;
> Read this, and you'll soon learn to know it,
> I'm not your papa the great lyric poet.

Glimpses of the personality of Cooper in his later years are all too few, but such as they are, they serve to disclose the warmth of his character, and to illustrate the loving word portraits which his daughter has left us. "You allude to the *affection* he merited," wrote Susan to Rufus Griswold a few weeks after her father's death,[3]

> Ah, Sir, there indeed he was sorely misrepresented! No man had warmer sympathies, stronger affections, or a more social temper. Yet with the exception of those who knew him intimately, he was no doubt usually considered as a gloomy, disappointed cynic—a character wholly foreign to his nature, as you must be well aware, from your own intercourse with him. But I shall be led too far, though less I could not say.

The letters to his wife, which have been published, and those from his wife to him, most of which have not, give further proof of the depth of his sympathies. If anything,

[3] Griswold, *Correspondence,* pp. 277–78.

he was too much a man of family for his own good. His uxoriousness and his devotion to his children might be cited by certain schools of modern thought as impediments to the full development of his powers. Whatever their effects on his thoughts and actions, their presence in his character is undisputed.

Much of his time, however, was spent during these years on business trips to New York and Philadelphia. In the latter city he had few friends, but in New York there were always many people to be visited and much gossip to be exchanged. His friendship for Dunlap, Cruger, Dr. Francis, and innumerable others seems not to have waned in the least, and Francis may well have sat for the portrait of that admirable physician, Dr. McBrain, in *The Ways of the Hour,* Cooper's last novel.

Financial problems seem to have given him much cause for worry during these years. The panic of Jackson's administration had left its mark on the country, and unsettled political conditions, coupled with the northwestern boundary dispute, the Mexican War, and the social unrest resulting from Westward expansion and the slavery issue, all helped to stave off a period of national prosperity. These circumstances were doubtless reflected in Cooper's private affairs, but even more serious was the decline in his popularity. Not only were his returns from the sale of British rights cut to a quarter of what they once had been, but his American publishers were becoming more and more cautious. The need of realizing more substantial rewards for his work led to many negotiations of a strictly business nature, but it never influenced him to change an opinion or to write a book merely because of public demand.

This was the period in which Poe, Willis, Lowell, and other American authors were beginning to abandon book publication for the more lucrative annual and magazine. Cooper felt the force of the tendency, and his miscellaneous contributions to periodicals soon settled to a regular contract with *Graham's*. "The Autobiography of a Pocket Handkerchief" appeared in this journal in 1843, to be followed by the series of lives of naval officers, and finally by serial publication of *Jack Tier* under the title "The Islets of the Gulf: or Rose Budd."

His relation with the Carey firm in Philadelphia came to an end with the publication of *Ned Myers* in 1843. The next novel, *Afloat and Ashore,* was published by the author in Philadelphia, and its sequel, *Miles Wallingford,* was issued in New York for the author by Burgess, Stringer and Company. With *Satanstoe,* Cooper adopted an arrangement with the latter firm which held for all of his remaining novels but the last. The manuscripts were bought from the author outright and issued in paper-covered volumes for 25 cents each. Cooper tells us that by this method he was able to reach a large public and to obtain a reasonable financial return for his work in spite of hostile reviews and journalistic contempt. But there is a certain irony in this cheapening of his novels in conformity with the levelling influences of the new democracy against which he was maintaining so offensive a warfare. The influences of the times were inescapable even for their most bitter enemy.

In the face of such circumstances, it is somewhat surprising to discover that the decade fom 1840 to 1850 marked, beyond doubt, the highest point in Cooper's literary attainment. Opening with *The Pathfinder* and

The Deerslayer, which are his most finished and balanced romances, the period produced sixteen works of fiction in addition to *Ned Meyers,* the *Lives of Naval Officers,* and a vast amount of controversial writing. The qualitative level of his work at this time is almost as impressive as its quantity. To one who is willing to waive or to concur in the opinions which are so frequently stated in these pages, there is much pure romance to be enjoyed and much revelation of American men and manners to be studied. In addition to the Leather-Stocking and the sea tales already discussed, *Afloat and Ashore, The Sea Lions, Jack Tier, Satanstoe,* and *The Chainbearer* are all excellent stories of action, and the Littlepage trilogy is one of the most thorough studies of the social life of an American state that has ever been written.

It is significant also that, although many of his romances have been dramatized by others, the only original play he ever wrote, *Upside Down; or Philosophy in Petticoats,* produced unsuccessfully during June 1850, was apparently a comedy of manners.

Some of these novels are introduced frankly as novels of purpose, others as romances. *The Two Admirals, The Redskins,* and *The Ways of the Hour* contain the most direct discussion of specific problems in their prefaces, but the element of purpose is as clearly marked in a number of the others as it is in these. *The Crater* belongs with *The Monikins* as social allegory of satirical intention, and *Satanstoe* is referred to by its author, in so many words, as a chronicle of manners. The difficulty of reconciling romance with moral or social purpose in fiction worries his readers more than it did Cooper. He was still experimenting with his art when he finally laid it aside in 1850.

Not having a highly cultivated æsthetic judgment, he could not distinguish his failures from his successes. His interests remained divided in two: a love of action for its own sake and a conviction that a novel should convey a moral ideal along with its capacity for amusement.

Through his long list of experiments, however, one may trace at least one legitimate development in the novel of purpose. This is the chronicle of manners, tried first in *Home as Found*, laid aside for the controversy which resulted, and taken up again five years later in the *Pocket Handkerchief*. This slight work, never included in the collected edition of its author's novels, is significant chiefly for its place in the history of his development. When it appeared, it was greeted as both a decided success and as a complete failure. It is a story of society, with its principal scenes laid in New York City during 1830–32. In it, Cooper continued that discussion of the types of Americans which he had undertaken in the early chapters of *Home as Found*, and he turned the motives of his story upon class distinction.

We find him therefore, in 1843, when his suits on the Effingham libels and the naval history were coming toward their close, ready to undertake a more serious and more comprehensive study of the social factors underlying the Three Mile Point Controversy: namely, the problems of ownership and inheritance of property in the American democracy and of those flexible distinctions between social classes which seemed to him essential to a civilized state. But he had by now thought beyond the immediate issues of his own property rights or of his own good name in the world. He saw himself as his father's son, as his wife's husband, as a property owner, as the head and founder of a family of his own, as himself a man of culture and reasonable wealth. There were others like him, others who had even more of the social qualities by which he had learned to put so much store, more land, more inherited wealth, more worth, and more culture. Of such men must the new society of America be constructed. The alternative was mass rule, the tyranny of the majority.

This line of thought now became the central motivating force for all his writings, the extremes of romance excepted. In *Wyandotté,* he returned once more to the problem of Dutch and English land grants, and he explained the methods of obtaining, inheriting, and holding property in New York State in the colonial and the early national times. In his second experiment with the double novel, *Afloat and Ashore,* he undertook the careful examination of the social consequences of this background on one Miles Wallingford, in many respects just such a man as himself. And finally, in the Littlepage trilogy he studied the social structure of New York State in all its aspects; first, in the problem of the founding of families and land fortunes in the new world in *Satanstoe;* second, in the problem of the New England squatter in *The Chainbearer;* and finally, in the problem of the Anti-Rent War and the threatened dissolution of all landed estates in *The Redskins. The Ways of the Hour,* with its discussions of the rights of landlords in a court of law and of the evil of the jury system, provides a final footnote to the discussion. Cooper had become the voice of conservatism, of tradition, of values in culture and in wealth, crying out against the standardizing tendencies of American materialism and middle-class rule. A Jefferson, living in 1845, might well have followed the same course; the will of the people seemed a nobler force in theory than it was proving itself in fact. Between the *Notions of the American* and *The Redskins* there is the distinction which separates deluded idealism from disillusioned experience.

With *Afloat and Ashore,* Cooper succeeds in establishing for himself the objective approach necessary to the social chronicler. "Everything which can convey to the human mind distinct and accurate impressions of past events, social facts, professional peculiarities, or past history, whether of the higher or more familiar character, is of use," he offers in justification. "All that is necessary is that the pictures should be true to nature, if not absolutely drawn from the living sitters."

Cooper adopts in this novel the autobiographical mode which adds a feeling of veracity to historical or pseudo-historical work. The first chapter is a detailed record of his ancestry and the means of the Wallingford family, possessors of the modest estate of Clawbonny in Ulster County, New York, on the Hudson, since 1707. The narrator is Miles Wallingford, who had succeeded to the estate in 1794 at the age of eleven through an accident to his father, a one time sea-captain. His widowed mother and sister look to him as the head of the family and to Mr. Hardinge, an Episcopal minister, as executor, for their solace and support. Mr. Hardinge has a son and daughter, and the plot of the story concerns itself with the growing-up of these children and with the romances which develop among them. The Hardinges, although poor, are of more aristocratic stock than the Wallingfords, and when Lucy inherits a fortune, her romance with Miles is both facilitated and complicated. It is not hard to read into the Wallingford-Hardinge romance the social factors which must have operated in the Cooper-DeLancey romance of 1811. And Miles with his blunt honesty and forthrightness, his recognition of social differences without snobbery or false humility, his love of the sea, and his love for Lucy, is as much James Fenimore Cooper's idea of James Fenimore Cooper as the gentle, intelligent womanly Lucy is his idea of Susan DeLancey.

The "afloat" part of the story, which occupies a good half of both the volumes, is as full of action as the best of its author's sea romances, but the "ashore" part reveals an entirely new Cooper. "We had orchards, meadows, and ploughed fields all around us," writes this chronicler in describing the ancestral farm of his hero,

> while the barns, granaries, styes, and other buildings of the farm were of solid stone, like the dwelling, all in capital condition. In addition to the place, which he inherited from my grandfather quite without any incumbrance, well stocked and supplied with utensils of all sorts, my father had managed to bring with him from sea some fourteen or fifteen thousand dollars, which he carefully invested in mortgages in the county. He got twenty-seven hundred pounds currency with my mother, similarly bestowed; and two or three great landed proprietors and as many retired merchants from York excepted, Captain Wallingford was generally supposed to be one of the stiffest men in Ulster County. I do not know exactly how true was this report, though I never saw any thing but the abundance of a better sort of American farm under the paternal roof, and I know that the poor were never sent away empty-handed. It is true that our wine was made of currants; but it was delicious, and there was always a sufficient stock in the cellar to enable us to drink it three

or four years old. My father, however, had a small private collection of his own, out of which he would occasionally produce a bottle; and I remember to have heard Governor George Clinton, afterward Vice-President, who was an Ulster County man, and who sometimes stopped at Clawbonny in passing, say that it was excellent East India Madeira. As for clarets, burgundy, hock, and champagne, they were wines then unknown in America, except on the tables of some of the principal merchants, and here and there on that of some traveled gentleman of an estate larger than common. When I say that Governor George Clinton used to stop occasionally and taste my father's Madeira, I do not wish to boast of being classed with those who then composed the gentry of the state. To this, in that day, we could hardly aspire, though the substantial hereditary property of my family gave us a local consideration that placed us a good deal above the station of ordinary yeomen. Had we lived in one of the large towns, our association would unquestionably have been with those who are usually considered to be one or two degrees beneath the highest class. These distinctions were much more marked immediately after the War of the Revolution than they are today; and they are more marked today, even, than all but the most lucky or the most meritorious, whichever fortune dignifies, are willing to allow.

The social ideals and habits intrinsic to this description belong to another world than the wilderness of Leather-Stocking or the sea lanes of the *Red Rover*. The difference in point of view is further emphasized when Cooper later interrupts his story to comment upon the social situations which he has been describing.

Perhaps no country [he writes] that ever yet existed has been so little understood, or so much misrepresented,

as this America of ours. It is as little understood, I was
on the point of saying, at home as it is abroad, and almost
as much misrepresented. Certainly its possessors are a good
deal addicted to valuing themselves on distinctive advantages that in reality they do not enjoy while their enemies
declaim about vices and evils from which they are com-
paratively free. Facts are made to suit theories, and thus
it is that we see well intentioned, and otherwise respectable writers, constantly running into extravagances in order
to adapt the circumstances to the supposed logical or moral
inference. This reasoning backwards has caused Alison,
with all his knowledge and fair-mindedness, to fall into
several egregious errors, as I have discovered while recently reading his great work on Europe. He says we are
a migratory race, and that we do not love the sticks and
stones that surround us, but quit the paternal roof without regret, and consider the playgrounds of infancy as
only so much land for the market. He also hazards the
assertion, that there is not such a thing as a literal farmer
—that is, a tenant who *farms* his land from a landlord—
in all America. Now, as a rule, and comparing the habits
of America with those of older countries, in which land
is not so abundant, this may be true; but as a literal fact,
nothing can be less so. Four-fifths of the inhabited portion of American territory has a civilized existence of half
a century's duration; and there has not been time to create
the long-lived attachments named, more especially in the
regions that are undergoing the moral fusion that is always
an attendant of a new settlement. That thousands of heartless speculators exist among us, who do regard everything,
even to the graves of their fathers, as only so much im-
provable property, is as undeniable as the fact that they
are odious to all men of any moral feeling; but thousands
and tens of thousands are to be found in the country, who
do reverence their family possessions from sentiment that

is credible to human nature. I will not mention Clawbonny, and its history, lest I might be suspected of being
partial; but it would be easy for me to point out a hundred families embracing all classes from the great proprietor
to the plain yeoman who owns and resides on the estates
of those who first received them from the hand of nature,
and this after one or two centuries of possession. What
will Mr. Alison say, for instance, of the Manor of Rensselaer? A manor, in the legal sense, it is no longer certainly, the new institutions destroying all the feudal tenures;
but, as mere property, the late patroon transmitted it as
regularly to his posterity as any estate was ever transmitted in Europe. This extensive manor lies in the heart of
New York, a state about as large and about as populous
as Scotland, and it embraces no less than three cities in
its bosom, though their sites are not included in its ownership, having been exempted by earlier grants. It is of
more than two centuries' existence, and it extends eight-
and-forty miles east and west, and half that distance, north
and south. Nearly all this vast property is held, at this
hour, of the Van Rensselaers, as landlords, and is farmed
by their tenants, there being several thousands of the latter.
The same is true on a smaller scale, of the Livingston, the
Van Cortlandt, the Philipse, the Nicoll, and various other
old New York estates, though several were lost by attainder
in the Revolution. I explain these things, lest any European who may happen to read this book, should regard
it as fiction; for, allowing for trifling differences, a hundred Clawbonnys are to be found on the two banks of the
Hudson at this very hour.

In *Afloat and Ashore,* Cooper's tone was temperate, his
point of view that of the impartial observer. But as the war
between the land owners and the tenants of his state

gradually became more intense in the years following the death of Stephen Van Rensselaer, "the last of the Patroons," in 1839, his attitude became more embittered.

The Anti-Rent War of the forties and fifties in New York State has by now dropped from the short histories of the United States and is remembered as an incident of little general significance. To Cooper, however, it seemed the ultimate test of American theories of government, the issue upon which hung the future welfare of the entire nation. His view of its importance was not mistaken, whatever the verdict of history, if we consider the problem as he did, in terms of social principles. The New York land-owners were fighting for a system which, if successful, would have fundamentally altered the status of landlord and tenant in this country. It was, in effect, a battle of an agrarian and feudal against an industrial and democratic system. Factors other than those in the immediate situation foredoomed the cause of the landlords. But in their threatened defeat, Cooper saw the decay of a sense of values in the American mind.

The Anti-Rent War originated and centered in the Rensselaer holdings, although most counties of north central New York State were infected by it. The original grant of the Manor of Rensselaerwyck was made by the Dutch in 1630, and extended from the Mohawk River at the Cohoes Falls on the north, twenty-four miles down the Hudson, extending eight miles inland on each side of the river. This tract was increased by an English grant obtained through Thomas Dongan, the Governor of New York from 1683 to 1688, to include almost all of the present Rensselaer County. This tract was settled on long-term leases, and the Patroon, Stephen Van Rensselaer, a descendant of Killian of the same name, was respected by his tenants. Rents were paid in wheat, fowls, and services with horses and wagons, in addition to "quartersales," which entitled the landlord to one fourth of the proceeds from sales by the farmers.

There was no trouble between the parties to this agreement until the death of the Patroon, in 1839, when the estate was divided between two of his sons. Fearing that these young men might abuse their powers in a way that their father had not, the tenants sent a delegation to the new owners to negotiate, if possible, a purchase of all the reservations in the leases and a termination of their tenure. They were refused.

Anti-Rent associations were immediately formed and popular indignation swept even conservative and satisfied tenants along with the discontented. Bands of men, disguised as Indians, created local havoc and some blood was shed. Through the powers of numbers the movement gained some political influence, and between 1842 and 1847 the new Anti-Rent Party succeeded in electing about one eighth of the members of the state legislature. The constitutional convention of 1846 was so far controlled by the Anti-Renters as to insert in the new state constitution a clause abolishing all feudal tenures and prohibiting the leasing of agricultural lands for more than twelve years. Other laws favoring the movement were passed by the state legislature during the following years, and, at least until many of the Van Rensselaer rights had been purchased by Colonel Walter S. Church, in 1854, there was little to stem the tide.

Cooper was entirely on the side of the landlords, even though his father and the Patroon had differed on the relative advantages of the systems of sub-dividing or leasing their holdings. The experiences and the ideas of the intervening years had convinced him, not that the Rensselaer theory was the only sound one, but that leases, of whatever nature, were sacred contracts and should be protected by law. Further, he saw in the landlords a class-consciousness and an appreciation of social values which were to him essentials of civilization.

The Littlepage trilogy was the result. The three novels are planned with a thoroughness not usual to him. He went down to causes, and devoted the first entirely to the problems of settlement. The period covered by the action extends from May 3, 1737, the date of the birth of Cornelius Littlepage, to October 1854, the date of his marriage to Anneke, daughter of Herman Mordaunt. The style is that of the preceding novel, the autobiography of meticulous detail. The action takes places at Satanstoe, a neck of land on the north shore of Long Island Sound, at Lilacbush, a small estate on the Hudson near New York, and at Mooseridge and Ravensnest, the wilderness patents of the Littlepage and Mordaunt families in the northern part of the state. Almost every possible system of land settlement and tenure is represented in these holdings, from the private estate held only for pleasure to the great tract divided by sales or rented on long leases.

In discussing the problem of leases with Corny Littlepage, Herman Mordaunt outlines the very foundations of old New York social organization.

You see [he explains] that my twenty thousand acres are not like to be of much use to myself even should they prove to be of any to my daughter. A century hence, indeed, my descendants may benefit from all this outlay of money and trouble; but it is not probable that either I or Anneke will ever see the principal and interest of the sums that will be expended in the way of roads, bridges, mills, and other things of that sort. Years must go by before the light rents which will only begin to be paid a year or two hence, and then only by a very few tenants, can amount to a sufficient sum to meet the expenses of keeping up the settlement, to say nothing of the quit-rents to be paid to the Crown.

Satanstoe is especially interesting as a study of the relationship of the Dutch and the English in early New York. In the person of Guert Ten Eyck, Cooper has drawn a faithful portrait of the honest, somewhat stolid, but courageous Dutchman whom Irving burlesqued so unmercifully. Guert has the stuff of aristocracy in him and we can appreciate Cooper's respect for his race as well as for himself. The English also in this novel fare exceedingly well, and, when writing of pre-Revolutionary days, he consistently expresses his belief in loyalty to the Crown. It is only in the days of later independence that he objects to a deference to English opinion.

The result is that his story is saturated with the feeling of old times and old customs. It conveys an impression of authenticity and yet it has the flavor of romance. There is no action scene in any of Cooper's novels quite so engrossing as the description of the ice flow on the Hudson, when Corny and Anneke, Guert and Mary Wallace, are caught in sleighs on the moving ice and saved only after an heroic struggle. The quiet tone of the introduction to the story, the sense of reality which the chronicle method has succeeded in conveying, and the intimate characterization of the principals, serve to off-set this exciting adventure far more effectively than the usual romantic background. *Satanstoe* is not the best of Cooper's novels for the younger reader, but it is his most thoughtful and his most representative work. More than anything he ever wrote, it is an answer to Poe's criticism that he was, in the final analysis, merely a popular writer of romance and not an author of artistic and intellectual worth.

In the next novel of the series, *The Chainbearer,* Cooper moves on to a second generation of his landlords and shows, in the person and the experiences of Mordaunt Littlepage, how the squatter from New England threat-ened the social organization which these early settlers were laboriously building up. The character of old Andries Coejemans, the chainbearer, and of his daughter, "Dus" Malbone, are among the most living of Cooper's por-traits. The story and the social problem in this novel, as in *Satanstoe,* are so closely integrated that they build together a genuine work of art, even though there is the usual repetition of ideas and the loquacity from which Cooper never escaped.

After the war, Mordaunt returned to Satanstoe where it was presumed that he would marry the nearest good-looking girl of his class, Priscilla Bayard. He might have done so if he had not decided to go north to look into the family estates in the forests. Mooseridge, which his father owned with Colonel Follock, was being settled by selling the land in fee to small farmers. Ravensnest was being developed on the Dutch patroon system of life and other long leases. Jason Newcombe, the former Con-necticut school master, had been the family agent there for many years and had built mills in his capacity of squire.

The first half of the book is devoted to a laying of the stage and a discussion of the two systems of land holding. With the arrival of Mordaunt at Ravensnest and the "raising" of the new meetinghouse, the action begins. He falls in love with Dus at first sight and the party start out on a journey to Mooseridge with Trackless, the Onondaga Indian, as guide. There they soon discover old Thousandacres and his family in their saw-mill, clearing the land on which they had squatted and selling the lumber to Jason Newcombe. Mordaunt and the Indian are held prisoner and argue the aristocratic *vs*. the so-called democratic theories of law and land tenure. Frank Malbone, the new agent and the brother of Dus, finally attacks the settlement and frees the prisoners, but only after both the chainbearer and Thousandacres have received mortal wounds. Dus marries Mordaunt, it developing that she comes from a good family, and Frank marries Priscilla Bayard. Ravensnest becomes the seat of the new Littlepage generation.

In the third novel, *The Redskins,* Cooper brings his narrative down to date and discusses the last phase of his problem, the revolt of the Anti-Renters. It is a much less pleasing work, and the story proves insufficient to float the weight of social purpose with which it is loaded. The principal characters are Hugh Roger Littlepage, second son of Mordaunt and Ursula, and his nephew of the same name, the son of Malbone Littlepage, and, being an eldest son of an eldest son, the inheritor of Ravensnest. Satanstoe had gone to his uncle, and Mooseridge and Lilacbush had been sold.

The two men are in Paris when the news of the uprising comes to them, and Cooper puts into the mouth of
the uncle his own belief in American "institutions," his
own dismay at American "facts." They hurry home and,
in the disguises of a German pedlar and a hurdy-gurdy,
they visit the estate and take part in the conflict, between
the "Injuns," the masqueraded tenants, and the landlords
supported by the true Indians.

The significance of this book lies not in its artistry, nor
even in the fact that it deals exhaustively with an historical
incident. Rather it is important because it completes
Cooper's statement of his social position and makes
finally clear and inescapable his conflict with his times.

> As democrats [he insists] we protest most solemnly
> against such barefaced frauds. . . . Democracy is a lofty
> and noble sentiment. It does not rob the poor to make
> the rich richer, nor the rich to favor the poor. It is just,
> it treats all men alike. . . . It is indeed, one of the proofs
> of the insincerity of those who are decrying leases, on ac-
> count of their aristocratic tendencies, that their destruction
> will necessarily condemn a numerous class of agricul-
> turists, either to fall back into the ranks of the peasant
> or day-laborer, or to migrate, as is the case with so many
> of the same class in New England. In point of fact, the
> relation of landlord and tenant is one entirely natural and
> salutary in a wealthy community, and one that is so much
> in accordance with the necessities of men that no legis-
> lation can long prevent it. A state of things which will
> not encourage the rich to hold real estate would not be
> desirable, since it would be diverting their money, knowl-
> edge, liberality, feelings, and leisure from the improvement
> of the soil to objects neither so useful nor so praiseworthy.
> The notion that every husbandman is to be a free-

holder is as utopian in practice as it would be to expect that all men were to be on the same level in fortune, condition, education, and habits. As such a state of things as the last never yet did exist, it was probably never designed by divine wisdom that it should exist. The whole structure of society must be changed, even in this country, ere it could exist among ourselves, and the change would not have been made a month before the utter impracticability of such a social fusion would make itself felt by all.

The status, as well as the imperative necessity, of gentlemen in the American democracy was now demonstrated. Cooper had completed the statement of his social philosophy. The rest of his novels are footnotes, the rest of his ideas are corollaries, to this central conviction.

Much has been said of Cooper's attitude toward women, of his antipathy toward New Englanders, and of his later religious dogmatism and his preference for the Episcopal Church. Each of these problems may be dismissed by reference to his social philosophy. Toward women he adopted the old chivalric code of protection and idealization; toward New Englanders he had an instinctive antipathy because he realized that the middle class ideal had been brought to America by the Pilgrim and Puritan fathers; and toward the Episcopal Church he felt an irresistible attraction because it was the religion most clearly integrated with the social traditions of which he was a part and of which he preached the doctrine.

Of his later novels, only the last demands special mention, chiefly because it illustrates how completely he had lost sympathy with the ways of the hour. The action of the story concerns itself entirely with a crime committed and with the consequent trial and conviction of an in-

nocent woman. Its main purpose is to show how a jury
may be prejudiced to a point where obvious justice is
impossible. Other favorite principles, the evils of divorce,
the rights of property, the justice of social distinctions,
and the ultimate submission of the human to the divine
will, are all introduced incidentally. In plot structure, a
pioneer of the modern mystery story, in characterization
more successful than many of the favorite romances, *The
Ways of the Hour* remains principally noteworthy as a
postscript to Cooper's earlier and fuller statement of his
social philosophy.

Cooper, in spite of his appearance of vigor, had not
been well for almost thirty years. In the summer of 1850,
Bryant met him in New York City and remarked upon
his robust personal appearance; in April 1851, he was again
in the city, this time to consult his old friend Dr. Francis.
The verdict was not promising. The inroads of the
disease were rapid and he died on Sunday, September
14, 1851. Eleven days later his friends and enemies assembled in the New York City Hall and held a meeting
in his honor, with Washington Irving in the chair. The
two men had never been friendly; their temperaments
were almost diametrically opposed. Irving has left some
tolerant remarks about Cooper; Cooper some caustic comments upon Irving. Between them they laid the foundations of a native American literature.

Among the manuscripts left at Cooper's death was the
beginning of an historical work on his beloved New York.
Most of this manuscript was destroyed by fire, but the
remnant of it was printed in a casual publication, *The
Spirit of the Fair,* in 1864. It is an invaluable summing
up of his position on national issues and of his warning

to the America which permitted the Civil War. He points to the dangers of commercialism and the uncontrolled concentration of wealth; to the evils of substituting party for national loyalty in the cultivation of the demagogue and the corrupt political machine; he denounces the theory of the sovereignty of states and reasserts his belief in that of the people, delegated to the federal government; he discusses slavery as a social rather than a political issue and recognizes the rights of the slave-holder to his property but the wrong of inflicting his social organization on other sections of the country; and he reaffirms his belief in democracy as the preferred among the imperfect social systems devised by man for his own government.

Nevertheless, [he concludes] the community will live on, suffer, and be deluded; it may even fancy itself almost within reach of perfection, but it will live on to be disappointed. There is no such thing on earth—and the only real question for the American statesman is, to measure the results of different defective systems for the government of the human race. We are far from saying that our own, with all its flagrant and obvious defects, will be the worst, more especially when considered solely in connection with whole numbers; though we cannot deny, nor do we wish to conceal, the bitterness of the wrongs that are so frequently inflicted by the many on the few. This is, perhaps, the worst species of tyranny. He who suffers under the arbitrary power of a single despot, or by the selfish exactions of a privileged few, is certain to be sustained by the sympathies of the masses. But he who is crushed by the masses themselves must look beyond the limits of his earthly being for consolation and support. The wrongs committed by democracies are of the most cruel character; and though wanting in that apparent violence and sternness that marks the course of law in the hands of narrower governments, for it has no need of this severity, they carry with them in their course all the feelings that render injustice and oppression intolerable.

This pessimistic criticism was probably written early in 1851. The state of the national mind has probably never been so low as it was at that moment. Clay's compromises of the year before had served to clamp the lid on a pot boiling with sectional and class conflicts. A self-made and unstatesmanlike man, Millard Fillmore, was President. Civil War was daily becoming more certain.

In this year Melville produced *Moby Dick* and lapsed into morose silence, with *The House of the Seven Gables* the art of Hawthorne foundered, and Mrs. Stowe began to publish her *Uncle Tom's Cabin* in the *National Era*. Poe had been dead two years and Lowell had turned from the melody of Tennyson to the dialect of Hosea Bigelow. Byrant had become a newspaper editor and Irving was living on for a few years to complete his *Life of Washington*. Literature in America was dying on the eve of its first maturity.

Cooper had lived to the end of a cycle of American social and cultural history, and he was fortunate not to see the next two decades. The foundations which Colonial and Revolutionary America had laid were not broad enough to support the new industrialism of the east and the westward expansion. New minds—Mark Twain, Walt Whitman—must deal with these problems in the making of a new American literature. Cooper had attempted to build a social philosophy on a discarded feudal agrarianism and to restore a contact with the traditional past in an epoch when his nation was preparing for new material conquests and adjustments. Culture can subsist only when economic factors are stable. The old process of settlement and adjustment had been completed, and, had there been no West, Cooper's convictions might have held firm, his art have matured and mellowed. But the nation was destined to start over again, on a larger scale, the process of its economic and cultural development.

There is much evidence that we have reached—or almost reached—today the completion of another cycle. Once more we may pause to take stock of our accomplishment over material obstacles, and to question the values in the *things* we have gained. With that questioning, there may come, as there came to Cooper, an appreciation of the amenities of life and an opinion that equality in all things—education, art, even society—is alien to the principle of quality in anything. It is once more a time for critics; a time for us to reconsider this most thoroughly critical mind that early America produced.

BIBLIOGRAPHICAL NOTE

The following bibliography lists only the more important sources for the study of Cooper's life and ideas. Footnotes in the text do not include references to such obvious sources as the works of Cooper themselves, the published *Correspondence,* or the more general histories which have been consulted.

A descriptive bibliography of Cooper's writings has been announced but has not yet appeared. At present the most satisfactory list is that in the appendix of *James Fenimore Cooper,* by Thomas R. Lounsbury (New York, 1882), pp. 290–99, which mentions the first American editions as well as some variant European titles and a few magazine and newspaper contributions. Carl Van Doren's bibliography in the *Cambridge History of American Literature* (New York, 1917), I, 530–34, lists also a few later editions and many biographical and critical works on Cooper. *James Fenimore Cooper,* by W. B. Shubrick Clymer (Boston, 1900), pp. 146–49, and a few of the special studies listed below, add a few titles.

The recent gift to Yale University by James Fenimore Cooper, Esq., of the manuscripts in his possession which relate to his grandfather adds substantially to the available source material for biographical studies. The importance of this gift is, however, not as great as it might have been had Cooper's daughter not followed his dying injunction and destroyed the more personal of his papers. The remaining documents include first drafts, in Cooper's own hand, of many of his works, a few letters by him and many to him from his family and friends, one or two brief diaries and account books, many contracts and other impersonal documents, and a few autographed volumes. The most interesting part of the collection was edited, with only a few excisions, by Mr. Cooper and published as the *Correspondence of James Fenimore-Cooper* (2 vols., New Haven, 1922). Cooper's letters and parts of his manuscripts are frequently listed by booksellers, and a few may be found in the Aldis Collection of Yale University, as well as in the collections of the Historical Society of Pennsylvania, the New York Historical Society, the Boston Public Library, the New York Public Library, the Morgan Library of New York, the State and Navy Departments in Washington, the Library of Congress, and private hands. Letters not included in the *Correspondence* may be found in *The Letters and Journals of Samuel F. B. Morse,* edited by E. L. Morse (2 vols., New York, 1914), *Memorials of Eminent Yale Men,* by A. P. Stokes (2 vols., New Haven, Conn., 1914), *The Life of Benjamin Silliman,* by G. P. Fisher (2 vols., New York, 1866), *The Diary of William Dunlap,* (3 vols., New York, 1930), *The Life and Letters of Washington Irving,* by Pierre M. Irving (4 vols., New York, 1862–64), and early biographies of John Murray, Rufus Griswold, Samuel Rogers, W. C. Bryant, and others. A collection of such letters was published as "New Letters from Rome and Paris, 1830–31," in *American Literature,* I, 131–148 (May 1929), and British Museum Add. MS. 33, 964, ff. 449–454 was printed with editorial comment in *The American Historical Review,* XXXV, 575–582 (April 1930).

Thomas R. Lounsbury was the first to collect the printed sources for Cooper's life and his is still the nearest approach to a "standard" biography, even though its attitude is unsympathetic. W. B. S. Clymer's shorter study is based upon Lounsbury and a few fresh sources; it is in many ways a fairer estimate. Miss Mary E. Phillips, in her *James Fenimore Cooper* (New York, 1913), was the first to attempt a portrait of Cooper, the man. Her innumerable illustrations increase the personal interest of her volume. *James Fenimore Cooper,* by Henry E. Boynton (New York, 1931), is written from the same point of view. Its value lies chiefly in the fact that Mr. Boynton had access to many of the manuscripts now at Yale. Neither of these last two biographies attempts critical estimates of Cooper's work.

All biographical study of Cooper must start with the "Discourse on the Life and Genius of Cooper," by William Cullen Bryant, published first in the *Memorial of James Fenimore Cooper* (New York, 1852), and reprinted in Volume I of the collected edition of *Cooper's Novels* (New York, 1859–61). Other biographical data are to be found in the entertaining and revealing, but not always reliable, reminiscences of the novelist's daughter, Susan Fenimore Cooper. These are included in *Pages and Pictures from the Writings of James Fenimore Cooper* (New York, 1861), which was republished as *The Cooper Gallery* (New York, 1865); in the published *Correspondence,* I, 9–72; in special introductions to the titles in the Leather-Stocking series and a few of the sea tales and later novels, published in Boston, 1876–1884; and in two articles in the *Atlantic Monthly* for February and October 1887. Other personal reminiscences were contributed by the writers of the letters in the *Memorial,* notably Dr. John W. Francis (pp. 94–103), by James Grant Wilson in *Bryant and His Friends* (New York, 1886), by G. W. Greene in *Biographical Studies* (New York, 1860), by Nathaniel Parker Willis in his *Pencillings by the Way* (New York, 1844), by G. Pomeroy Keese in *A Few Omitted Leaves in the History of Cooperstown* (n. p., n. d.), and by many other contemporaries and friends of Cooper.

In addition to the critical estimates contained in these biographies, a few essays are worthy of special mention. W. C. Brownell's estimate in *American Prose Masters* (New York, 1909) is perhaps the best, although Carl Van Doren's essays in the *Cambridge History of American Literature* and the *Dictionary of American Biography* are excellent. Percy H. Boynton and Brander Matthews are also among those who have written more or less unprejudiced commentaries. V. L. Parrington, in *The Romantic Revolution in America* (New York, 1927), stresses the significance of Cooper's social criticism, and *The American in England,* by the present writer (New York, 1926), discusses the European novels and critical prose. F. L. Pattee, Russell Blankenship, and H. S. Canby have also emphasized this phase of his thought.

The early criticism of Cooper was practically all biased. The praise of Balzac and the depreciation of Poe and Mark Twain are illustrative of the extremes to which such opinions could reach. Contemporary reviews and biographical notices which appeared after about 1835 are practically worthless for anyone but the literary historian. Exceptions may be noted in the essays of G. S. Hilliard in the *Atlantic Monthly* for January 1862, Francis Parkman in the *North American Review* for January 1852, and H. T. Tuckerman in the *North American Review* for October 1859. Articles on Cooper are also contained in *Prose Writers of America,* by R. W. Griswold (Philadelphia, 1847), and the *Cyclopædia of American Literature,* edited by E. A. and G. L. Duyckinck (2 vols., New York, 1852).

American scholarship has but recently discovered Cooper. The half-dozen or more theses or special studies now in progress may be noted in E. E. Leisy's current bibliographies in *American Literature. The "Effingham" Libels on Cooper,* by Ethel R. Outland (Madison, Wis., 1929), deals fully but inconclusively with the problem of the War with the Press. E. E. Leisy contributes some notes on the early novels in *The American Historical Novel,* etc. (Urbana, Ill., 1926). Studies on special problems relating to Cooper have been contributed by Gregory Paine, Tremaine McDowell, and others to recent issues of *American Literature, Studies in Philology,* etc. Preston A. Barba's *Cooper in Germany* (Bloomington, Ind.,

1914), and J. D. Ferguson's *American Literature in Spain,* (New York, 1916), deal with phases of his European reputation.

On the whole, foreign scholarship has been slightly more active than the American. Marcel Clavel has contributed occasional comments in the *Revue Anglo-Américaine* as a part of his comprehensive studies of Cooper's biography and of his reputation. Among other foreign studies are *"The Monikins" von J. F. Cooper in ihrem Verhältnis zu "Gulliver's Travels" von J. Swift,* by Willi Müller (Rostock, 1900), "Cooper e Loti," by C. Segré, in *Saggi Critici di Letterature Straniere* (Florence, 1894), *Goethe's Novelle; der schauplatz, Coopersche einflusse,* by S. Wukadinovic (Halle-a-S., 1909), *Fenimore Cooper et Edgar Poe, d'après la Critique Française du dix-neuvième siècle,* by George D. Morris (Paris, 1912), *Le Roman de Bas-de-cuir; étude sur Fenimore Cooper et son influence en France,* by Margaret M. Gibbs (Paris, 1927), and *Fenimore Cooper et le roman d'aventure en France vers 1830,* by G. C. Bosset (Paris, 1928). Rudolf Drescher has contributed articles on his own incomparable Cooper collection (principally of editions in German), and on aspects of Cooper's German reputation, to the Cooperstown *Freeman's Journal* (December 6, 1911, November 14, 1918, and February 13, 1929) and to newspapers in Hanau-a-M., Frankfurt, and Dresden.

The Cooperstown background is the subject of many reminiscences and studies. William Cooper's *Guide in the Wilderness* (Dublin, 1810), reprinted with an introduction by J. F. Cooper (Rochester, N. Y., 1897), is the earliest. Fenimore Cooper's *The Chronicles of Cooperstown* (Cooperstown 1838) was continued to 1886 by Samuel M. Shaw, and to 1929 by Walter R. Littell, being reprinted as *The History of Cooperstown* (Cooperstown, 1929). *The Legends and Traditions of a Northern County,* by James Fenimore Cooper (New York, 1921), contains many letters of William Cooper and other members of the family. *A Centennial Offering,* etc., edited by S. M. Shaw (Cooperstown, 1866), contains a biographical sketch by the Hon. I. N. Arnold, and other data. *The Proceedings of the New York State Historical Association,* XVI,(Albany, 1917), contains records and pictures of the annual meeting which was held that year at Lake Otsego. *The Home of Cooper,* by Barry Gray [Robert B. Coffin] (New York, 1872), and *The Story of Cooperstown,* by the Rev. Ralph Birdsall (Cooperstown, 1917), supply many facts and some gossip. Levi Beardsley's *Reminiscences* (New York, 1852) is a valuable early record. In addition to the histories of J. B. Hammond and of D. S. Alexander, *The Old New York Frontier,* by Francis W. Halsey (New York, 1901), and *The Decline of Aristocracy in the Politics of New York,* by Dixon Ryan Fox (New York, 1919), furnish material on the general history of the State.

Sectional histories and memoirs include *Valentine's Manual, History of the County of Westchester,* by Robert Bolton (rev. ed., New York, 1881), *History of Rye, Westchester County, N. Y.,* by C. W. Baird (New York, 1871), *Old New York,* etc., by John W. Francis (New York, 1858), *Literary New York,* by Charles Hemstreet (New York, 1903), and *A Sketch of Dr. John Smith Sage,* by Anna Mulford (Sag Harbor, L. I., 1897). In addition to the *Memorials* by A. P. Stokes, the early catalogues of Yale University, *Biographical Sketches of the Graduates of Yale College with Annals of the College History,* by F. B. Dexter (New Haven, Conn., 1912), and biographies of William Jay, Noah Porter, and other Yale graduates furnish information as to Cooper's probable life at college. His own naval history and biographies, as well as his *Ned Myers* and the sea tales, are the principal sources for his naval experiences, as are his *Gleanings in Europe* and his European novels for his experiences in Europe. In addition, the guide books and maps which he probably consulted are still available. Chief among them are Picot's *Statistique de la Suisse* (edition of 1819), Ebel's *Manuel du Voyageur en*

Suisse (Paris, 1826), which contained Keller's *Carte Itinéraire de la Suisse,* Marianna Starke's *Information and Guide for Travellers on the Continent* (7th edition, London, 1829), Vasi's *Itinéraire Instructif de Rome et ses Environs* (revised by A. Nibby, 1824), and Winkelmann's *Briefe an seine Freunde* (Dresden, 1777).

INDEX